SOLUTIONS
FOR
SINGERS

SOLUTIONS
~ FOR ~
SINGERS

Tools for

Performers and Teachers

RICHARD MILLER

OXFORD

UNIVERSITY PRESS

2004

OXFORD
UNIVERSITY PRESS

Oxford   New York
Auckland   Bangkok   Buenos Aires   Cape Town   Chennai
Dar es Salaam   Delhi   Hong Kong   Istanbul   Karachi   Kolkata
Kuala Lumpur   Madrid   Melbourne   Mexico City   Mumbai   Nairobi
São Paulo   Shanghai   Taipei   Tokyo   Toronto

Published by Oxford University Press, Inc.
198 Madison Avenue, New York, New York, 10016

www.oup.com

Oxford is a registered trademark of Oxford University Press

Library of Congress Cataloging-in-Publication Data
Miller, Richard, 1926–
Solutions for singers: tools for performers and teachers / Richard Miller.
p. cm.
Includes bibliographical references and index.
Contents: pt. 1. Breath management—pt. 2. Posture—pt. 3. Laryngeal and
intra-laryngeal function—pt. 4. Resonance balancing.
ISBN 0-19-516005-3
1. Singing—Questions and answers. 2. Singing—Instruction and study. I. Title.
MT820.M5993 2003
783'.04—dc21   2002041661

1 3 5 7 9 8 6 4 2

Printed in the United States of America
on acid-free paper

In Memoriam William McIver

ACKNOWLEDGMENTS

I wish to thank my friends and colleagues Carol Sedgwick, D.M.A., and Shirley Zielinski, Ph.D., for reading manuscript drafts and offering me sensible advice. Additional thanks are due final-draft peer evaluators, unknown to me, whose comments were exceedingly helpful. I am grateful to members of the editing and production staff of Oxford University Press for their ready assistance. To Richard Sjoerdsma, editor of *Journal of Singing,* my thanks for permission to rework some items I have previously touched on in a regularly contributed *sotto voce* column for that journal. My biggest debt is owed Mary, my wife, who continues to be my guiding light in this, as in all ventures.

PREFACE

Over several decades it has been my privilege to meet with singers and teachers in weeklong courses devoted to the art of singing, in which the correspondence of efficient physiologic and acoustic function to artistic expression is considered in detail. Half of each day is devoted to systematic technique, the remainder to master classes in communication. Several thousand teachers, students, and professional singers have participated. To ensure sequential information, and to avoid interruption of master class performances, observers are asked to write out questions as they occur to them. Questions are then codified and discussed in question-and-answer sessions at the close of the week. These inquiries often go to the heart of vocal pedagogy, pointing out watersheds that separate voice-training systems. This book deals with a number of them—some briefly, some in detail.

Recurring topics have been selected from more than fifteen hundred written questions. They deal with both technique and artistry. Falling into specific categories, they consider a single topic from several angles. I have tried to tailor my responses to the specifics of each question. Associated issues are assembled within overall categories; related questions have been joined together. Technical areas considered involve breath coordination, laryngeal function, resonator-tract response, resonance balancing, voice categorization, voice registration, linguistic articulation, vibrancy, matters of style, the enhancement of artistry and communication, pedagogic and professional attitudes and concerns, and healthy voice production. In answering variations on similar themes, for clarity and completeness, it has occasionally been necessary to revisit important facets of information.

Certain topics require at least some minimal anatomical and acoustical background. For that reason, a few illustrations have been included. The intent of this book, however, is not to detail the structure of the voice as an instrument (something I have previously attempted), but to engage in pragmatic tutoring, and to share historic and contemporary vocal philosophies with professional performers, students, and teachers. A glossary of terms for quick reference and a select bibliography are included. A reader may proceed sequentially or selectively. The book has been written in response to requests such as the following:

QUESTION
I appreciated the information supplied by the course on systematically approaching vocal pedagogy. But sometimes the most practical came from the concluding question-and-answer sessions where teachers raised specific problems they have to deal with in the studio. It would be very helpful to see a book of answers devoted to those specific problems. Why don't you write one?

RELATED QUESTION
In every master class I have ever attended, no matter who the teacher may be, I always come up with questions as to why certain approaches were taken rather than others. I understand that in order not to disturb the singer you are working with, you ask for written questions to be considered on the final day. These last day discussions are especially interesting, but the questions and the answers are not permanently recorded. Shouldn't they be in book form?

ANOTHER RELATED QUESTION
It would be great to have an entire course on nothing but singers' questions and answers! Since that may be impractical, why not compile the questions that have surfaced, together with the answers you have given? If you do it, please deal with each question separately and don't wad them all together in one comprehensive answer. As you can tell from the questions asked, people look at a topic from different angles, and they want more than a generalized response.

YET ANOTHER RELATED QUESTION
When are you going to write a text offering solutions to common, and not so common, problems that we as performers all deal with?

COMMENT
Here it is! Answers will not please every reader. My responses are at times knowingly controversial, but I am emboldened to toss them into the great steaming pedagogic cauldron, because it is my conviction that these answers originate

in the mainstream of historic vocalism developed over several centuries, here viewed in the light of current factual information. The suggested solutions are traditional and reside in the pedagogic public domain; they do not originate with me.

I have largely avoided responding to medical questions and to many dealing with vocal health, because I am convinced that teachers of singing should teach voice and not practice medicine, just as I believe that medical doctors and researchers do best when diagnosing and prescribing, not when teaching voice. Some other questions that were submitted in courses have not been included in this book because I do not have sufficient expertise to deal with them. There is unceasingly much more to discover, and sharing experiences is itself a form of learning. I wish to thank the many performers and teachers who have had the insight and curiosity to raise issues that constitute the essence of voice pedagogy. I hope my comments will be of help.

CONTENTS

2   POSTURE

3   LARYNGEAL AND INTRALARYNGEAL FUNCTION

8 HEALTHY SINGING

9 PEDAGOGY ISSUES

10 PERFORMANCE CONCERNS

SOLUTIONS
FOR
SINGERS

When it comes to singing it was God's little joke to place the larynx, the hard surfaced kernel of the voice containing the vocal cords, just out of sight of any normal visualization of what is going on in the throat during vocalization.... No wonder that singing seems to be accomplished by magic.

ROBERT RUSHMORE

Every art consists of a technical-mechanical part and an aesthetic part. A singer who cannot overcome the difficulties of the first part can never attain perfection in the second, not even a genius.

MATHILDE MARCHESI

It is the province of knowledge to speak, and it is the privilege of wisdom to listen.

OLIVER WENDELL HOLMES

Who dares to teach must never cease to learn.

ANCIENT PROVERB

BREATH MANAGEMENT

APPOGGIO VERSUS BELLY BREATHING (*BAUCHAUSSENSTÜTZ*)

QUESTION
Is there a difference between the appoggio technique you advocate and what some writers call belly breathing?

COMMENT
Before addressing the question more directly, some comment about the appoggio is essential. The term is not narrowly related to the management of airflow during singing. It encompasses a complete system of structural support, during which the muscles of exhalation and those of inspiration maintain an antagonistic balance, inciting a stable but dynamic relationship among the intrinsic muscles of the larynx, which in turn are fully supported by the external laryngeal frame-support system. An axial body posture and a relatively low larynx allow the resonator tract above the larynx to function freely. In short, during execution of the appoggio, as part of this physical complex the abdominal-wall musculature not only controls the speed at which the air exits but also and simultaneously induces proper responses directly at the level of the larynx, and in the vocal tract above the larynx.

Belly-breathing advocates probably know that the breath process cannot be controlled by the belly. Perhaps they mean to stress that the abdominal-wall musculature plays an important role in managing the breath for cultivated singing. Yet a check through the pedagogic literature reveals that belly-breathing proponents tend to practice the *Bauchaussenstütz* technique (outward-belly position) common to one large segment of the German school. This breath-management system does not equate with the appoggio of the historic international school. In appoggio technique, the sternum and the pectorals remain relatively stationary, without induced rising or falling. The rib cage stays well positioned, and the costals remain near the position of inspiration. A steady internal-external muscle balance is maintained. Expansion is felt at the base of the rib cage, at the front and sides of the torso, between the tenth rib and the crest of the iliac (upper surface of the hipbone), and in the back at the eleventh and twelfth ribs. There is no pressing down or out against the viscera, either at inhalation or during sustained singing.

So-called belly breathers often resort to singular physical devices. One maneuver is to place an object (one source suggests a pint bottle) on the "breathing muscle," and to press outward against it during inspiration and phonation. A related stratagem is to lie on the back while thrusting the belly upward against weights (books or other objects) placed on the abdominal wall. Another favorite exercise is to sit with a fallen chest and the abdomen dropped downward on inhalation, then protruded for the duration of the phrase. In the *Bauchaussenstütz* system the epigastrium and the abdominal wall are actively distended on inhalation and retained there during phonation. Breath is then renewed from the same induced position. However, if during singing the rate of airflow is not retarded beyond what is appropriate for speech, pulmonary volume is quickly diminished, and the singer either runs out of breath or must resort to high levels of resistance in order to inhibit the rapid exit of breath. Pushing outward on the abdominal wall in the region of the belly forces the rib cage to move inward and the sternum to fall. *Bauchaussenstütz* blocks the exit of air by increasing resistance at the larynx.

In contrast to belly breathing, the appoggio avoids excessive outward distention of the epigastrium and hypogastric (pelvic, lower abdominal) regions during both inhalation and phonation. At complete inspiration, the lower torso expands laterally, dorsally, and frontally. For most of a sung phrase, the large, flat muscles of the abdomen (transverse abdominis, internal oblique, and external oblique) can be trained to remain relatively stable, near the inspiratory position. (See figure 1.1.)

Breath renewal, silently taken without perceptible chest displacement, reestablishes abdominal expansion, and at the same time assures that the larynx remains in a stabilized position. Complete abdominal contraction occurs rarely; it is restricted to the termination of exceedingly long phrases. Instrumentation that measures both chest and abdominal movement during singing verifies that among singers trained in the appoggio technique, minimal displacement is registered in either the chest wall or the abdominal wall. The term *appoggiare* means "to lean against, to be in contact with, to support," and accurately describes the interaction of muscles of the anterior/lateral abdominal wall. Neither outward pushing nor in-

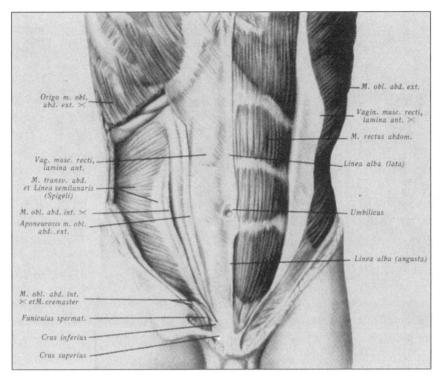

FIGURE 1.1. Muscles of the abdomen. (From Wilhelm Lubosch, ed., *Topographische Anatomie*, 13th ed. Munich: J.F. Lehmanns Verlag, 1935.)

ward pulling takes place during the singing of a phrase. A nearly imperceptible inward motion occurs only toward the conclusion of a moderately long phrase; conscious inward thrusting is averted. During short phrases there is little or no discernible movement in the anterior epigastric area or in the hypogastric region.

Through gradual development of the appoggio system, lateral abdominal expansion equals or exceeds that of the frontal abdominal area. Breath renewal is silent, occurring within a split second. Or it is possible to pace it slowly, over several seconds, without raising or lowering the larynx. While remaining in the noble posture, which keeps the head, neck, and torso in alignment, it is difficult to push outward on the belly, as happens in the *Bauchaussenstütz* method. Above all, appoggio technique avoids rapid chest displacement. As the lungs' air supply becomes naturally depleted, the rib cage and abdominal wall must eventually change their contours; but the performer who retains the greatest degree of torso stability is the best manager of the breath. This is the contribution of the appoggio.

Because laryngeal action cannot freely function when forced visceral distention or contraction takes place, outward and downward stretching of the belly

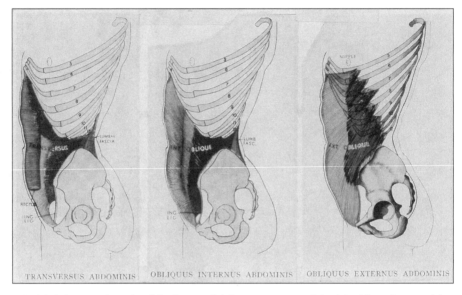

FIGURE 1.2. Internal muscles of the thorax and abdomen: transversus abdominis, obliquus internus abdominis, obliquus externus abdominis. (From *Illustrations of Regional Anatomy,* Section III, 6th ed. Edinburgh: Darien Press, 1946).

induces heavy voice production, and encourages a slow vibrato rate, which is characteristic of some segments of the German school. The chiaroscuro ideal is disturbed because the *oscuro* (dark) aspects of the spectrum come to dominate the *chiaro* (bright) factors. (See Chiaroscuro.) Among internationally recognized singing artists, the appoggio technique is the main route for breath management. (See Protruding the Stomach Wall.)

PROTRUDING THE STOMACH WALL

QUESTION
Isn't tension created in the stomach region when you try to hold it out for the appoggio? Won't that action produce a tight, held tone?

COMMENT
    In the appoggio technique, the stomach is neither pushed out nor held in. The three main muscles of the lower abdominal wall—transverse abdominis, internal oblique, and external oblique—originate in the pelvic and hip regions. These muscles expand laterally during deep inspiration and assist in managing the breath for singing. (See figures 1.1 and 1.2.)

Segments of these muscles insert upward into the ribs of the upper torso, as far as the fifth costal (rib), and dorsally into the eleventh and twelfth costals. Together with the rectus abdominis, they provide muscular abdominal contact that keeps the rib cage expanded and the diaphragm at its lowest, thereby delaying the reflex impulse for early breath renewal. These muscles, developed through appoggio drills that delay expiration and retard the reflex breath-renewal syndrome, can be trained to remain in contact with each other over longer periods of time than is customary during speech. The appoggio modifies accumulating vocal-fold tension by remaining close to the initial inspiratory abdominal-wall expansion. Subglottic pressure levels are reduced. Pouting the stomach outward causes laryngeal tensions by inducing excessive resistance to the exiting air. (See Appoggio versus Belly Breathing [*Bauchaussenstütz*].)

HOW LONG SHOULD IT TAKE TO ACQUIRE THE APPOGGIO?

QUESTION
How long should it take a singer to acquire the appoggio technique?

COMMENT
Acquiring reliable information on how the singing voice functions is essential for every singer and teacher of singing. Such fundamental information is available to any person of average intelligence who is willing to take the time to acquire it. This means not relying solely on experiential circumstances, but on identifiable, communicable, specific data. On such information is the appoggio built. The more fully it is understood, the quicker is its assimilation.

The time it takes to acquire security in any area of voice training is dependent on a singer's pedagogic history and current levels of overall skill. On being introduced to the appoggio exercises, some singers undergo an almost immediate improvement in breath management, while others require weeks or months. In all cases, it is essential to comprehend how airflow, a freely vibrating larynx, and the resonator tract can be brought into unity by the appoggio.

ROUTINING THE ONSET, SILENT BREATHING EXERCISES, AND THE FARINELLI MANEUVER

QUESTION
How do you teach the repeated onset, what some people call the "attack"? Can silent exercises be helpful?

You had a singer do a silent breath-control exercise that you called
the Farinelli maneuver. I didn't follow its purpose. What is it, and
what is its value?

COMMENT

The term "onset" is often substituted for the aggressive-sounding "attack."
Mastering a well-balanced tonal onset is the key to discovering an optimal breath
system. Clean abduction (parting) of the vocal folds produces the precise onset
and sets the stage for the subsequent phrase. There is no perception of "holding the
breath." Silent breath-management exercises develop early awareness of the appoggio. The Farinelli maneuver consists of breath-cycle segments: (1) paced inhalation;
(2) retention of the inspired breath; (3) regulated exit of the breath; (4) immediate,
silent replenishment of the breath. Mentally count to four—about one second per
count—or rhythmically tap out the counts during each part of the Farinelli silent
breath-pacing exercise:

1. Slowly pace quiet inhalation over a count of four
2. Remain in the inspiratory position for a count of four
3. Pace the exit of breath over a count of four, without audible
   exhalation.

Increase numbers gradually, equally pacing the three portions of the breath cycle.
Through sequentially increasing the numbers, a count of ten eventually becomes
a comfortable goal. As counting mounts, do not take in a larger quantity of air than
was inhaled during the lower numbers. Each inhalation, no matter what its duration, is a complete breath without becoming a crowded breath. In the third and exhalation phase, minimal contraction of the abdomen occurs very slowly and gradually. Each of these parameters can be monitored through awareness of activity in
the lateral/anterior abdominal wall and in the musculature of the torso. (See Leaning on the Breath.) Repeat the process a number of times. Oral tradition attributes
the origin of this exercise to Nicola Porpora, who assigned it to Carlo Farinelli for
daily use. It is traditionally called "Farinelli's exercise." Farinelli was known as
"the silent breather," and was lauded for his ability to sustain exceedingly long
phrases at all dynamic levels, even during competition with trumpets.

A second useful nonphonatory exercise is based on a short group of quickly
executed unvoiced sibilants /s–s–s–s–s/, produced consecutively on one breath
in rapid staccato sequence. Undertake numerous repetitions of this pattern, each
group followed by silent breath renewal.

A third unvoiced device, the fricative /f/, executed in imitation of the rapid
blowing out of five candles, in an /f–f–f–f–f/ pattern, serves a similar purpose. It

should be repeated serieswise, silent breath renewal separating each series. Be aware that although there is mild articulatory bouncing in the epigastrium, there is no need for inward abdominal thrusting.

A fourth unvoiced exercise involves a barely audible escape of breath while producing a prolonged sibilant /s/, perceivable only by its producer (or by a listener's closely positioned ear). It is executed through extremely slow air emission. The abdominal wall is retained in the inspiratory position until near the completion of expiration. Even as the abdominal wall finally moves inward at the depletion of the breath supply, the chest does not undergo visible displacement. This protracted exhalation can, with practice, be extended to nearly a minute's duration. Begin with twenty seconds, gradually increasing the expiratory phase to higher counts. Placing the hands at the sides of the abdomen, between hip and rib cage, note the continuing contact among muscles of the lower trunk, inward contraction coming only at the last moment.

In routining these exercises, the great flat muscles of the abdominal wall (transverse abdominis, internal oblique, and external oblique), through their synergistic antagonism acquire fine tonus over time, resulting in greater firmness and strength. The rectus abdominis, although perhaps less directly involved in controlling breath retention than are the other three flat muscles of the abdomen, will also become activated.

With regard to developing the muscle groups that manage the tripartite (breath/ phonation/resonation) vocal instrument, distinctions must be made between muscle groups that can be consciously developed and those which cannot. Maneuvers that advance and maintain muscle tonicity of the torso are of value; exercises that try directly to develop control over the internal laryngeal mechanism are not. Fine-tuning of intrinsic and extrinsic laryngeal muscle function for singing comes through the coordinated mechanics of breathing, not through nonphonatory laryngeal exercises.

Nobility of stance and carriage must be the overriding postural goal. They permit full cooperation among breath mechanism, larynx, and resonator tract. Laryngeal freedom and optimum resonance are dependent on the manner in which the breath-motor source is brought into play. The head, neck, and torso must be well aligned in order for the rib cage to assume an ideal position for quiet breathing, and to ensure the avoidance of a falling sternum and a correspondingly quickly rising diaphragm. It is not possible for the musculatures of the thoracic region and those of the abdominal wall to experience the appoggio if the neck and head are distended forward or elevated upward, the pectorals flaccid, the spine limp, or the abdominals slack. (See Always Noble and Axial?)

The appoggio is not simply a quick fix. It may require months of concentrated attention in its early stages, and continuous daily execution for its fuller development. However, even within a few weeks of daily association with the appoggio, a disciplined student may show marked improvement in stabilizing the breath and in an optimal laryngeal response. (See How Long Should It Take to Acquire the Appoggio?)

THE SHORT ONSET

QUESTION

Why do you put so much emphasis on the short attack? Most phrases are much longer than the brief "Ha–ha–ha–ha–Ha!" exercises you start with. Wouldn't it be more logical to teach the student to immediately handle long single notes and phrases of the kind of duration met in the standard repertoire?

COMMENT

How a singer begins the sound determines the degree of freedom in the rest of the phrase. To request sustained phonation from a singer who lacks coordination of larynx and breath is to invite problematic vocalism. Only when the onset is precise, the sound vibrant, the vowel well defined, and breath renewal reflexive, can free vocalism emerge. The reason for using the short onset, to be followed somewhat later by a sustained phrase, is that the cumulative problems of extended phonation are put aside until the most basic of all technical skills has been addressed. (See Routining the Onset.) With the aspirated onset (prefaced by a quick /h/), the vocal folds are not occluded until the appearance of the subsequent vowel. In the glottal onset, the vocal folds are already closed. A quick, nearly inaudible /h/ allows only a minuscule amount of initial airflow, permitting rapid but nonpressed vocal-fold closure.

APPOGGIO DELLA NUCCA

QUESTION

You stress the importance of the support given the larynx by the musculature of the back of the neck. Please explain further.

COMMENT

Proper neck posture guarantees an axial body stance. If the chin and head are erroneously raised, the front of the neck feels lengthened and the back of the

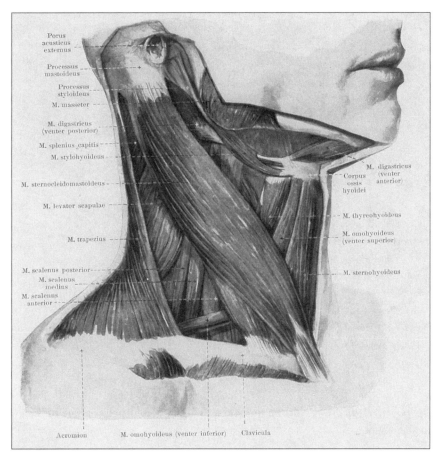

Porus
acusticus
externus

Processus
mastoideus

Processus
styloideus

M. masseter

M. digastricus
(venter posterior)

M. splenius capitis

M. stylohyoideus

M. sternocleidomastoideus

M. levator scapulae

M. trapezius

M. scalenus posterior
M. scalenus
medius
M. scalenus
anterior

M. digastricus
Corpus   (venter
ossis   anterior)
hyoidei

M. thyreohyoideus

M. omohyoideus
(venter superior)

M. sternohyoideus

Acromion   M. omohyoideus (venter inferior)   Clavicula

FIGURE 1.3. External-frame support of the larynx. (From Werner Spalteholz, *Handatlas der Anatomie des Menschen,* 13th ed., Vol. 2. Leipzig: S. Hirzel-Verlag, 1933.)

neck shortened. By contrast, in order to maintain the external-frame support of the larynx, the back of the neck should feel long and the front of the neck, short.

A number of structural muscles of the neck influence laryngeal positioning and function. These muscles assist in positioning the sternum and rib cage. Sternocleidomastoid, scalenus, capitis, and trapezius muscles originate in the region of the mastoid, with insertions in the front and back regions of the torso. (See figures 1.3 and 1.4.) The larynx lodges between the two great sternocleidomastoid muscles. If the larynx is to remain stabilized—neither rising nor falling during respiration and phonation—it requires firm support from the surrounding external musculature. Associated muscles of the back of the head and pharynx are part of this laryngeal support system, identified in the historic Italian school as

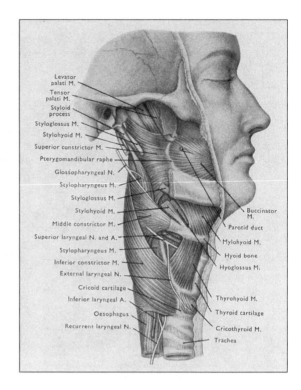

FIGURE 1.4. Lateral view of the constrictors of the pharynx, and the muscles of the face and throat regions. (From *Cunningham's Manual of Practical Anatomy,* revised by G.J. Romanes, vol. 3. London: Oxford University Press, 1967. By permission.)

l'appoggio della nucca. It is an important part of a complete technique of breath management.

EXPLAINING THE APPOGGIO TO JUNIOR AND SENIOR HIGH SCHOOL STUDENTS

QUESTION

How would you explain the appoggio to junior high and high school students? How would you work on it with them?

COMMENT

There is no reason why junior high or high school students cannot comprehend the primary mechanics of breathing, if those concepts are properly explained. An accurate understanding of the principles requires far less time to acquire than do the academic subjects that students of this age group are expected to master. An explanation of the actions of the musculature of the torso lies well within the comprehension of youthful singers. A few noncomplex anatomical illustrations may help. (See figures 1.1 and 1.2.)

Young people enthusiastically undertake the onset and the agility exercises that bring about the appoggio. These are within the competence of any healthy individual. By identifying and drilling these natural processes, development of the musculature requisite to the appoggio begins. Flexibility replaces tension; the singing timbre improves; phrase duration is extended. Motivated young minds and bodies can grasp and assimilate the concept as readily as can those of their elders. Youngsters and high schoolers are younger, not dumber, than the rest of us!

LA LOTTA VOCALE

QUESTION
What is meant by *la lotta vocale?*

COMMENT

In keeping with the historic Italian school, both Francesco Lamperti (fl. 1860) and Giovanni Battista Lamperti (bridging the nineteenth and twentieth centuries) advocated the older appoggio technique in opposition to the then emerging Germanic-oriented belly-breathing system. With the appoggio, the singer learns to stay in the position of inspiration for as long as possible. A frequent admonition from the Lamperti school: "The muscles of inspiration must not immediately give in to the muscles of expiration. Silent renewal of the breath takes place within postural quietude." *La lotta vocale* (French, *la lutte vocale*) describes the vocal contest during which muscles of inhalation endeavor to retain their initial extension in opposition to expiratory forces. Around 1860 Francesco Lamperti gave the classic definition of this engagement:

> To sustain a given note the air should be expelled slowly; to attain this end, the respiratory muscles, by continuing their action, strive to retain the air in the lungs, and oppose their action to that of the expiratory muscles, which is called the lotta vocale, or vocal struggle. On the retention of this equilibrium depends the just emission of the voice, and by means of it alone can true expression be given to the sound produced.

Appoggio technique results from breath retention, during which the inspiratory muscles do not early lose their tonicity. It makes certain that neither excessive airflow nor too much resistance to the exiting air is offered by the vibrating vocal folds. This can be described as *la lotta vocale.*

RIGIDITY IN THE SUPPORT MECHANISM

QUESTION

Can the support mechanism lock itself? I sometimes think that my students and I become rigid in trying to support the breath. How can this error be determined and prevented?

COMMENT

The two poles of bel canto are the ability to move and the ability to sustain the voice. A successful breath-management system cannot be constructed on rigidity. When stiffness prevails, the sound is not free. Isometric contact among the flat muscles of the abdomen remains intact during coordinated breathing, but at the same time, that musculature must be flexible. A fully resonant and vibrant voice avoids holding in any part of the instrument. Giovanni Battista Lamperti and the Italian School insisted that controlled singing ought to feel uncontrolled. Agility promotes flexibility in the abdominal wall.

Tension intrudes when a singer tries to control the breath process directly at either the abdomen or the larynx. As corrective measures, turn to hummed laughter, to quiet panting, to short velocity patterns, and to onset patterns with almost imperceptible silent breath renewals following each segment. Gradually attach sostenuto phrases to the same short agility phrases, retaining a sense of flexibility. These two abilities—agility/sostenuto—are complementary poles of cultivated vocalism.

Do not overdo the commendable premise that one should remain for as long as possible in the inspiratory position. Maybe the rubric might better read "Stay as long as possible in the inspiratory position, but only so long as is comfortable." Do not try to force expansion of the abdominal wall. Not all bodies are in identical condition. There may be a problem in trying too soon to increase phrase lengths; take a more gradual approach to the sustained portions. Perhaps "Don't try so hard!" would be a useful studio axiom.

RESONATOR/LARYNX/BREATH

QUESTION

You say the fundamental pitch is determined by the frequency of the vibrating vocal cords, and that the vocal tract above the larynx (supraglottic resonator system) serves as an acoustic filter that selects which harmonics will be prominent; all that helps determine formant balance. Doesn't it sometimes seem that shapes of the resonator system itself influence breath control and even freedom within the larynx?

COMMENT

What a perceptive query! The singer or teacher posing this question is aware that the singing instrument is tripartite, consisting of the motor (breath management), the vibrator (the larynx), and the resonator (the supraglottic vocal tract). The questioner is examining the symbiotic relationships among these three parts.

Technical proficiency in the singing voice requires (1) sufficient energy generated by the breath management (the motor) to match the degree of resistance offered by the vocal folds (the vibrator) and (2) vocal-tract configurations (the resonator) that produce the exact acoustic characteristics dictated by the phonemes. Put another way, each vowel has its own laryngeal and acoustic configuration, and a correspondingly specific resonator-tract shape must match that configuration; airflow excites the larynx into vibration, an action that activates responses in various regions of the vocal tract. Appoggio activity, laryngeal configuration, and vocal-tract shapes must be in agreement. Sometimes a singer may think that faulty breath control is the cause of inconsistent vocal timbre, when in actuality the resonator is not in sync with the breath supply; that is, breath management cannot become efficiently operative because laryngeal events are not being matched by vocal-tract postures.

A recurrent pedagogic message in these pages is that the voice of singing and the voice of speaking are complementary aspects of the same physical instrument. It is not necessary to abandon speech principles in order to build a singing voice. If the phonetic aspects of the phrase are distorted, laryngeal freedom is impossible. If lip, jaw, zygomatic posture, faucial-arch activity (including the velum), tongue position, and the location of the larynx itself are not in accordance with phonetic definition, breath management will not be optimum; there will be discomfort at the level of the larynx. The buccopharyngeal (mouth/pharynx) resonator plays a feedback role in laryngeal action. Relying on the functions of spoken phonation (while avoiding regional or pathological speech mannerisms, of course) permits natural coordination among phonatory components. The questioner wisely indicates that interplay among the three parts of the vocal mechanism (motor, vibrator, resonator) produces a synergistic relationship enabling freedom in singing.

SINGING ON THE GESTURE OF INHALATION

QUESTION

You sometimes tell a breathy singer to think of singing on the gesture of inspiration. What, exactly, are you advocating?

COMMENT

It is clear that unless the singer is indulging in abnormal voicing, phonation cannot take place during inhalation. "Sing on the gesture of inhalation" paraphrases a Giovanni Battista Lamperti concept, expressed over a century ago and frequently encountered in Italian studios of the mid-twentieth century. It counteracts the false notion that there must be consciously induced breath emission over the vocal folds in order to produce a singing tone.

At inspiration, subglottic pressure is at its lowest level and lung volume at its highest. During singing, the rate of expiration has to be retarded beyond that appropriate to speech. Staying as long as possible in the position of initial inspiration gives a sensation of singing on the gesture of inhalation rather than on that of exhalation. This concept is often helpful in maintaining the appoggio and avoiding breathy phonation, especially during extended sostenuto passages.

ATMOSPHERIC PRESSURE AND THE SINGING VOICE

QUESTION
What effect does atmospheric pressure (changes in location) have on singing?

COMMENT
At sea level, atmospheric pressure is exerted at approximately fifteen pounds per square inch. At inhalation, subglottic pressure rapidly falls below atmospheric pressure, and the volume of air in the lung is expanded. As air in the lungs diminishes, internal pressure below the glottis gradually rises, eventually surpassing atmospheric pressure. Remaining as long as possible in the inspiratory position, the singer retards the phases of the breath cycle (inspiration/phonation/ exhalation) by reducing the rates of breath emission and adjusting laryngeal resistance to the airflow, thus increasing the ability to sing long phrases. In techniques that do not adequately retard breath exit, there is a more rapid return to atmospheric pressure levels, followed soon by mounting subglottic pressure. (See Singing on the Gesture of Inhalation.)

Because of strong changes in atmospheric pressure, singers sometimes find that it takes time to become acclimatized to singing in locations of high altitude. At first, they may feel slightly short of breath. Generally, adaptation is relatively quick. A skillful singer will adjust normal appoggio procedures to meet the new environment.

THE BREATH-MANAGEMENT CANDLE TEST

QUESTION
What do you think of holding a candle about five inches in front of your mouth while you sing, to see if the flame stays straight or if it flutters?

An Italian teacher recommended that to me years ago. The flame was supposed to stay steady. Is that a foolish, old-fashioned notion?

COMMENT

The device described is centuries old. As a check on airflow levels, it is based on solid ground. When the appoggio is operative, there is minimal fluttering of the candle's flame during the singing of vowels, because most of the exiting breath is turned into tone by the efficiently vibrating larynx. A breathy tone production will produce marked fluttering of the candle flame. (For some singers, the front vowels are less problematic than the back vowels.) Even for a singer who remains well *appoggiato* (connected with the breath), the steadiness of the flame alters when plosives and fricatives are sung. For that reason, phrases which include nonpitch consonants are not suitable. If this trial is used, the singer should not clasp the candle in a hand, but place it on a solid surface free of air currents, about twelve inches away from the mouth, at a height directly in line with the mouth. I do not make use of the candle-flame test. It does not feel comfortable to have a burning candle positioned so close to the face, and the heat and odor are not conducive to carefree vocalism. There are better ways to monitor breathy production.

A related centuries-old feedback technique is to place the palm of one hand an inch or two in front of the mouth while singing a melodic phrase on a single vowel. A vowel sequence on a single pitch then follows. If a high level of breath emission occurs, warm exhaled breath registers on the palm of the hand. Little warmth from exhalation is felt if the exiting air is properly turned into tone by the vibrating larynx. Again, unvoiced consonants—in which the vocal folds are parted—give a strong response of warm air on the hand. This examination is a considerably friendlier procedure than the candle test. Although I do not consider it a major studio device, from time to time I have used it with good results.

More effective testing for nonbreathy phonation than either candle-flame or palm-of-the-hand monitoring is to place a hand mirror quite close to the mouth while singing. If there is high breath condensation on the mirror, the production is clearly breathy; a clean production of tone, free of a high rate of air expulsion, will show reduced condensation. Once again, nonvoiced consonants register high levels of airflow and are not appropriate to the test. Such a check may be useful in illustrating the principle that breath emission requires special, learned regulation during singing. I make occasional use of this stratagem with breathy singers.

Degrees of breath emission in singing can be measured by electroglottography (EGG), instrumentation that displays percentages of breath emission in breathy, normal, and pressed phonations. Modern voice research is in tune with centuries-old voice pedagogies that made use of whatever tools were available to provide feedback information on breath emission during singing. Candle, palm-of-the-hand, mirror, and EGG are related tests. The ultimate aim of each is to identify the differing degrees of efficiency in breathy, pressed, and normal phonations. Proficient airflow for singing is best developed by routining onset exercises that conclude with sostenuto phrases. (See Routining the Onset.)

EXPELLING AIR FROM THE LUNGS

QUESTION
I had a teacher who was very influential in my early training and whose ideas are still hard for me to get rid of. We practiced using up total lung capacity on every phrase. If any breath was left over, I had to expel it before taking a new breath. Otherwise, he said, I would be singing on stale air and injure my vocal health. Were these true or false assumptions?

COMMENT
The person who presented you with this hypothesis appears to have been misinformed about the actual events of the breath cycle. Vital capacity includes complemental, tidal, and supplemental breath. It is measurable by several spirometric instruments. (A spirometer registers the maximum amount of breath that can be quickly exhaled after forced inhalation.) Lung volume is dependent on individual physical structure; the way in which breath is efficiently used is determined by acquired breath-cycle habits. Although suddenly emptying the lungs in forced breath expulsion is a recognized method for measuring vital capacity, that maneuver does not contribute to managing the breath for singing. For example, vital capacity has nothing to do with the ability to sustain long phrases. A small soubrette may sing as long and as energetically as a barrel-chested baritone. What is important is how one paces the exit of breath to meet the requirements of extended phrases, not how much air can be inhaled or gotten out during expiration. This balance is achieved by retaining flexible antagonistic contact among the large muscles of the torso, which was established at the moment of deep inspiration. (See Appoggio versus Belly Breathing [*Bauchaussenstütz*]).

There are those who erroneously believe that exercises based on rapid breath expulsion alert a singer to the source of breath management: inhale deeply, then expel the breath in one quick, noisy action. This concept is not a part of the historic international technique, because it has no relationship to controlled breath management. Instigating early exhalation is detrimental to the pacing of airflow for the tasks of the literature to be sung. The appoggio technique of breath management is devoted to retention of the breath for as long as possible, not its induced, rapid emission. As is well known, the diaphragm, in cooperation with the intercostal muscles, is the chief organ of breathing. However, contrary to some assumptions, during singing the diaphragm is not consciously engaged as a means for pulling in new breath, nor is it used as an upward-driving piston for the expulsion of breath. Its upward motion is retarded by the musculature of the torso.

Abetting breath expulsion raises subglottic pressure; breath retention, appropriately applied, minimizes mounting subglottic pressure. This gradually acquired expertise becomes the earmark of skillful singing. Don't try to empty your lungs as you exhale, or as you sing, because it is not physically possible to do so; some residual breath always remains in the lungs. Instead, learn how to slow down the exit of the breath.

LEANING ON THE BREATH

QUESTION
Some teachers speak of "leaning on the breath" or of "the lean of the breath." Do you know what they mean? I don't.

COMMENT
Recall that the Italian verb *appoggiare* means "to lean on," "to be in contact with," or "to support." I do not use the expressions "leaning on the breath" or "the lean of the breath." But I can imagine that users of those terms may have in mind inducing proper muscle antagonism among the major flat muscles of the abdomen that are essential to the extended regulation of airflow in singing. Specific information as to how breath-management maneuvers can be accomplished through coordination of these muscles should be communicated to the singer. Only if a subjective pedagogic expression is precisely explained and demonstrated can exact information be conveyed. Although the above two expressions may indirectly refer to the appoggio maneuver, they lack specificity. What can they really mean without an explanation of how breath management works?

HOLDING THE BREATH

QUESTION
In terms of body sensations, how does holding the breath feel different from experiencing the appoggio?

COMMENT
"Hold the breath" is an unfortunate pedagogic admonition that encourages conscious stoppage of the breath at some point within this respiratory system, inciting laryngeal and abdominal tensions. Trying to hold the breath produces overly firm glottal closure and impedes flow phonation. An efficient technique of breath management produces exactly the opposite: breath flow is not held back but pragmatically paced (1) at its inhalatory inception, (2) during phonation, (3) at the mo-

ment of the release of the sound, and (4) at the replenishment of the breath. In free singing, nothing should be "held." To tell a student "Hold back the breath," "Hold onto the support," "Hold the high note," "Hold the long note" is to use counter-productive language. References to holding the breath are best eliminated from the pedagogic vocabulary. (See Rigidity in the Support Mechanism.)

NATURAL BREATHING

QUESTION
You have demonstrated different techniques of breath control from various teaching methods. My old teacher insisted I should never give any more thought to breathing for singing than I do for living. So what really is wrong with just plain old natural breathing?

COMMENT
In normal speech, phonation on a single respiratory cycle is generally of brief duration, seldom exceeding more than five or six seconds. The Shakespearean actor learns to elongate the phonation cycle, as does the professional public speaker. However, it is the elite singer who needs to be able to produce extended phrases at all tessitura and dynamic levels. Breath-management requirements for artistic singing far surpass those of speech.

Jussi Bjoerling could sing a fifteen-second passage in upper range, followed by a second phrase of equal duration, with only a split second between them available for breath renewal. The tenor who sings the long "Il mio tesoro" melisma on *cer–ca–te* in one breath will do so over thirteen to fifteen seconds (depending on the tempo insisted upon by the conductor and on the country in which the tenor is performing!). Leontyne Price, as evident in her famous *Voice of Firestone* video rendition of "O patria mia," produced one immense sustained phrase after another. Current classically trained singers aim for similar long-phrase ability.

Are these incidents of natural breathing? No. Although it is in accordance with natural function, natural breathing as employed for speech is not adequate to the tasks of cultivated singing. Breathing for singing is based on natural processes but must be enhanced in order to accommodate extended duration and intensity. *Homo sapiens* will drown if thrown into deep water, unless taught to swim. Swimming is based on learned physical skills made possible by adherence to natural laws; so it is with breathing for singing.

The reason for examining the several approaches to what is often termed "breath support" is to discover how they coincide with, or how they violate, the physiologic bases that permit natural functioning of the breath cycle, and to abandon premises that are inept or harmful. It might be assumed that only a breath-management system which accords with extended natural processes would be universally thought acceptable. However, some systems are founded on misinformation and false hypotheses as to how the breath mechanism works. These assumptions are often imaginative but not in accordance with what is known about physical function. "Natural breathing" then becomes an unnatural process for the singing tasks at hand. Perhaps in reaction to some of these false approaches, your teacher has stressed natural breathing. Yet, breathing for singing is not like breathing for mundane daily activity.

When the body is at rest, the breath cycle is about four seconds long, one second for inhalation and three seconds for exhalation (at times the inhalation/exhalation components of the cycle are nearly equally divided). The respiratory rate is not uniform from person to person, and it can be consciously varied. During speaking or singing, subglottic pressure rises, approaching atmospheric pressure. In sustained phonation, subglottic pressure achieves levels higher than those of atmospheric pressure; then the breath cycle, in response to reflex events, recommences. (See Atmospheric Pressure.)

Additional space does not have to be made in the vocal tract in order to renew breath supply, nor is air forcibly pulled in. Like water, air seeks the lowest possible level. When subglottic pressure falls at the moment of inspiration, air freely enters the vocal tract, the trachea, the bronchi, and the lungs. There is no mysterious column of air located below the lungs and diaphragm in need of being moved upward. The "column of breath" is immediately available, and is not sent to the larynx from the abdomen!

In order to extend breath-management capabilities, learned controls must be mastered. To achieve this, various procedures have been devised, some less efficient than others. It should be the purpose of comparative vocal pedagogy to examine the validity of premises that motivate these systems and to weigh each one against the rule of functional efficiency. A number of controversial breath-management techniques violate natural function. Most of these, influenced by regional or parochial tonal aesthetics, have origins in nineteenth-century national schools. Although numerous and varied, these contradictory techniques generally fall into three categories:

1. Internal abdominal thrust ("in-and-up" approach)
2. Hypogastric (pubic) distention ("down-and-out" approach)
3. International appoggio system of breath management.

Neither (1) nor (2) is physiologically tenable. In the first, proponents erroneously believe the diaphragm can be fixated in its lowest position by inward motion of the lower abdominal wall. The fallacy of this technique is at once apparent: the diaphragm is not located in the umbilical and hypogastric regions of the body. Indeed, the central tendon of the diaphragm is attached to the pericardium, in which the heart is housed. The central tendon of the diaphragm lies relatively high in the torso, approximately at the fifth rib; it can be topographically located by the origins of the mammillae (nipples) of the breast in both genders. The diaphragm follows the lateral anterior contour of the rib cage. It is not located at the navel. Diaphragmatic descent at inhalation, determined by the size of an individual's torso, is often less than two inches. It does not plunge some great distance downward to be grasped by muscles of the lower abdominal region. Inward thrusting of the lower abdominal wall forces an early ascent of the diaphragm, reducing the volume of the lungs and increasing subglottic pressure. Nor does the diaphragm descend for low notes, and rise for high notes, as some pedagogies claim.

Downward and outward thrusting of the abdominal wall actuates tensions in the lower trunk, generating sphincteral action not only in the lower trunk but also at the level of the larynx. Pressed phonation is a result. Pushing down on the abdomen causes the ribs to move inward and the sternum to fall. Further, low-abdominal outward thrusting reduces contact of the abdominal musculature with the eleventh and twelfth ribs in the low dorsal area. These actions diminish lung volume and contribute to the rate of rising subglottic pressure.

The most effective management for extending the normal breath cycle beyond normal speech requirements is to elongate the several phases of the cycle. In what is appropriate to quiet respiration and normal speech, the rib cage expands on inhalation, and gradually collapses on exhalation; the sternum begins to lower during phonation. Contrariwise, a skillful singer remains in the inspiratory position for as long as possible, maintaining a relatively high sternal position (taking care not to elevate it in military-parade manner), allowing muscles of the lateral abdominal wall to stay close to the position of inhalation and consequently delaying early rib cage collapse. Of course, something must eventually move—either the chest wall or the abdominal wall. Retarding these movements depends on an acquired, disciplined breath-management technique.

A technique of lateral abdominal-wall retention and the noble, elevated sternum has for centuries been known as the appoggio. Clearly, one cannot continue to inhale while phonating, but the singer can retard the upward surge of the diaphragm and the collapse of the rib cage by training the musculature of the abdominal wall, in cooperation with the pectoral musculature, to delay normal collapse of the breath mechanism. (See *La Lotta Vocale,* and Singing on the Gesture of Inhalation.)

Historic *attacco del suono* exercises, in which short phonatory onsets are sequentially repeated, reestablish low subglottic pressure levels. (See Routining the Onset.) Appoggio is an extension of the natural breath process, not a substitute for it. In this international technique, normal breath function is schooled to a degree that goes far beyond the "natural breathing" appropriate to spoken phonation.

TANKING UP FOR LONG PHRASES

QUESTION

I have several students who in the past used an approach they jokingly call "tanking up," recommended as necessary for long phrases. How can I get them to let go of the tension this excessive inhalation causes in the chest and rib cage?

COMMENT

Because we are air breathers, it is not unusual to want to "tank up" for heavy-duty activity. In every case, such hoarding of the breath operates negatively. Young children learning to swim, when first requested to put their heads under water, will "tank up." Subsequently, they must quickly expel the air in sudden explosion when they bring their heads up out of the water. Anyone engaging in this kind of forced inhalation falls prey to the Herring/Breuer syndrome: overcrowding the lungs induces a faster rate of breath expulsion. Singers who unwittingly "tank up," breathe clavicularly, indulging in what Herbert Witherspoon described as "the breath of exhaustion." G. B. Lamperti gave this advice: "Breathe to satisfy the lungs, not to overcrowd them."

There should be no visible chest displacement (or so minimal as to be scarcely perceptible) during inhalation, at phonation, or for breath renewal. During singing, the chest ought to retain its noble, nonrigid position throughout the breath cycle. (Watch videos of Leonard Warren or Eleanor Steber for superb examples.)

Your tanker-uppers probably are also noisy breathers. Insisting on quiet breath renewal helps eliminate clavicular breathing. Sometimes the silent breath renewal feels like no breath replenishment has been taken. Breathe slowly and quietly through the nose (see Nose Breathing), then transfer the same breath process to noiseless mouth breathing. The most practical way to discourage tanking up is to return to short onset exercises, outlawing all grabbing or holding of the breath. Building new responses takes time and persistence. (See Routining the Onset.)

PRESSED PHONATION

QUESTION

I'm a twenty-one-year-old tenor, a conservatory junior, and I have been told I am going to have a large operatic voice. This past summer I auditioned and was admitted to [a well-known program for college voice majors and advanced performers], and accepted to study with a famous teacher who teaches there in the summer. She told me that I have a problem because my top voice is pressed. It is true that there are times when it does feel tight when I sing up there, and it is never as easy for me to sing above high G or A♭ as below, except at forte level. This teacher put me on a series of sighing and yawning exercises starting in falsetto that were supposed to make my larynx relax and get rid of the pressed sound she heard. After about four weeks, I either had to go completely into falsetto in upper range or come back to what I had been doing before with my old teacher, with whom I thought I had been making a lot of progress.

I saw no improvement, after six weeks of falsetto singing in my upper voice, with the summer teacher. She also said I should leave my old teacher and transfer to the city to continue work in her private studio or at one of the schools where she teaches. I came back to my regular campus teacher this fall—against the summer teacher's advice. My old teacher tells me that it is okay to do some falsetto relaxation stuff, but he thinks that I need to go back to working half-step by half-step through the *passaggio* area, using normal [as opposed to falsetto, it appears] male resonance. I am confused. What do you think?

COMMENT

[In what follows, the term "falsetto" designates the imitative female timbre in the male voice, recognized in historic voice pedagogy as distinct from male *voce piena in testa*—full head voice. It does not, as in certain current pedagogies or speech therapy systems, consider falsetto as everything that lies above modal or chest register.]

Learning optimal coordination of laryngeal response to exiting breath, particularly in the upper range of a sizable young tenor voice such as you apparently have, cannot be accomplished over a summer. Nor does an ethical teacher recommend changing studios on the basis of such a brief encounter. Keep in mind that after auditioning you, she clearly liked your voice. She thought you sang well enough to admit you to her summer program and to invite you into her studio, a suggestion she has made, by the way, to a number of other exceptionally talented singers studying elsewhere.

In attempting to find the right balance between relaxation and energy, there may be times when you undergo excessive vocal-fold resistance to airflow (too long a closure phase of the folds within a vibratory cycle). That may be a temporary result of the search to find balance between energy and freedom.

Except for loud calling or yelling, males are unaccustomed to making sounds that lie above habitual speech-inflection levels. Many young tenors and baritones tend to grip and grunt as they sing beyond the speech range. Falsetto may sometimes prove helpful in momentarily reducing vocal-fold tension in the *zona di pas-*

saggio (passage zone) and in upper range. In light falsetto, the folds are properly elongated for the required pitch, but vocal-fold closure is not yet complete. Although falsetto may be used as a pedagogic device, relying chiefly on falsetto for upper-range production will not provide a satisfactory solution for achieving this balance. (See The Role of Falsetto in the Tenor Voice.) Work to coordinate energy and relaxation, step by step, throughout and above the *zona di passaggio,* in the manner your college teacher seems to be suggesting. I'm on his side!

INCREASING ENERGY BUT NOT VOLUME

QUESTION
When you advise to increase the energy but not the volume, what do you mean?

COMMENT
"Undersinging" is as destructive as "oversinging." Tonicity in every athletic endeavor must be commensurate with demands. It is not easy to achieve an appropriate balance between freedom and energy. Too often, there is little awareness of the degree of athleticism it takes to accomplish the advanced tasks of professional vocalism. By no means does this imply an increase in decibels. If sufficient technical skill is present, proper balance in the *chiaro* and the *oscuro* aspects of the chiaroscuro timbre can be produced at all dynamic levels. Energy is increased as the exiting breath is turned into tone by the vibrating vocal folds, in exact accordance with the requirements of vowel, tessitura, and intensity. As pitch ascends, the vocal folds elongate, and the ligament (the innermost edge of the vocal fold) becomes tauter, while the influence of the vocalis muscle is altered. Vocal-fold stretching presents greater resistance to exiting air. To avoid excess of mounting airflow, as well as to avert slackening of vocal-fold closure, the abdominal wall remains near its inspiratory position. Comfortably retaining, and at times increasing, natural antagonism among the transverse abdominis, the internal and external obliques, and to some extent the rectus abdominis, engenders high levels of energy. A skillful singer learns to increase energy without augmenting decibels.

UPPER-DORSAL BREATHING

QUESTION
I was taught that there should be a space/stretch sensation between the shoulder blades when singing. Is this true?

COMMENT

Stretching muscles of the shoulder girdle during inspiration, and retention of it for singing, follows a clearly identifiable tenet known as upper-dorsal breathing. It is advocated in a segment of the traditional English School. It yields slightly raised and rounded shoulders, with torso, head, and neck positioned forward. As the clavicles rise and fall, sensations in the trapezius and related shoulder-girdle muscles can readily be mistaken for increased inspiratory action. In battling what he considered a false pedagogic viewpoint, noted baritone and prominent voice teacher Herbert Witherspoon termed such breathing "the breath of exhaustion." The uppermost fibers of the trapezius muscles, in cooperation with sternocleidomastoid and scaleni muscles, can extend the neck. This method causes chest displacement and loss of contact between upper and lower torso muscle groups. It is not possible then for the transverse abdominis, the internal oblique, the external oblique, and the rectus abdominis muscles to remain in suitable relationships. Clavicular breathing is noisy and labored.

In contrast to Witherspoon's sage warning against clavicular breathing, John Newburn Levien, noted English voice teacher/author, advised singers to move the elbows outward from the sides of the torso, and to raise the shoulders "before the drawing in of breath." He postulated that this action would allow the upper part of the lungs to be filled with air, an admonition that clearly induces high-chest breathing and is patently without basis in cumulative pulmonary action.

William Shakespeare, outstanding English singer, teacher, and author, is a continuing major influence on British voice pedagogy. He suggested in his *The Art of Singing* (1921) that a singer should breathe "as high as possible" without giving up elasticity of the points of the shoulders. He requested ample expansion of the upper back, to be felt under the shoulder blades. He further advocated a sense of muscle interlocking under the shoulder blades. William Vennard, in his unique and invaluably comprehensive volume on the mechanics of singing, *Singing: The Mechanism and the Technic* (revised 1967), correctly pointed out the error of Shakespeare's hypothesis: Shakespeare deceived himself. He advocated using shoulder muscles for inhalation, pulling shoulders forward. In so doing, this British tenor/teacher was allied with long-held, recurrent English pedagogic viewpoints.

Only in compensatory breath-renewal methods that produce both chest and abdominal wall displacement are the muscles of the shoulder girdle consciously activated during singing. In contrast, the system of the historic international school ensures quietude of shoulder girdle, chest wall, and sternum, accomplished through retention of the inspiratory position of the abdominal wall. From practical studio and performance standpoints, singers who try to make space in the upper-back region ("space/stretch") inevitably decrease tonus of the pectoral muscles. They diminish the stabilization offered the laryngeal scaffold by the sternocleidomastoids, the scaleni, and the capitis muscles (the system of external-frame support).

Breath renewal cannot occur silently in clavicular breathing. As a result, most upper-back spreaders have high rates of breath emission, often in conjunction with straight tone. Upper-dorsal breathing is found among nonoperatic British singers who adhere to the "cathedral-tone" aesthetic, and far less frequently among those who pursue operatic careers. Although fading somewhat in popularity, this technique can still be found in England, Australia, New Zealand, and parts of North America—wherever the Anglican choral tradition continues to flourish. Parenthetically, it is remarkable that a talented singer with a good ear and musical sensibilities may manage to negotiate performance demands despite adhering to compensatory technical maneuvers. A logical question: "Why continue to do them when there are easier and better ways to sing?"

NOSE BREATHING

QUESTION
Why, in a number of slow, breath-pacing exercises, do you ask the student to breathe through the nose?

COMMENT
Breathing silently through the nose retards arrival at full breath capacity. It allows the singer to pace the inspiratory gesture over a period of time. Further, nose breathing induces relaxation of the vocal tract: the body of the tongue lowers slightly, as does the larynx, and the zygomatic muscles elevate the fascia of the cheek region. As a result, the velum is slightly elevated, even though velopharyngeal closure does not take place until a nonnasal phoneme is produced. This slow gesture of inhalation ideally positions the vocal tract, the larynx, and the musculature of the abdominal wall, enabling *la lotta vocale*. (See *La Lotta Vocale.*) Noisy breathing, with rising and falling torso, is a major problem. When noise accompanies inhalation, the vocal tract is not relaxed. Breathing through the nose while maintaining an axial position diminishes the propensity toward chest displacement and brings tranquillity to the breath process. The same kind of silent breath, fast or slow, is then taken through the mouth.

Breath-pacing exercises should be done rhythmically. For example, in a comfortable range, devise an onset measure of quarter notes to be sung at moderate tempo, with a silent breath after each note; conclude with a brief sustained phrase. Pacing can be shortened or lengthened to correspond to intervals of rest between phrases. Over time, the technique will ensure the avoidance of breathy onsets, and prevent the holding of the breath in advance of the next phrase.

AIR PRESSURE LEVELS IN HIGH AND LOW SINGING

QUESTION
Does it take more breath pressure to sing high than to sing low? I have noticed in my own singing, and in that of my students, that after singing high for a while, it is sometimes difficult to feel free when coming back into middle range. The voice feels as though it has too much breath pressure behind it. How can I work this out?

COMMENT
The question concerns adjustment of breath-energy levels when moving directly from high range to low range. (Loss of volume in low range, as a result of singing extensively in high range, is a different matter. See Low-Range Loss in the Female Voice after High-Range Singing.) It takes more concentrated breath energy to sing in upper range than in lower range. With ascending pitch, gradual adjustment of the vocal folds for the elongation process, and the increase of vocal-fold resistance to airflow, occur. In a descending scale, it is sometimes difficult to regulate reduced levels of breath energy to match vocal-fold shortening. Breath pressure then remains too high. The singer should learn to gradually relax the energy rate. (A just as frequently encountered related matter concerns reducing breath energy too quickly.)

Go from moderate tempo to adagio sostenuto exercises that bridge middle and upper ranges, as in 1−5−1−5432−1−5−1 patterns; gradually carry them upward, then downward, in shifting key sequences. Slightly increase the "support" factor on the short upward intervallic leap and cautiously diminish it on the downward interval from upper range to middle range. Make certain that the descending passing notes undergo step-by-step energy adjustment. For ironing out discrepancies in energy levels from one range to another, use upward and downward octave intervals, moving to neighboring keys by semitones. No matter how efficient the technique, excessively aggressive work in upper range can contribute to vocal fatigue that manifests itself upon the return to middle and low ranges.

CORRECTING HIGH-BREATH EMISSION LEVELS
IN YOUNG FEMALE VOICES

QUESTION
I have an eighteen-year-old female student with unusually breathy phonation. She has been checked by an ENT and has no vocal-fold pathologies. How can I address this?

COMMENT

Young women often exhibit higher levels of slack breath emission than do young males. Young men frequently suffer from the opposite defect: pressed phonation. These characteristics may in part be attributable to role expectations society dictates for the genders, with their marked differences in laryngeal size and structure. Most males feel the need to increase energy for pitches lying above the speech range. As she ascends the scale, a young female may hesitate to augment the energy level for singing beyond her usual speech level, because in heightened speech or laughter, many upper pitches are already easily accessible to her. In the question posed, there is no indication that excess breath is limited to upper-middle or upper range, areas of the scale where lack of energy is most marked in many young female voices. Since the student has no evident voice pathologies, it is safe to assume that the problem is technical.

Breathy singing in any category of voice results from high levels of airflow passing over less than fully adducted vocal folds. Breath should be turned into tone by the vibrating larynx. If there is meager resistance by the vocal folds to the exiting breath, breathy phonation results. What's important is not how much breath one can get out of the lungs, but how one paces the release of the breath. With breathy female voices, the aspirated onset is best replaced temporarily by the light glottal attack—not to be confused with the heavy *coup de glotte*. The glottis is lightly closed in advance of phonation, so that airflow is retarded. Another useful device for correcting breathiness in the onset is use of the unvoiced consonant /k/, which restricts airflow until the vowel is sung. Its paired voiced consonant /g/ produces similar results. The /m/ hum also is helpful in eliminating excess airflow, because the lips are closed and the sound emerges less directly, by way of the nose. The more securely the appoggio is established, the sooner excess breath emission will disappear.

SINGING ON THE BREATH

QUESTION
Do I understand you to say that you do not use the common expression "Sing on the breath?" What are your objections?

COMMENT

High airflow rates that precede phonation elicit breathy timbre. A hallmark of good singing is the exactitude of prephonatory tuning in which precise vocal-fold approximation and breath energy levels meet. The historic *attacco del suono* (attack of the sound) achieves onset precision. Subjective expressions such as "Sing on the breath" are perilous. Singers told to sing on the breath often misunderstand that expression to mean they must initiate a flow of air on which tone is then introduced ("Ride the tone on the breath"). Some teachers believe that such language helps the singer to stay *appoggiato,* or that it avoids vocal-fold resistance to airflow. However, if loose breath is passed over the vocal folds before adding tone, the activity of the abdominal wall in its air-retention role is slackened, and efficient glottal closure is negated. It is far better to be specific about how to routine the regulation of airflow. (See Resonator/Larynx/Breath.)

BREATHY SINGING IN YOUTHFUL FEMALE UPPER RANGE

QUESTION
Please address breathiness in the high register of many young females. Why, when there isn't a breathy sound in the middle and low ranges, should the upper range sound breathy?

COMMENT
As pitch ascends, the vocal folds elongate. This stretching process becomes more marked in pitches beyond speech level, increasing the degree of vocal-fold tension during the vibratory cycle and causing the closure phase of the vocal folds to last longer. With mounting pitch, an increase in breath energy accompanies this longer duration of vocal-fold closure. Breathiness among underenergized young females (and some males) often occurs at the *secondo passaggio,* because the vocal folds have increasingly elongated and breath resistance is rising. The way to correct disequilibrium between these two contingencies is to discover a proper balance between mounting pitch and rising energy. (See *La Lotta Vocale.*)

ENERGY LEVELS IN TENOR AND BARITONE VOICES

QUESTION
Does it take more energy for a tenor to sing in upper range than for a baritone to do so? Does it require greater energy for a tenor with a substantially big voice to sing high A, B, or C than for a lighter tenor? Can a tenor extend his performable upper range by incorporating falsetto into performance? I have a fairly big tenor voice. I think I use more energy than many baritones.

COMMENT
In considering differences in technical procedures among categories of male voices, we must take into account the physical size and the speaking range of

the individual instrument. The *primo passaggio* (first register pivotal point) of the tenor occurs about a minor or major third above the *primo passaggio* of the baritone. The *secondo passaggio* (second passaggio) lies roughly a fourth above the *primo passaggio* in each voice.

When the *primo passaggio* is reached, breath energy needs to increase beyond that appropriate to normal speech. A gradual augmentation becomes more marked in the *zona di passaggio.* (This "passage zone" covers the approximate scale segment of a fourth, lying between *primo passaggio* and *secondo passaggio* demarcations.) Further increases in breath energy and vocal-fold elongation are required for pitches that lie above the *secondo passaggio,* the *voce piena in testa* of international voice pedagogy, commonly known as "head voice." Corresponding vowel modification (*aggiustamento*) is dependent on the location of individual *passaggi* pivotal points.

Were vocal literature concentrated in identical ranges for the tenor and the baritone, the question regarding shifts in degrees of energy would be less significant. However, the tenor generally has tasks of tessitura extension and of energy application that outweigh those of his baritone colleague. For example, with the *La bohème* score in hand, compare range requirements for baritone Marcello and for tenor Rodolfo. Rodolfo's *zona di passaggio,* assuming a lyric tenor voice of good size, lies between D_4 and G_4; Marcello's passage zone is located roughly a third lower: $B\flat_4/E\flat_4$. (See Appendix I for pitch designations.) It becomes apparent upon leafing through the Puccini score that Marcello has relatively few notes above his *secondo passaggio,* whereas Rodolfo has note upon note above that point in his comparable scale.

Significantly, it is not easier for a tenor to sing above his *secondo passaggio* than for a baritone to do so above his. Rodolfo's vocal folds are more frequently elongated and his breath-energy levels remain repeatedly higher than Marcello's. In regard to the performance literature for the two vocal categories (from the mid-nineteenth century onward), many opera, oratorio, and song literatures support findings similar to those cited from *La bohème.* However, the baritone who sings the Rossini Figaro, Rigoletto, and the Leoncavallo *Il prologo,* will also have a more than average share of notes to be sung above his *secondo passaggio.*

What of light versus heavier instruments within each general category? Again, the answer is relative to where *passaggi* events occur for any voice within the comprehensive categories; heavier voices have slightly lower *passaggio* events; lighter voices, higher. It takes less energy for a *tenorino* or *leggiero* tenor to sing $F\sharp_4$ or G_4 than for a large lyric or *spinto* tenor, because the *tenorino* and *leggiero* are still slightly below their *secondo passaggio* points, whereas the ample lyric and the *spinto* are already at or above theirs. In similar fashion, because of differences in registration events, it requires less skill for a lyric baritone to sing an $E\flat_4$, or an E_4 than it does for a dramatic baritone, a *basso cantante* or a *basso profondo.* The underlying density of orchestral scoring, and the size of other dramatic voices around one, contribute to the need for enhanced energy.

Although less marked, similar events pertain in female instruments. A soubrette or a soubrette coloratura has a far less daunting task in sustaining B_5 than does the *spinto* soprano, the dramatic soprano, or the dramatic mezzo-soprano. The ease with which the lighter female voice negotiates the extreme upper range is not necessarily due to better technical facility than that of heavier-voiced colleagues, but to the fact that those pitches lie in less demanding relationships to her *passaggi* events.

One of the problems in training tenor voices comes from a misconception that the tenor voice is a high, light instrument, quite distinct in character and timbre from that of the baritone. In nonprofessional quarters, it is sometimes fallaciously assumed that in upper range the tenor should aim only for an easy "head" sound, as though all high-lying pitches in every male voice were to be delivered with no greater energy than is used in the execution of pitches lying an octave below. Neither "relaxing" nor "placing the tone in the head" is a solution for the successful production of upper range; it is the appropriate tonicity among the muscle groups involved in the ascending scale that produces the free *voce piena in testa.* To treat tenor voices as though they were all *tenorino* or *leggiero* instruments is to induce passionless, tepid, unsupported vocalism.

The inexperienced teacher of tenors may assume that upper range is but an incorporation of the falsetto timbre that almost every male is capable of producing. In actuality, the tenor makes no more use of traditional falsetto in performance circumstances than does the baritone. Although there are distinct and important uses for falsetto in developing ease for the negotiation of vocal registers in male voices, it plays no role in professional public performance, except in comic imitation of female vocalism. No major premier tenor publicly sings his upper range in traditionally designated falsetto quality. Persons who resort to falsetto as a performable upper extension of the tenor voice generally do so out of an inability to achieve proper freedom in upper range, or because of false premises as to how male registers are produced. Timbre terminology for the singing voice is further obfuscated by misapplication to the singing voice of modal/falsetto definitions appropriate to speech therapy.

Baritones and tenors must be capable of vital vocalism as well as of introspective timbres. A tenor who incorporates falsetto into upper range as a performance timbre is unable to perform the standard repertoire with its demanding high-lying tessitura in *voce piena.* Energy levels ought to be high enough to produce balanced spectra in all ranges of the voice. There are rare moments of purposeful vocal coloration in the lied or the *mélodie* where falsetto production may be acceptable, but in singing the *cavatina* or the *cabaletta,* at either *p* or *f* dynamic levels, falsetto is not viable. (See The Role of Falsetto in the Tenor Voice; Pressed Phonation; Falsetto and Airflow; More on Falsetto.)

PRECISION IN THE RELEASE

QUESTION

I think I do the right thing when starting most phrases, but I feel like something goes wrong when I release the last note of a phrase. Even if I am not out of breath, I experience an increase in tension and a change of voice quality. Any help?

COMMENT

You raise an important technical point. Breath management has to do with five specific components:

1. Quiet initial inhalation (paced inspiratory gesture)
2. Clean inception of sound (the onset)
3. Duration of phonation (the phrase length)
4. Precise termination of sound (the release)
5. Immediate breath replenishment (silent renewal of the breath).

If the release of the phrase is not precise, subsequent breath renewal lacks freedom. Regardless of the length, shape, or dynamic contour of a phrase, it must be completely sung to its point of termination (the release). Regardless of dynamic changes or phrase contour, there should be no letting down of tonal consistency or of breath energy at phrase termination. Regardless of the rapidity with which ensuing phrases occur, the release of the breath must be as clean as the onset. A primary rubric: Energize throughout the phrase to the point of release. The release itself becomes the renewal of the breath. Return to exercises that combine mastering clean onset, sustained phonation, precise release, and silent pacing of breath renewal. (See Routining the Onset, and Singing on the Gesture of Inhalation.)

SENSATION ASSOCIATED WITH MELISMATIC MOVEMENT (THE BOUNCING EPIGASTRIUM)

QUESTION

Is the bouncing epigastrium that we read and hear about, here and there, a fallacy?

RELATED QUESTION

What should be the sensation in the abdomen when I sing a lot of fast notes in a run? I'm wondering what the abdominal muscles do and what they should feel like when they do whatever it is they do! Does the abdomen accentuate every note by a small movement, or is that done with the throat? I hope something happens in the throat, because I have trouble making my abdominal muscles move that fast.

COMMENT

Vocal phrases often include turns, shakes, and longer groups of running notes. A short pattern (usually three, four, or six notes) is termed a *gruppetto*. Melismas, roulades, and runs generally consist of series of *gruppetti*. Quickly occurring articulated passages can be accomplished in either staccato or legato mode. In either, abdominal wall movement, not conscious throat action, should be the germinating source.

In velocity patterns, the extent to which abdominal articulation is felt depends on the degree of swiftness, emotion, or bravura of the passage. An irregularly oscillating abdominal wall indicates a lack of firmness, with slack breath management. Singing must never be consciously controlled from the throat. However, in the execution of agility passages, if each individual note of the melisma is delivered by aspirated /h/ articulation, the singer may get the impression that the throat has participated. In considering these questions, both aspirated and nonaspirated articulation must be examined.

Natural, flexible abdominal-wall action takes place in stifled laughter. Recall the schoolchild mirthfully rocking behind teacher's back, hand over mouth so that no sound escapes. Epigastric/abdominal-wall bouncing in suppressed laughter can be felt and minimally seen. The same kind of movement occurs in audible panting. Place the hands on the anterior/lateral abdominal wall during several seconds of stifled laughter, and while silently panting, note the gentle, flexible action that takes place in the epigastric/umbilical area and at the sides of the torso.

As a practice device, it is helpful to establish awareness of this action by executing a single pitch in comfortable speaking range on a rapid *Hm–hm–hm–hm Hm!* sequence. Then with the lips open, use a sixteenth-note pattern, as though engaged in quiet laughter, concluding with a quarter note. This articulated *gruppetto* has a slight aspiration (/h/) before each note. Next, raise it to higher pitch and dynamic levels. Now, apply *Ha–ha–ha–ha–Ha!* to a quickly descending 5–4–3–2–1 motif. In all maneuvers, the abdominal-wall, epigastric, and umbilical regions—remaining engaged—evidence slight articulatory movements. This exercise serves well as a device for initiating articulatory sensations in the abdominal wall.

Next, execute the same patterns without the assistance of /h/, as in *Ah–ah–ah–ah–Ah!* The glottis automatically closes in advance of each onset. Abdominal-wall articulation happens while the singer remains *appoggiato* (that is, retains the basic inspiratory position that occurs initially during the breath cycle). There is a gentle, almost imperceptible epigastric bouncing action during the articulatory drill, but no inward pulling or outward pushing. This technique should become normal performance procedure for both articulated legato and staccato passages.

Because of the depletion of breath capacity, the abdominal wall eventually must move inward at the conclusion of an extremely long phrase. This inward motion is not necessary in phrases of average length or during the execution of brief agility *gruppetti.*

Turn to brief, rapid agility patterns built on scale passages (e.g., 123——1234—–12345) in comfortable low-middle range, first in staccato fashion, then legato. For either, the nonaspirated onset (*ah,* as opposed to *ha,* is now used). Alternation of quick staccato and legato modes follows. Using an aspirated agility pattern alerts the singer to abdominal-wall action. But as soon as this agility energy source has been located, articulated legato (no /h/ insertions permitted) should become the aim. The small articulatory movements that occur in singing staccato are then retained in the legato. A good pedagogic rubric: Sing the pattern in staccato; repeat it immediately in legato, while retaining identical articulatory action.

Whether in staccato or legato, abdominal wall movement is the generator of melismatic articulation. Radiologic examination indicates that the diaphragm responds to these diminutive articulatory motions by providing impetus for the precise apportionment of measured, exiting breath. The vocal folds react by turning the minute puffs of air into tone. One has the feeling that there is an immediate and precise correspondence between minimal airflow and vocal-fold approximation.

After several short patterns have been mastered, longer passages such as an ascending/descending nine-note scale should be introduced. Traditional triadic and arpeggiated patterns ought to be adapted to these alternating staccato and legato styles. In summary, whether singing staccato or legato, the same articulatory motions take place in the anterior/lateral abdominal wall.

Excerpted passages from familiar sources of the performance literature serve as splendid melismatic vocalises. For soprano: Handel's "Rejoice Greatly" and "O Had I Jubal's Lyre"; for mezzo-soprano, Purcell's "Iris, Hence Away!" and Rossini's "Cruda sorte"; for tenor: Handel's "Ev'ry Valley" and Mozart's "Il mio tesoro"; for the low-voiced male, Handel's "See the Raging Flames Arise!" and the triplet passages from Mozart's *Le nozze di Figaro,* "Hai già vinta la causa!" Based on portions of each, short melismatic vocalises of several bars may be constructed. Transposed sequentially, they serve as excellent drills for establishing articulatory movement. In literatures for all voices, some agility passages require only slight articulation, while others demand marked accentuation. The degree of articulatory action determines the extent of discernible epigastric movement. To be avoided at all costs is an artificial impulsing (shaking) of the abdominal wall as a means for generating either articulatory movement or vibrato.

Because bel canto literature is based on the ability both to sustain and to move the voice (note the *cavatina/cabaletta* juxtapositions of innumerable arias) in systematic voice training, the agility factor should be early introduced. Indeed, until velocity facility is acquired, sostenuto singing will never be totally free. As previously stated, melismatic passages can be accomplished through the aspiration of each note, a favorite device among some choral conductors who hope to obtain clean melismas though the constantly inserted /h/. Such melismatic technique is exceedingly inefficient because of breath loss at each aspiration. The maneuver has no place in the solo literature, and a doubtful one in choral music. However, consecutive velocity patterns are sometimes so rapid (as in many Rossini arias) that it may prove temporarily helpful to introduce the first note of each *gruppetto* with a slight aspiration. However, singing bel canto pyrotechnical arias in constant "Ha–ha–ha–ha–Ha!" manner is neither stylistically correct nor aesthetically pleasing.

For all singers, agility patterns should be part of the daily technical routine. Because of their freedom-inducing nature, they ought to be among the first exercises in every warm-up session. They are intended not solely for voices singing literature that calls for frequent coloratura and fioritura passages, but for voices of every *Fach* (category).

ABDOMINAL-WALL MUSCLE CONTACT

QUESTION
I have noticed that when I do my best singing, my abdominal muscles seem to gently contact each other. That is, the deeper muscles seem to feel they are being pushed out a little—more toward the sides than directly in front—and the muscles of the outside wall resist them. It doesn't feel tight, but it does feel like the muscles are firmly balanced against each other. I assume this must be necessary to sustain an even air pressure without blowing everything out all at once. When I sing this way, long phrases are much easier. Hey! Is this the appoggio?

COMMENT
Francesco Lamperti would say that you are properly keeping the muscles of inspiration from giving in too soon to the expiratory gesture. You are remaining as long as possible in the inspiratory position without holding your breath. You are harnessing natural antagonism among the abdominal muscles. You have a very good grasp of the appoggio process and of sensations that accompany it. (See Appoggio versus Belly Breathing [*Bauchaussenstütz*].)

POSTURE

ALWAYS NOBLE AND AXIAL?

QUESTION
You speak of being "axial" and "noble." How can a singer remain axial
and noble while responding to all the stage business that opera and
music-theater directors demand of us?

COMMENT
Regardless of the performance medium, it is neither possible nor desirable
to hold to a rigid, static body posture. In fact, there are no physical movements or
body positions that a stage director may request that cannot be accommodated
(unless bizarre contortion is required at high vocal climaxes). However, because
the relationship between breath management and phonation is fundamental to
solid technique, physical alignment must become standardized procedure. Maintaining a noble position does not mean that it is never varied to meet dramatic ob-
ligations. Head, neck, and torso alignment can pertain in standing, walking, dancing, fencing, bowing, kneeling, sitting, or lying down. In fact, all can be ideal for
singing. Stage movement benefits vocal freedom (not to be mistaken for rhythmic
weaving and bobbing). Because of the body alignment it induces, a number of
singers find lying down on stage can actually be beneficial to vocalism. In any postural stance, the head can be turned to either side without disturbing the basic axial

posture. But all movement during skilled vocalism must be based on initial axial relationships.

In extreme ranges or exceedingly difficult passages, if the singer is requested to assume various body positions, a stage-wise singer knows how to handle them. In the opening passages of "Ecco ridente in cielo," while serenading Rosina, Almaviva must gaze up to her balcony. But as he approaches his *secondo passaggio,* or when singing above it, a clever count looks back at his mandolin, thereby reestablishing an axial posture. Pelleas must look upward to Melisande's tower as he reaches for her hair, but he will wisely return to a noble position in approaching the subsequent dramatically intense high-lying passages, thereby avoiding laryngeal elevation.

For Romeo, dawn does not break with an overhead sun. Rusalka's moon need not shine directly above her so that she has to look at the ceiling while executing demanding passages of high tessitura. The eyes of both Rusalka and Romeo can be focused at the near horizon. Suor Angelica's highly emotional imploring of heaven's help is technically disadvantaged if she stares upward in search of spiritual sustenance. God and the Saints listen at all levels. He, they, and we will appreciate Angelica's vocalism better if she maintains a noble petitioner's position, allowing her to sing out toward the house rather than to the last row of the topmost balcony. Experienced singing artists learn to maintain optimum vocalism while complying with dramatic stipulations.

BREAKING STANCE AND SHIFTING THE BODY WEIGHT

QUESTION
Describe more fully what you mean by breaking stance and shifting one's weight.

COMMENT
Inexperienced singers, trying to keep erect posture, tend to cement themselves to the floor of the stage. They stand with feet firmly planted and move only from the waist as they attempt to communicate the text; the torso typically sways slowly back and forth in response to rhythm or to phrase length, but the feet never move. This rigid fixation of legs and of feet bears no relationship to the body language of spoken communication. How often does a speaker sway from side to side? Never, except to portray distress or madness. In speaking privately or publicly, we do not weave rhythmically back and forth from the waist, but we do make slight alterations in our stance. We do not separate the body into two parts—the lower half consisting of the hips and the legs, the upper half of the torso and the head. We remain axial, but from time to time we shift our weight.

During singing, the weight of the torso should be seldom equally distributed on both legs for long periods of time, unless we are being as statuesque as the Commendatore, or pretending to be invisible. Body language is altered now and again by shifting from the right leg to the left leg; then the reverse process. Arms are relaxed, occasionally making small emotive movements, as in narrative speech, while avoiding meaningless gesticulation. As a new thought or emotion arises in the text or music, while remaining axially poised, we occasionally shift the body—a nearly imperceptible half-step forward or half-step back—while still retaining noble posture. At a later moment, we return to the original position. During the singing of a lied, a *mélodie,* or an art song, such occasional shifting of stance is in response to the drama or mounting emotion. On the opera and music theater stage, the performer finds independence from rhythmic servitude. Accommodating the varied pace of the drama, one learns to walk out of rhythm, to make predetermined movements that appear free of the musical structure. The technique of altering body language through weight-shifting is an integral part of producing a believable stage persona.

Intermittent shifting of stance produces performance freedom and dramatic authenticity. It places an audience at ease as well. Stance alteration removes the artificiality of singing an hour's recital, appearing like a statue attached to the crook of the pianoforte or being rigidly positioned center stage for the aria. Occasional weight-shifting also avoids the wiggling, jiggling, and meaningless gesticulations that seem, like a communicable disease, to beset some solo and group performers. But don't overdo it.

THE SWAYBACK SINGER

QUESTION
How can I get my student not to have a concave curve in her back; that is, how can I correct her swayback posture? When she stands erect to speak or sing, her spine is not straight; it curves inward.

COMMENT
Without meaning to appear facetious, the briefest reply to that question may well be "Are you certain that you want to try to straighten her spine?" The human spine is not constructed in a perpendicular line. There is a natural series of inward and outward curves of the spinal column that serve to balance the head, the neck, the shoulders, and the sacroiliac region. This system extends even to the calves and ankles. Attempts to force the flexible spine into a perpendicular axis is foreign to balanced human body alignment. There is no need to improve on the natural design of the human spinal column for singing.

As a bipedal creature, *Homo sapiens* does not go on all fours with a luxuriant tail to be flicked about to express anger or pleasure, or to help maintain balance while leaping from tree limb to tree limb. Nor do our necks and snouts extend forward, as is the case with most members of the animal world. We have no need to swallow and smell at the same time, in order to ward off predators, nor do we have to keep our bellies close to the ground while stalking. Our mandibular and buccal musculatures are not adapted to the same functional needs as the epiglottic/laryngeal constructions of other mammalian species. The spinal columns of even extinct *Homo erectus* and Neanderthal Man were differentiated from those of the higher apes by greater axial alignment. There is no need for today's soubrette to imitate her household pet by adopting a condition predating the evolution of the curvaceous human spine. Why should any voice pedagogy recommend such postures?

Concern for straightening the spine has led to eccentric vocal hypotheses. One is the tilt-and-tuck method, in which the request is to tuck the buttocks in, and to tilt the pelvis forward, in order to place the spine in a position appropriate to your four-footed golden retriever. In humans, this tilted posture forces the sternum lower, so that the pectoral muscles lose their tonicity, the ribs move inward, and the diaphragm ascends more rapidly. Although tilting and tucking may place the spine on a perpendicular axis, human locomotion undertaken during such a body misalignment can offer some amusing results, especially on stage. The related "gorilla posture," advocated by one segment of voice pedagogy, is meant to negate spinal curvature. Bending the legs slightly outward at the knees, to straighten the spine and find relaxation, is another questionable practice. Throwing the shoulders backward in a military posture will inordinately sway the back, as will excessive elevation of the sternum.

Contrary to what is sometimes assumed, rarely does problematic swayback occur among singers, although some performers with little natural tendency toward spinal curvature may exaggerate axial balancing by inducing swayback. Having the singer stand on one foot while balancing the body, then move to the other foot, with head, neck, and torso in alignment, helps eliminate any tendency to forced curving of the back.

Unwarranted concern for the shape of the spine is based on questionable physiologic assumptions, including the notion that all heads fit exactly the same way on all shoulders, and that every head is placed in an upward, direct line from the shoulder girdle. Regardless of how straight the spine or how round the shoulders, the back of the neck should feel long and the front of the neck short, not the other way around. The ears ought to seem lined up with the spine, with the weight of the torso carried to the balls of the feet, producing natural curvature of the spine. Attempts to straighten the spine reveal how the art of singing can be impaired when limited physiologic information is applied. If the noble position produces a normal amount of "swayback," so be it!

THE FALLING STERNUM

QUESTION
I teach that the sternum should remain relatively high to allow full expansion of the ribs. Some of my young students seem to be able to retain that position quite well, but with others, the sternum begins to fall fairly early in a long phrase. Then, of course, the next breath is noisy and incomplete. Any suggestions?

COMMENT
The answer for a falling sternum lies in coordinating all of the musculatures of the torso: pectoral, epigastric, umbilical, and abdominal. It is not a matter of trying to keep the sternum up or of holding out the ribs. Chest displacement during long phrases is a common problem for young singers not yet thoroughly grounded in stable breath management. I find that the best way to eliminate this problem is to break long phrases into briefer segments and to initiate each portion by short onsets. Finally, the segments are reunited. This helps to maintain something close to the inspiratory position of the torso, engendering quietude in the region of the pectorals and sternum, even during longer phrases.

THE GARCIA POSITION

QUESTION
What, exactly, is the Garcia position you recommended to several singers, and what does it accomplish?

COMMENT
Late eighteenth-century and early nineteenth-century treatises on singing often point out the need to assume a noble position before breath inhalation, and to continue it throughout a song or aria. Breath is renewed while postural elegance is retained. This position ensures that the sternum is relatively elevated, the shoulders are comfortably back and down, while an exaggerated military stance is avoided. Then the rib cage remains nearly stationary throughout all phases of the breath cycle; there is little visible evidence of chest displacement or abdominal-wall instability during any phase of the cycle. A technique for perpetuating this position consists of the singer crossing hands, palms outward, at the lower dorsal (back) area, just below the twelfth rib (bottom of the cage). This is called the Garcia position, because Manuel Garcia advocated its use as a practical device for assuring

optimal posture during singing. Although Manuel Garcia *fils* is usually credited as its originator, the procedure had already been described by Manuel Garcia *père* in the early nineteenth century (c. 1825). It was later favored by members of the Lamperti School, and recommended by Mathilde Marchesi (1826–1913) in her 1901 practical vocal method. The noble pose it produces is the main route of current international vocalism.

Crossing the hands at the sacroiliac, palms outward, brings the pectorals into proper relationship with the clavicles, the sternum, and the rib cage. When the rib cage is thus poised, the muscles of the lower abdominal wall are free to expand on inhalation. This posture stands in direct opposition to techniques that falsely recommend a lowered thorax and shoulder girdle as necessary to "relaxed" breathing. The Garcia position avoids outward abdominal thrusting of the belly, practiced by one segment of the German school. (See Appoggio versus Belly Breathing [*Bauchaussenstütz*].) It also distinguishes itself from conscious inward abdominal pulling on the epigastric/hypogastric areas advocated in several late nineteenth-century and early twentieth-century regional European techniques. The Garcia maneuver assures normal curvature of the spine, elevates the thoracic cage and the pectoral muscles, and balances the stance. (See The Swayback Singer.)

Paired pectoral muscles, each with clavicular heads attached to the collarbone and sternal heads attached to the breastbone, configure the rib cage so that it can reach full expansion. Inasmuch as the lungs are housed in a pleural sac within the rib cage, full breath capacity is achievable only when the ribs are fully extended and the diaphragm is allowed to make its limited descent. Although other muscles of the torso, such as the serratus, the trapezius, and the latissimus dorsi, are not breathing muscles but postural muscles, their structural help is necessary for proper rib-expansion posture.

The pectoral muscles, originating in the upper-chest region, extend downward, covering much of the costal region. Upon deep inspiration the abdominal muscles expand, engaging in antagonistic contact. (Muscle antagonism is the mechanical principle on which most physical action depends.) Constituting the outward abdominal wall, these muscles have sources on the pelvis and hipbone, extend upward, and terminate as insertions in the ribs as high as the fifth rib (level of the nipple of the breast). Muscles of the torso form a structural unit, the pectoral muscles coursing downward and the abdominals running from the pelvis and the hipbone to the sternum.

The torso is not divided into lateral segments of pectoral, epigastric, umbilical, and hypogastric regional muscle functions, each under separate control, as is sometimes assumed. There is cooperation among the perpendicular, large, flat abdominal muscles that cross the body from bottom to top, and the pectoral group that runs from the clavicles nearly to the bottom of the rib cage. In the historic international school, the muscles of the upper and lower torso synergistically delay chest displacement, thus avoiding early rib-cage collapse. However, it must not be assumed that during a lengthy phrase it is possible to remain completely in the inspiratory position. At phrase termination, the umbilical/epigastric musculature gradually moves slightly inward, but the sternum, the rib cage, and the lateral abdominals remain near their initial inhalation position. The Garcia posture is a pedagogic tool that tends to bring these muscle systems into natural convergence. Of course, no singer should keep hands crossed at the back during performance; the device is only an occasional practice assist. The Garcia position induces quietude of the torso. It can be combined with other freedom-inducing maneuvers such as sitting, kneeling, or walking. (See Physical Movement during Singing.)

SINGING IN THE SUPINE POSITION

QUESTION
It seems bizarre when you have a singer lie down to sing. What does this achieve?

COMMENT
Lying on the back places the entire body, head to toe, in alignment, and the sternum is dissuaded from falling. In the supine position, the head, neck, and torso remain axial, and problems of laryngeal positioning, voice registration, and clavicular breathing are avoided. Without modifying the axial line, the subject moves the head freely from side to side, but head, chin, and larynx are not elevated.

When singing while lying on the back, it becomes even clearer that the lateral/anterior abdominal wall is the source for managing the breath. First, breathe in and out normally, without thinking about singing. Note that the sternum remains stationary during both inspiration and expiration, and that the rib cage expands without pectoral displacement. No tension is present in the hypogastric (low pubic) region. Next, momentarily experience the inefficient effects of pulling inward on the abdominal wall or of pouting the wall outward or downward. Notice the extent of rib-cage displacement in both of these defective actions.

The breath-pacing maneuver performed in the supine position makes the appoggio process fully apparent. Follow a series of Farinelli breath-pacing exercises with groups of onset motifs, agility patterns, and sostenuto phrases. (See Routining the Onset, Silent Breathing Exercises, and the Farinelli Maneuver.) Because of increased awareness of contact among the flat muscles that cross the abdomen, any tendency to pull inward or to push outward on the abdominal musculature can be sensed and eliminated. Entire songs and arias can be sung from the supine position.

Lying down while singing is the first in a series of technical maneuvers. Next, sit tall, cross the legs, and place the arms in the Garcia position while executing the same group of exercises or phrases that was undertaken while lying down. Axial posture must be perpetuated. Then sing identical series of vocalises or literature phrases from a kneeling position, still remaining axial. Rise and sit well balanced on a desk or table, feet not touching the floor. Again assume the Garcia position as the same patterns are sung. Finally, stand and repeat the phrases or exercises. In all of these positions, an axial body posture should be sustained. While singing, walk backward and forward, then remain in place. (See Garcia Position.)

SITTING OR STANDING TO VOCALIZE?

QUESTION
I do a fair amount of vocalizing while seated at the piano. Does it matter whether I sit or stand when I sing?

COMMENT
Physical position doesn't matter as long as you keep the head, neck, and torso aligned. Because of a feeling of compactness when one is seated, some singers gain an additional perception of secure breath management. If you teach, or do vocal modeling for your students, while seated at the piano, guard against turning the head to one side. When you do your own daily technical work, avoid always vocalizing from one static position. Stand, sit, move about; assume the postures of normal activity. Remember that in stage productions the position of the body must be adjusted to the requirements of the dramatic situation. Do not become accustomed to singing only when seated. It should not supplant the standing posture as chief performance position.

PHYSICAL MOVEMENT DURING SINGING

QUESTION
I am curious why you sometimes ask people to walk slowly backward, then forward at the same pace, as they perform a song or an aria.

COMMENT
Posture and stance are important determinants for establishing an optimal physical framework for singing. The vocal instrument is not simply the larynx but the entire body. Surrounding the larynx is a muscle system that can balance the

head and neck on the torso. A number of these muscles have origins in the region of the mastoid bone, located just behind the ear. Among the strongest and more important is the sternocleidomastoid pair. They originate at the sternoclavicular joint at the anterior base of the neck, where the clavicles (collarbones) and the sternum (breastbone) connect. They terminate in the posterior mastoid region. The trapezius, as its name implies, has a trapezoidal shape, with origins in the back of the neck, from which it descends to cover much of the upper dorsal region. Turning the head sharply to the side delineates three observable triangles at the front and sides of the neck, in an area formed by the sternocleidomastoids and the trapezius muscles. The larynx lodges between the strong, supportive sternocleidomastoid muscles. At the nuchal region (back of the neck), the scaleni muscles (singly, the scalenus) have their origins at the mastoids. These muscles progress downward and attach to the first and second ribs, and act as rib-cage positioning agents. Other torso/neck/head alignment muscles are the capitis and the spinalis, which originate in the nuchal area. They attach to the cervical and thoracic vertebrae.

Not infrequently, when performing emotive, dramatic music or when trying to increase audience communication, some singers lose body alignment, leaning forward from the trunk or raising the head upward and forward, taking away natural external-frame support of the larynx. Even in stationary upright position, a less than fully skillful singer may lose contact between the pelvis and the rib cage if the sternum drops, the pectoral muscles lose their tonicity, or the head migrates upward and forward. By elevating the larynx and shortening the vocal tract, these postures cause muscle imbalances and resonance distortions. There are several devices for helping a singer to reestablish body alignment:

1. Walk slowly backward while singing. It would then be unusual to thrust the head and neck forward and upward, or to position the head and the larynx downward.

2. Sit axially erect, the firmly planted buttocks forming a foundation and the torso lifting upward from it. The spine has a natural sacroiliac inward curvature, and the shoulders do not slump. The head remains in a normal speech-communication position, neither raised nor lowered. Practicing onsets in this position ensures good breathing habits. Sing series of onsets and several phrases from the sitting position. Rise gradually to a standing posture, maintaining the same axis that prevailed during sitting. (See Sitting or Standing to Vocalize?)

3. Sing from a kneeling position on both knees; the torso feels more compact. While slowly singing 1–5–1, 5–4–3–2–1 patterns, alternate kneeling, standing, and backward walking, followed by walking forward, then kneeling and standing again, all at unhurried pace. Such movements ensure good posture regardless of physical activity. As with all technical maneuvers, these devices can be adjusted to the individual

singer's need. Their use should be judiciously applied. (See Garcia Position; and Singing in the Supine Position.)

NECK TENSION

QUESTION

Some of my students develop a lot of tension in the back of the neck as they sing. It seems as though they do not have enough strength in their necks, particularly when going into upper range. Are problems of neck tension fairly common, and what can be done about them?

COMMENT

A number of teachers agree with me that most tensions in singing that are not related to breath management, occur in one or more of three locations: tongue, jaw, and neck. In every case, while singing brief phrases, small freedom-inducing movements restricted to the specific region are recommended. Sometimes neck tension occurs especially in high-lying phrases. Have the student, while singing, move the head from side to side in very small motions while keeping a perfect alignment of head, neck and chest, thus inducing looseness in the neck. The torso remains quiet, except for the minuscule side-to-side head movement. Then eliminate the movements, retaining the sense of freedom in the back of the neck. (Similar quick, side-to-side shaking movements can be applied separately to tensions of the tongue or jaw.)

The external-frame support structure of the larynx includes the muscle system at the nape of the neck, where the nuchal muscles lodge. Much neck tension can be traced to weakness or slackness in the neck musculature. To strengthen this muscle group, without singing, turn the head slowly sidewise—left to right, then right to left—until the sternocleidomastoid muscles offer resistance (that is, until the head cannot be turned farther). This maneuver exercises and strengthens the posterior muscles of the neck. Do these movements for thirty or forty seconds at a time, then roll the head on the shoulders in circular fashion several times. Finish with a series of quick, easy side-to-side shakes of the head. These exercises ought to be done daily. (They are not for persons with cervical disk or spinal problems.) Pull-up exercises also develop the nuchal as well as the pectoral muscles.

There are "bobble heads" among singers, people who raise and lower the chin and the larynx in response to phrase direction. These imperfections vitiate the *appoggio della nucca*. Working with two mirrors (hand mirror observation of the body profile in a full-length mirror) alerts the singer to such unwanted actions. (See *Appoggio della Nucca*.)

CAN THE HEAD BE HELD TOO LOW?

QUESTION
One of my teachers advocated raising the head in order to free the larynx. You seem to be opposed to lifting the head in general during singing, and especially at high pitches. Isn't there also a reverse problem? I have seen some public performers, males in particular, who keep the head very low all the time. Their production sounds heavy. Is there a head position that you consider too low for efficient production?

COMMENT
Indeed there is a low head position unfavorable to the singing voice. There is no need for what I sometimes term "turtleing," a low head position that presses the submandibular muscles downward on the larynx. The head should be held neither high nor low, but remain in the communicative position of normal speech. Above all, the head must not elevate for ascending pitch nor lower for pitch descent. Mostly, problems of laryngeal choreography that occur during pitch change have to do with neglect of posture and a lack of skill in negotiating the *passaggi* pivotal points.

NECK PROTRUSIONS DURING SINGING

QUESTION
What does it mean when sometimes even quite good singers show veins and arteries in the neck region, particularly at the end of long phrases and in upper range? The sides of the neck seem to enlarge. It looks like the performer is straining, even when it doesn't sound that way.

COMMENT
Some singers of slight, thin, ectomorphic build, when speaking or singing, show surface activity in the neck. Their long, slender necks are thinly padded. Heftier, somatotonic bodies have wider and thicker neck structures that do not readily display external structures as subglottic pressure is increased. During quiet breathing, the glottis opens; there is no vocal-fold resistance to airflow. In phonation, the vocal folds engage the exiting breath stream. As the fundamental pitch is raised and breath energy is added, resistance increases. An augmentation of vocal-fold resistance to airflow during long, sustained breath cycles makes the exterior neck structure more visible, as does heavy-duty lifting, pulling, or related isomet-

ric activities. Elevated subglottic pressure affects both the cardiovascular system and the muscle systems of the neck. Muscle antagonism in any part of the body brings clearer muscle definition, but enlargement of the leaders of the neck at phrase endings, or in high-lying passages, may be indicative of excessive subglottic pressure or of excessive muscle antagonism. Protuberance of the sternocleidomastoid muscles is sometimes mistaken for enlargement of the external jugular vein. These robust muscles show greater definition if there is excessive resistance to airflow in long, high-lying phrases. (See *Appoggio della Nucca,* and Neck Tension.)

Females with long, slender necks display more observable movement than do more sturdily built women or most males. In fair-skinned, slightly built persons, a related phenomenon is occasional heightened color in face and neck. In some females, spots of insignificant flushing on the neck and on the uppermost regions of the chest become visible. (See Flushing of the Face and Neck.)

LARYNGEAL AND
INTRALARYNGEAL FUNCTION

MYOELASTIC/AERODYNAMIC SOURCES OF VOCAL-FOLD VIBRATION

QUESTION
What is myoelastic/aerodynamic voice production?

COMMENT
Janwillem van den Berg, noted Dutch scientist and researcher, in his seminal article "Myoelastic-Aerodynamic Theory of Voice Production" (*Journal of Speech and Hearing Research* 1: 227–244, 1958), convincingly promulgated the hypothesis that vocal-fold vibration is produced by the coordination of muscle tension and breath pressure. He did so in rejoinder to Raoul Husson's neurochronaxic principle, which suggested vocal-fold vibration is determined by events initiated by rapid excitation of cells of the recurrent nerve that consequently place the vocal folds into vibration. Van den Berg declared the now generally accepted premise that the vocal folds provide a muscle (myoelastic) response to airflow (aerodynamic) events. In contrast to nonvoiced sound, voiced phonation in speaking and singing is dependent on the vibratory action of the vocal folds in response to airflow that sets them in motion.

Much of voice pedagogy is directed to the adroit coordination of the vibrator (larynx) and the motor (breath mechanism). A reliable breath-management technique assures proficient myoelastic-aerodynamic collaboration for the tasks of

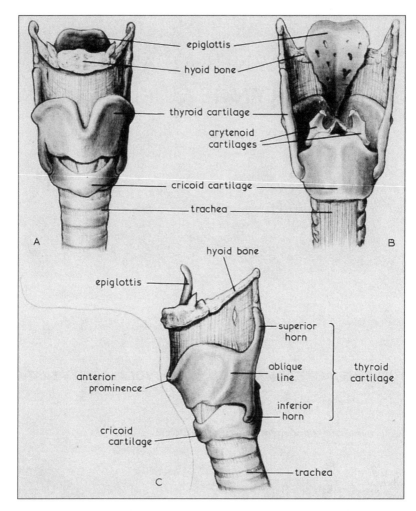

FIGURE 3.1. The hyoid bone, cartilages, and muscles of the larynx. (From Meribeth Bunch, *Dynamics of the Singing Voice*. New York: Springer-Verlag, 1982. By permission.)

singing. The age-old appoggio pedagogic system illustrates the practical application of van den Berg's myoelastic-aerodynamic theory of voice production. Figure 3.1 shows the relationships among muscles and cartilages of the larynx.

ABDUCTION AND ADDUCTION

QUESTION

What do abduction and adduction mean with reference to what the vocal cords do in singing?

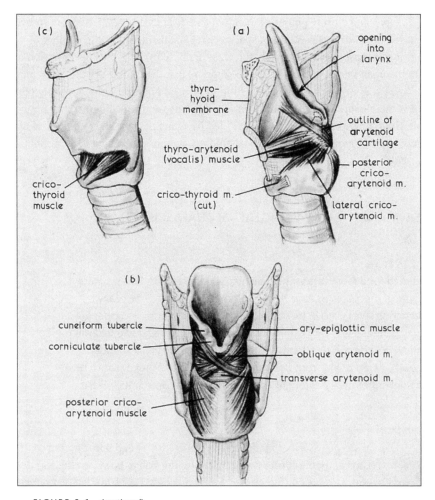

FIGURE 3.1. *(continued)*

COMMENT

Abduction is movement away from an established median line, as in the opening of the glottis in quiet breathing. Adduction is the drawing toward a median axis, as in glottal closure. During heavy-duty activities such as lifting or pulling, and in normal pitch-based phonation, the vocal folds are adducted. For the voice of singing, both heavy and slack glottal closure should be avoided.

In a proficient voice technique, at the moment of inspiration, the vocal folds swing cleanly away (abduct) from the median position. At phonatory onset, they approach the median line (adduct), initiating the vibratory cycle that produces tone. The number of cycles per second of vocal-fold approximation determines the fundamental pitch. For example, at A-440, the folds approximate 440 times per second (See Appendix I for pitch designations.)

Open and closure phases of the glottis are balanced in nonpathologic speech. That relationship pertains during speech-level vocalism, but as the number of vibrations increases for rising pitch, the closure phase of the glottis becomes longer than the open phase. A danger for the singer is that the glottal-closure phase may become excessively prolonged, resulting in pressed phonation. An opposing peril is that the closure phase will not sufficiently increase, producing breathy phonation. Both potential defects can be avoided by managing the right amount of airflow for the appropriate level of vocal-fold resistance, subtly adjusted throughout the scale.

HEAVY AND LIGHT LARYNGEAL MECHANISMS

QUESTION

I studied for a few years with a teacher who insisted on two separate laryngeal mechanisms, one heavy and the other light. The heavy mechanism was used in low voice; the light mechanism, in upper voice. My experience was that this registration technique never allowed me to achieve a unified scale. (I am a baritone.) Before my voice sounded smooth, when going from one range extreme to another, I had to give up thinking of heavy and light mechanisms. Your comments, please.

COMMENT

Speech science ascribes modal and falsetto to lower and upper regions of the voice, respectively. In the professional male singing voice, however, falsetto designates a specific timbre (differentiated from *voce piena in testa*) that is produced by less than complete vocal-fold closure. Except for use by the countertenor, it is generally not a viable performance timbre. In traditional voice pedagogy, modal voice is termed "chest voice" (*voce di petto*), and upper range is designated as "head voice" (*voce di testa*). A few teachers refer to these two functions as heavy and light mechanisms. Most singers find a region between chest and head, the *zona di passaggio,* where a mixture of "chest" and "head" takes place. While in modal (chest) register, the folds are thickest and fattest, whereas in traditional head register (*voce piena in testa*) the mass reduces as the folds elongate, while timbre remains vital. It is generally conceded that the weightiness of the lower range ought not be carried into the upper range. This is probably what the teacher who described light and heavy mechanisms was hoping to achieve, rather than requesting two distinct scale segments.

What distinguishes the sounds of these two main regions of the scale? A young male may be able to call out pitches loudly, or shout them in the *zona di passaggio* (registration passage zone), but he should not do so because of continuing vocalis influence as the vocal folds attempt to elongate for higher pitches. His voice may "break." Prolonged shouting in upper range causes vocal discomfort and invites pathologies. As pitch rises, the vocal folds are stretched and their mass diminishes. Heavy/light mechanism terminology leaves an impression of distinct either/or function. Wrong interpretation of heavy mechanism/light mechanism terminology can be detrimental to a unified scale. That seems to have been the questioner's experience. Every note in an ascending/descending scale produces slightly shifting relationships among the muscles involved in pitch change. This is particularly the case in upper-middle and upper ranges of the male voice. An even scale depends on the process of *aggiustamento,* a graduated adjustment, not on choosing between two opposing mechanical agencies.

FALSE VOCAL FOLDS

QUESTION
Where are the false vocal cords located? Are they ever used in singing? Do they produce falsetto?

COMMENT
The false vocal folds (ventricular folds) are part of the larger muscle complex that includes the true vocal folds. The false folds are not operative in normal, nonpathologic phonation. When the vocal folds are viewed laryngoscopically, the false vocal folds appear to lie just above the true vocal folds. (See figures 3.2 and 3.3.) The underside of the false folds forms the roof of the sinuses of Morgagni (ventricular sinuses, or laryngeal sinuses) that lodge between the false and true vocal folds. Inasmuch as the false vocal folds are not used in normal phonation, it may be wisest to refer to them as ventricular folds rather than false folds, and to call the pair of sinuses that lodge between the ventricular folds and the true vocal folds, the ventricular sinuses.

Questions as to the possible role the ventricular folds might play in phonation are frequent among singers, particularly when several late-twentieth-century sources incorrectly state that falsetto timbre is produced by the false vocal folds. The ventricular folds are involved only in pathological phonation that produces a hoarse, raspy quality which may deliver several noisy phonations simultaneously. The result is sometimes described as the "Louis Armstrong sound." (There is no certainty that Armstrong actually produced his unique vocalism by involving the ventricular folds.)

In schooled singing of an ascending scale, the true vocal folds elongate and

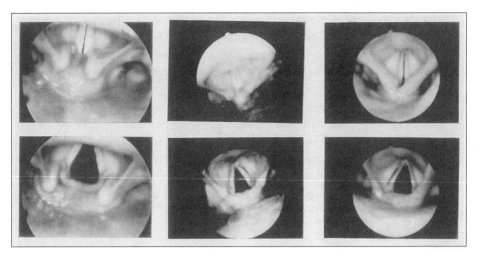

FIGURE 3.2. Vocal folds of three professional sopranos during singing; upper row in phonation, lower row in inhalation. (From Vocal Arts Center, Oberlin Conservatory.)

their mass diminishes; the ventricular folds retract so that the dimension of the sinuses of the larynx (ventricular sinuses) is increased. In unskillful singing, the ventricular space becomes diminished as the true vocal folds move upward toward the false vocal folds. Tomograpic studies of the larynx of a professional operatic tenor singing series of vowels on pitches A_2, A_3, and A_4 (low A, middle A, and high A) indicate that the ventricular sinuses of the larynx are an integral part of the trained singer's resonation system. As the true folds elongate during the singing of high pitches, the ventricular folds tend to retract, producing more space in the ventricular sinuses. In the case of an amateur tenor singing the same protocol with a consistently high laryngeal position (*Knödel, voce ingolata,* throaty voice, or necktie tenor), the ventricular sinuses nearly vanished in upper range, and the ventricular folds approached the true vocal folds. Ventricular contribution to resonance was nearly eliminated, and the resultant quality was thin, edgy, twangy, and pinched. It is a timbre, joined with nasality, sometimes heard among popular vocal entertainers.

The same phenomenon has been observed in forms of belting. Space between the true vocal folds and the ventricular folds is greatly diminished, so that the ventricular sinuses are reduced as contributors to vocal resonance. During many forms of belting, the larynx is in an elevated position, thereby inhibiting the normal rocking/gliding maneuvers of the thyroid and cricoid cartilages as pitch ascends; "chest" voice prevails. This seems to affirm that in such systems, the mass of the vocal fold cannot as readily be reduced for rising pitch, as can occur in skilled, elite vocalism. Elevating the larynx and reducing the space between the false and true vocal folds is considered a register violation in classical

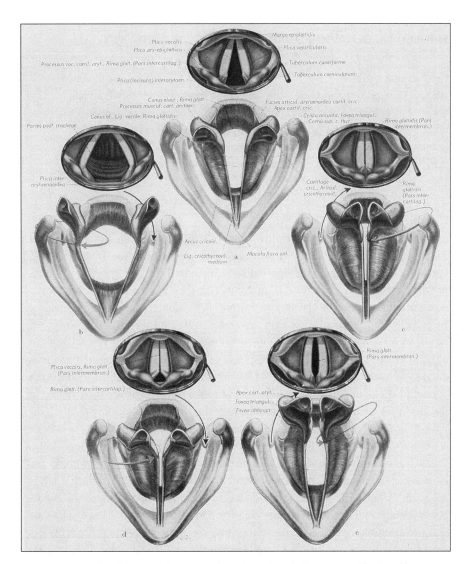

FIGURE 3.3. Glottal shapes, with correspondent schematics to indicate arytenoid action: (a) at rest, (b) in complete inhalation, (c) in phonation, (d) in a form of whispering, and (e) in one type of falsetto singing. (From Eduard Pernkopf, *Atlas der topographischen und angewandten Anatomie des Menschen,* 3rd ed. Munich: Urban & Schwarzenberg, 1987. By permission.)

singing but appears to be considered acceptable in some belting techniques. (See Belting.)

The term "falsetto" does not universally enjoy a single definition, having diverse meanings in the scientific and historic voice teaching communities. (See More on Falsetto.) However, there is general recognition in both the scientific and the performance worlds that falsetto singing does not involve the ventricular folds. Any published source maintaining that they do is not reputable.

EPIGLOTTIC BEHAVIOR DURING SINGING

QUESTION

We saw in your X-ray and fiberoptic films that some singers showed a fair amount of epiglottic movement when going from front to back vowels, while with other singers (those most of us judged as being best), the epiglottis stayed relatively stable, not obscuring the vocal folds from view. What conclusions as to technical skill can be drawn from that information? Can a singer learn to control epiglottic movement?

COMMENT

The observant questioner draws attention to an intriguing current question for all persons interested in voice pedagogy: epiglottic behavior. In swallowing, the epiglottis lowers, guiding ingested substances to the esophagus, thus protecting the larynx and trachea from intrusive matter. (See Figure 3.1.) During phonation, the epiglottis moves in response to vowel definition, its posture determined by tongue mobility. Normally, in a front-to-back vowel sequence, as in /i–e–ɑ–o–u/, laryngoscopic view of the vocal folds is unimpeded on the front vowels, but the epiglottis lowers over the larynx in response to the tongue's movement for the production of back vowels. In vocal-fold examination, the laryngologist requests the patient to speak or sing the vowel /i/, because the vocal folds are then visible in the laryngeal mirror. That is why in a laryngeal mirror examination, the laryngologist pulls the patient's tongue forward and requests a high, sustained "ee" (/i/).

In front vowels, the foremost portion of the tongue is in its highest position, producing more space in the pharynx. In back vowels, the tongue lowers in the front and rises in the back, thereby lessening pharyngeal space. (See Early Covering in the Young Male Voice.) It could be assumed that similar physiologic events occur during singing, as indeed they do for a majority of singers. However, as the questioner correctly observes, there are some singers who define the vowels exceedingly well while exhibiting limited epiglottic movement (other than that associated with vibrato) during vowel-defining changes. Further, they often are singers of high-level performance capability. Yet none of our subjects were taught to locally control the epiglottis.

With singers who engage in heavy "cover," the epiglottis lowers severely, at times approaching the swallowing position. Although there are no specific exercises for directly controlling the epiglottis, emerging evidence suggests that in phonations which display a good balance among the fundamental and the formants— producing the chiaroscuro—the epiglottis tends to move less during vowel change. At this moment, reliable conclusions cannot be drawn, because controlled studies have not been undertaken, nor has a sufficiently large population of subjects at varying levels of accomplishment been assembled. Plans for a study that compares speech and singing modes are under way.

THE TRACHEA AS A RESONATOR

QUESTION
Is the trachea part of the resonator system? Can a singer learn to bring
tracheal resonance into the tone, or to exclude it? Is it involved in chest
voice?

COMMENT
The trachea (windpipe) is the channel through which air passes into the
lungs, by means of tracheal bifurcation, at which point the bronchi lead into the
lungs. Because the lungs are composed of spongy material, they cannot serve as
resonating cavities; the lungs themselves make no contribution to subglottic resonance. The term "chest," when used to describe the low singing range, is largely
based on bronchotracheal responses and on low-range sensations produced by
sympathetic vibration delivered through bone conduction and experienced in the
region of the sternum and the rib cage. William Vennard (*Singing: The Mechanism
and the Technic,* pp. 86–89) cited studies on bronchotracheal resonance conducted
by Weiss, Wilcox, Scripture, Stanley, and van den Berg. He concluded: "Every
time a compression wave is created above the glottis, the pressure below the glottis is decreased: that is, a rarefaction wave is formed; and vice versa, the pattern
that goes up also goes down. The fact that it is in reverse makes no difference, the
frequencies are the same." Zenker and Zenker, investigating "tracheal pull" in the
mid-1960s, described a form of fixed resonance associated with low pitch. Recent
researchers propose theories as to the extent tracheal and bronchial resonance can
be induced in so-called chest register, and have speculated as to how subglottic
resonance may affect vocal-fold behavior, but no uniformity of viewpoint prevails.
Because the trachea cannot be consciously controlled, it is doubtful that information on its role has extensive practical application for the singing artist.

ELEVATING AND LOWERING THE LARYNX

QUESTION
I have read that a singer can raise the larynx to produce one kind of
timbre and lower it for another. How does that fit in with your insistence
on a stabilized laryngeal position during singing?

COMMENT
From the early 1940s to the mid-1960s, laryngeal depression for singing
was a relatively popular pedagogic concept in North America. It was based on the
notion that elongation of the vocal tract (through extended laryngeal lowering)

would produce beneficial resonance by increasing the strength of the first formant. (See Maintaining the First Formant [the Oscuro Factor].) This hypothesis still has a minority of adherents on both coasts of the North American continent, in some segments of Nordic/Germanic schools, and even within a few widely spread voice-therapy systems. Of course, if a high laryngeal position causes pathological problems for the speaking voice, therapeutic devices that lower the larynx may temporarily improve phonation. On the other hand, requiring the healthy speaking or singing instrument to assume an abnormally lowered larynx may induce other pathological behavior.

Unintentional laryngeal elevation during singing often happens at register pivotal points. However, one twentieth-century American pedagogue of note advocated the "sword swallowing position" for the head and neck as a means of "freeing the larynx," thereby purposely inducing a high laryngeal position. High laryngeal position is also present in prevalent pop-vocal styles where thin, twangy, reedy timbres are encouraged. Some segments of the French school still teach that raising the head and larynx achieves a favorable posture for singing. Many untrained singers, including "the untrained professional," produce a thin timbre when the larynx is high.

The larynx is but one component of the tripartite vocal instrument: (1) the motor (the breath mechanism), (2) the vibrator (the larynx), and (3) the resonator (the vocal tract). These components do not operate independently of each other. Unconscious internal and external muscle synergy, as well as airflow levels, dictate vocal-fold behavior and vocal-tract filtering. The larynx is lodged in a cartilaginous house between the two strong sternocleidomastoid muscles, and is supported by a composite muscle group that operates within a complex system. (See figure 1.3.) An additional group of nuchal (nape of the neck) muscles are part of the external frame that stabilizes the larynx during strenuous singing tasks. They include the scaleni, the capitis, and the trapezius muscles. (See *Appoggio della Nucca*.)

In classical singing, the larynx ought to remain as stable as possible, neither rising nor lowering appreciably for pitch change or breath renewal. The larynx should not pop up at the release of a sung tone or phrase; breath renewal must take place without inducing fundamental changes in laryngeal position. Even if the singer is a tall bass or bass-baritone, with long neck and large laryngeal prominence displayed by the thyroid notch, external laryngeal movement with pitch change should remain nearly indiscernible.

For an intentional disembodied, ethereal tone, or for a mysterious interpretative effect, male singers occasionally produce a timbre known as *voce finta* (feigned voice), with the head slightly elevated. This head position, in turn, raises the larynx. Because the length of the vocal tract is decreased, the strength of the first formant is reduced. This timbre is not a product of falsetto. It can become a legitimate *mezza voce* timbre as soon as the singer lowers the head, returning to an axial posture. (See *Voce Finta*.)

In leaving the speech range, less skillful singers tend to raise the larynx and to choreograph pitch changes with upward or downward movements of the head and neck, whereas singers of international stature show minimal head and laryngeal adjustments during pitch changes or at intervallic leaps between ranges. Bobbing heads and jumping larynges produce noticeable timbre distortions in any range of the scale. Habitual raising of the head is equally unwise for the female singer. If a female raises her larynx, she changes relationships among formants by diminishing the acoustic value of the first formant. During pitch ascent, major female artists do not lose the acoustic strength of the first formant—the depth of the sound. Indeed, the first formant tends to grow in importance. In some quarters, there remains a question as to the appropriateness of laryngeal elevation for the female's highest notes. It is postulated by some investigative research that elevation of the female larynx befits the highest register because it shortens the vocal tract. While it is true that many young, inexperienced sopranos demonstrate laryngeal elevation when singing their uppermost pitches, it is equally the case that they thereby weaken the acoustic value of the first formant. Timbre becomes thin and shrill. By contrast, spectral analysis of live and recorded performances by great sopranos of the past and present reveals that in singing high pitches there is an increase, not a diminution, in the strength of the first formant. (See Maintaining the First Formant [the Oscuro Factor] in Female High Range.)

To suggest that alternate laryngeal postures should be used for negotiating pitches in diverse vocal ranges is to invite a segmented vocal scale. (Yet, as the above question verifies, some current voice researchers recommend so doing.) There is ample acoustic evidence that changing the laryngeal position drastically alters spectral integrity. It may distort the vibrato rate and cause tonal imbalances. In the technical assignments that the elite singing voice encounters, laryngeal stabilization is the only certain route for securing timbre consistency throughout an equalized scale.

Techniques that concentrate on conscious muscle control over the laryngeal cartilages, and that recommend elevation or lowering of the larynx for timbre changes, violate healthy voice function. They rely on isolated fragments of pseudoscientific speculation that peaked during the middle decades of the twentieth century, when modern voice science was relatively new. As a result of subsequent research, these influences have declined. A practical evaluation of pedagogic assumptions must conclude that in the long run, summoning up birds, clouds, chimneys, funnels in various locations of the head, noncontributive sinuses, and imaginary sources of resonance unknown to the medical community may be less detrimental to healthy singing than pedagogies that misapply physiologic information. At least, images of birds and clouds do not bring pain or injury. Finally, a healthy voice technique does not embrace conscious or manual laryngeal manipulation. (See Separating the Thyroid and Cricoid Cartilages?)

SEPARATING THE THYROID AND CRICOID CARTILAGES?

QUESTION

A teacher once told me that I must learn to separate my thyroid and cricoid cartilages. He would try to insert his index finger between these two cartilages to manipulate my larynx, to make it function freely. I found it painful. I was also to practice pushing my larynx rapidly back and forth with my forefinger and thumb. Another exercise of his consisted of quickly wiggling the larynx up and down without singing, something I actually learned to do quite well. Several of us males used to have contests! These movements were to develop the laryngeal muscles. But none of it seemed to have any positive effect on vocal improvement. Would you comment?

COMMENT

The pitch-changing mechanism is partly dependent on concerted movements of the two great single laryngeal cartilages, the thyroid and the cricoid. The paired arytenoid cartilages, to which the vocal folds are attached at the laryngeal processes, swivel to open and to close the glottis. (See figures 3.2 and 3.3.)

Adam's or Eve's apple (the larynx) can be externally palpated, and the thyroid and cricoid cartilages slightly displaced, at least in some long-necked structures. These maneuvers are alleged to achieve localized control over the cricoid and thyroid muscles. Cricothyroid behavior is part of a concerted action that does not separate the two cartilages but brings them closer together, particularly in the vocal-fold elongation process. Neither cartilage is an autonomous actor. Nor do the muscles that move these two major single cartilages operate independently of each other. Pitch change is partly dependent on the concerted movements of these two great single laryngeal cartilages. (The epiglottis is the third single laryngeal cartilage.) The paired arytenoid cartilages, to which the vocal folds are attached, perform a swiveling action that opens or closes the glottis. (See figure 3.3.)

Laryngeal manipulation, cricoid separation, and conscious laryngeal depression and elevation prohibit free function. All parts of the vocal instrument function interdependently. As registration pivotal points are reached in an ascending scale, an automatic rocking and (in the upper ranges) a gliding of the two large cartilages contribute to the changing longitudinal shape of the vocal folds. These actions happen below the level of conscious control, in response to pitch ascent.

Many short-necked tenors have larynges that sit almost on top of their sternoclavicular joints. One such tenor will long remember an experience during the coaching of an operatic role he had been contracted to sing at a major American house. Without warning, a listening voice teacher/coach tried to insert her forefinger between the tenor's thyroid and cricoid cartilages (which in this particular singer's case are closely positioned), to substantiate her contention that she heard good mobility between the cricoid and thyroid cartilages. She just wanted to verify why she felt he was singing well. Following this remarkable, unsolicited pedagogic incident, the tenor, already well over a decade into a professional career, was unable to sing for several days. Needless to say, he did not return to that studio for further coaching. Such a traumatic experience is not likely to be recommended to others!

On another point raised by the questioner, oscillating the larynx rapidly up and down, independent of sound, may be a neat parlor trick, but does not contribute to the art of singing. Whether practicing such a questionable pedagogic drill may contribute to laryngeal instability is an open question. Further, there is no factual evidence that manually moving the larynx back and forth, or rapidly shaking it up and down, strengthens the surrounding musculature or renders the larynx capable of more flexible action. Indeed, at no time during healthy phonation should the larynx be made to shift from side to side or up and down. The best advice is to ignore any and all suggestions that advocate localized laryngeal control. What happens below and above the larynx is manageable; what happens within the larynx should not be subjected to attempts at direct control.

FLOW PHONATION

QUESTION
What do you mean when you advocate "flow phonation"?

COMMENT
The main, and at times most elusive, goal for a singer is to stay free while altering degrees of breath energy. In pressed phonation, airflow is too energetically resisted by the adducting vocal folds. In breathy phonation, there is insufficient resistance by the vocal folds to the air that sets them into vibration. Flow phonation, sometimes termed "free-flow phonation," refers to appropriate levels of airflow that match the requirements of the task at hand.

Although useful, the term is not universally well understood. There are advocates of flow phonation who risk reducing vocal-fold resistance to such a point that breathiness intrudes; hooty, breathy vocalism is the outcome. Scientific information without profound understanding of the nature of the professional voice is as dangerous as ignorance regarding function. Some persons who advocate free-flow phonation themselves demonstrate a nonprofessional timbre far removed from the *voce completa* of the trained performer. They admire the "relaxed sound" of the amateur, the folksinger, and the nonprofessional chorister, who show high incidences of breath admixtures. The sturdy, operatic voice often displeases advocates of "flow phonation."

Properly understood, flow phonation describes the process that permits the chiaroscuro tone: breath is never consciously held back at the laryngeal level, yet the vocal folds offer sufficient resistance to the exiting breath. (See Chiaroscuro; Adding Air to Pressed Phonation; and Singing on the Breath.)

ADDING AIR TO PRESSED PHONATION

QUESTION

Can adding a small amount of breath to the tone help get rid of pressed phonation?

COMMENT

On the face of things, asking for an increase of air in the tone may seem a logical way to relieve excessive laryngeal pressure. There may even be rare occasions when, as a momentary corrective device, sighing is in order. (The sigh increases the rate of exiting breath.) Yet consciously introducing higher airflow levels as a palliative to vocal-fold pressing is at best a compensatory solution that may produce problematic side effects.

The human body possesses a number of sphincters. Squeezing one of them, as in holding the breath, heavy lifting, or grunting, transfers tension to the others, including the vocal-fold sphincter. Experiencing tautness in epigastric and hypogastric regions of the abdominal wall, costals, or buttocks will incline the laryngeal sphincter to increase resistance to airflow. Singers who indulge in pressed phonation generally mostly do so in upper-middle and upper ranges because they mistake effort for energy; they induce too firm a laryngeal sphincteral response. This is particularly true of males.

Pressed phonation is largely an offspring of faulty breath coordination. The intrinsic muscles of the larynx attempt to resist a high level of subglottic pressure driven over resisting vocal folds. Remedial instruction should stress that there must be no greater sensation in the larynx during singing than in clear, energized speech. As a corrective device, short syllables should be spoken in low and lower-middle voice at relatively high dynamic stage levels, on patterns such as "A-ha!," "Oh, yes!," and "Hello!" Then the same expressions are sung in a corresponding range with comparable intensity. The singer with pressed production will thus be made aware of the sound and feel of free timbre as it occurs in the energized speaking voice, in contrast to tension inherent in manufactured, pressed, sung phonation. Return immediately to well-balanced, slightly aspirated brief onsets, gradually increased in length. Short agility patterns that stress flexibility over breath damming ought to follow.

Correlating breath emission and vocal-tract filtering of the laryngeally generated sound is the proper cure for pressed phonation. As is always the case, component parts of the vocal instrument (motor, vibrator, and resonator) must not be asked to act independently of each other. Introducing excess airflow as a means of alleviating pressed phonation is a Band-Aid solution, not a permanent correction.

DAMPING

QUESTION

What is damping in the singing voice, how is it done, and what does it accomplish?

COMMENT

Damping is not a consciously controlled laryngeal event; it produces no unique sensation within the larynx. It results as the main body of the vocal fold augments resistance to the increased air pressure. The process is both physiologic and acoustic: the cessation of vibration in a large segment of the vocal fold. With vocal-fold elongation and reduction in the mass of the vocal folds that regularly occurs for upper-range pitch adjustments, damping takes place. As pitch mounts, the posterior portion of the vocal folds undergoes progressive damping, so that in the uppermost pitches, it is largely the anterior portion of the folds that remains in vibration. Topmost pitches of the female flageolet range cannot be produced unless the vocal folds are heavily damped. High pitches of male voices also undergo degrees of damping. Excessive damping at upper levels in the already energized male voice can quickly deteriorate into pressed phonation.

RESONANCE BALANCING

THE VOCAL TRACT

QUESTION
What is meant by the vocal tract?

COMMENT
The vocal tract is the supraglottal resonator system, extending from the internal laryngeal lips (vocal folds) to the external lip bastion. (See figures 4.1 and 4.2.) It is a flexible, nonfixated system that responds to the articulatory demands of speaking and singing. In its response to the vibrating larynx, it influences the timbres of the singing voice.

CHIAROSCURO

QUESTION
You seem to be very fond of the expression "chiaroscuro." I understand what it means in the visual arts. What does it mean when applied to singing?

COMMENT
Universally used as a voice-pedagogy term, the expression "chiaroscuro" comes from the international school, and is featured in practical exercises from

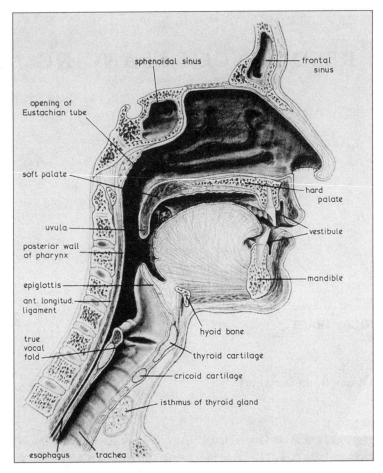

FIGURE 4.1. Midline section of the head and neck, showing structures of the left half. Note (1) the communication of the nose and mouth with the pharynx; (2) the crossing of pathways for air and food; (3) the extensive area of the tongue facing the pharynx, normally invisible from the mouth. (From Meribeth Bunch, *Dynamics of the Singing Voice*. New York: Springer-Verlag, 1982. By permission.)

historic treatises. "Chiaroscuro" means much the same thing in voice timbre as it does in the visual arts: the balancing of bright and dark aspects of color, and degrees of shading. In vocalism, "chiaroscuro" specifically refers to the equilibrium of acoustic strength manifested by an ideal distribution of lower and upper harmonic partials (overtones), clustered in formants.

Modern spectral analysis has verified the chiaroscuro (clear/dark timbre) concept, a balance of forces among the formants that represent acoustic peaks in

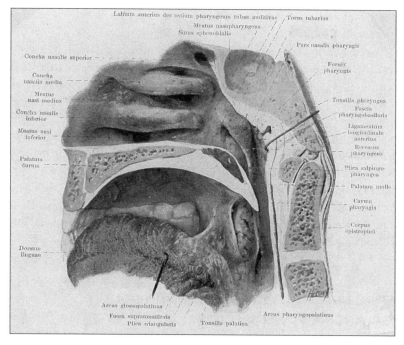

Labium anterius des ostium pharyngeum tubae auditivae
Torus tubarius
Meatus nasopharyngeus
Sinus sphenoidalis
Pars nasalis pharyngis
Concha nasalis superior
Fornix pharyngis
Concha nasalis media
Meatus nasi medius
Tonsilla pharyngea
Concha nasalis inferior
Fascia pharyngobasilaris
Meatus nasi inferior
Ligamentum longitudinale anterius
Recessus pharyngeus
Palatum durum
Plica salpingo-pharyngea
Palatum molle
Cavum pharyngis
Corpus epistrophei
Dorsum linguae
Arcus glossopalatinus
Fossa supratonsillaris
Arcus pharyngopalatinus
Plica triangularis
Tonsilla palatina

FIGURE 4.2. Sagittal section of the nasal cavity and mouth. (From Werner Spalteholz, *Handatlas der Anatomie des Menschen,* 13th ed., vol. 2. Leipzig: S. Hirzel-Verlag, 1932.)

voiced phonations. These relationships are clearly visible in spectral analysis of the singing voice. Almost every recorded major past or present singing artist displays chiaroscuro. Amateurs and unskilled singers do not.

VOWEL DEFINITION AND THE IPA SYMBOLS

QUESTION
You keep plugging use of the International Phonetic Alphabet symbols for defining vowels in singing. What are its advantages? Doesn't familiarity with the languages suffice? Won't such concentration on each individual sound inhibit expressive singing?

COMMENT
Vowel definition is a chief distinguishing characteristic of modern language communication. Each vowel produces its own vocal-tract shape. Much of voice training consists of ensuring linguistic articulation while maintaining the chiaroscuro tone, and this is attainable only when the shape of the vocal tract corresponds

to the vowel being defined. International phonetic symbols assist in describing these sounds.

No matter the language, clean vowel definition is the result of vocal-tract shapes that correspond to what the larynx is "saying." It is essential to be aware of the consistency of vowel formations from language to language. Most professional singers cannot fluently speak all of the languages encountered in the performance literature, yet they are expected to sing them accurately. The IPA vowel system is a great assist in achieving phonetic exactitude. Learning how to use the International Phonetic Alphabet no more impedes artistry than does learning music symbols for pitch and rhythm. It is an efficient device for achieving subtleties from language to language, and is of special value to the English-language speaker, who must be taught to avoid diphthongization and transition sounds. Appendix II offers model words for vowels in four languages, as well as for semivowels and for the French nasal vowel sounds.

KEEPING UNIFORMITY OF TIMBRE THROUGHOUT THE CHANGING VOWEL SPECTRUM

QUESTION

One of my many (well, about half a dozen!) voice teachers told me that my jaw should remain pretty much in the same dropped position during all vowel changes, and that only the tongue should move for vowel definition. This was to make certain that a uniform quality would remain, regardless of the text being sung. What is your opinion?

COMMENT

What you describe is a recognizable pedagogic approach that at first blush might appear to be in keeping with uniform resonance balance, regardless of pitch or vowel change. But it has no basis in the phonetic processes of the human voice. Voice timbre is not the product of a more or less fixed resonator system, which is to a large extent characteristic of the flute, the horn, and the trumpet. The filtering process of the supraglottic resonators of the vocal mechanism depends on constant alteration of relationships among vocal-tract spaces. To hold the jaw or mouth in a single shape while attempting to define vowels is contrary to normal, uncontrived vocal-tract response to laryngeally generated tone. It is in direct conflict with the adage of the historic international school, *Le parole sempre sulle labbra* (the words always upon the lips). If the mandible is retained in one low position, all vowel sounds share a common quality of distortion. The changing postures of the lips, the tongue, the jaw, the fascia of the zygomatic region, the velum, and the larynx determine flexible articulation. No one of these contributors, including jaw and tongue, can be held in a set position without inducing strain and distorted voice quality.

Because of the increase in energy demanded, the larynx naturally adopts a slightly lower level for singing than for speech, a position achieved with every complete breath renewal. The hung-jaw maneuver unites excessive laryngeal depression with the yawn, causing a drastically depressed larynx. A contrasting technique, promoted here, is based on a verifiable acoustic rule: There is no one ideal position of the mouth or jaw for speaking or singing; the vowel, the tessitura, and the intensity determine shapes of the vocal tract.

When singing within the speech-inflection range, *si canta come si parla* (one sings as one speaks). *Chi pronuncia bene canta bene* (who enunciates well sings well). Some teachers, with late nineteenth-century and early twentieth-century Germanic/Nordic orientations, continue to favor the low, immobile jaw, but are increasingly a minority in both Europe and North America. (See Elevating and Lowering the Larynx.)

VOCE APERTA AND VOCE CHIUSA

QUESTION
Please address the distinctions between *voce aperta* and *voce chiusa*.

COMMENT
Respective literal meanings are "open voice" (*voce aperta*) and "closed voice" (*voce chiusa*). *Voce aperta* is also termed *voce bianca* or *voix blanche* (white voice), because its "open sound" strikes the listening ear as colorless and white. Choosing the "open" side of the vowel produces a distorted vowel targeting. For example, /e/ becomes /ɛ/ or /æ/, /ɑ/ becomes /a/, and /o/ becomes /ɔ/. In contrast, *voce chiusa* selects vowel formations that migrate toward front-vowel resonances, and avoids open, dull, or spread sound. Resulting timbre has been subjectively described as pursuing the "high side" rather than the "open side" of the vowel.

Voce aperta is always a pejorative term. *Voce chiusa* is favorable, being closely allied with *copertura* (cover) and *aggiustamento* (adjustment or modification) skills. *Aggiustamento* makes possible the carrying of chiaroscuro timbre throughout all ranges of the voice. Subtle adjustments of *copertura* and *aggiustamento,* which together produce *voce chiusa,* account for much of the technical registration work of the elite singer.

THE ROLE OF SENSATION IN SINGING

QUESTION

Can a singer depend on sensation to ensure that correct resonance is present?

COMMENT

A singer has three ways to self-monitor his/her singing: (1) How does it sound? (2) How does it feel? and (3) How does it look? Identifying and selecting a basic concept of sound from among numerous possibilities provides a permanent and dependable tone-nucleus model. When a clear image of balanced resonance has been established, the sensation it produces becomes a reliable model. Because the psyche of each singer is a distinct entity, singing sensation is uniquely individual. It cannot be imposed on any singer, but must evolve as an individual, proprioceptive matter. Attempting to transfer a teacher's sensations to the student almost always results in technical complications.

Learning to recognize the new sensations experienced during well-balanced singing leads to replacement of previous perceptions. The singer may earlier have erroneously trusted responses induced in violation of freely produced tone. Eliminating those perceptions requires the substitution of one kinesthetic remembrance pathway for another. At first the singer may say "But I feel a lot less is going on!" or "But I'm not *doing* anything!" Letting go of superimposed controls changes how singing feels. (Once again, recall the dictum of Giovanni Battista Lamperti: "Controlled singing feels uncontrolled.")

Although we do not hear our voices as others hear them, we are fully capable of differentiating among sounds. The voice is the body; it is not hidden from observation. How do differences in voice production sound, look, and feel? Juxtapose examples of the old and the new sounds. (Feedback from mirror and video recording makes awareness much more possible.) Sensation associated with the chiaroscuro tonal balance is identifiable, repeatable, and above all, freedom-inducing. Taken together with companion perceptual parameters—hearing and seeing—feeling the ideal tone becomes a reliable monitor.

SYMPATHETIC VIBRATION

QUESTION

What do you mean by sympathetic vibration? Does it differ from vocal resonance? If so, how? How do you teach it?

COMMENT

Resonance, the result of an acoustic alliance between vibrating bodies at an identical fundamental pitch, can be either sympathetic or forced. The sounds of singing are the result of sympathetic resonance. Bony structures of the head can be set into sympathetic vibration, but not into actual resonance; they do not contribute to the complex tone the listener hears. Nonetheless, the sensations they produce are realistic to the singer, becoming reliable indicators of resonance balance. Sympathetic vibration (as opposed to resonance per se) can be illustrated by firmly grasping the music rack of the pianoforte while playing a low note, pedal down. The hand registers sympathetic vibrations on the woody surface, but the music rack itself can be removed and placed on the floor without perceivable difference in the quality of the instrument's sound. Many traditional pedagogic notions on "placement" stem from attempts to induce sensations in the head. Unfortunately, most placement attempts are unrealizable, because tone cannot be placed. Sinuses, cheeks, foreheads, occipital bones, and other structures do not contribute to the actual resonance of the voice, nor does resonator filtering of laryngeal tone include areas of the skull. It is restricted to the vocal tract, conjoined with the nasal cavities only for nasal phonemes. Bone, like wood, is a remarkable conveyor of sympathetic vibration.

One of the ways the sounds of singing can be monitored by the performer is through experiencing sympathetic vibration. (See The Role of Sensation in Singing, and Internal and External Listening.) When the spectral balance is complete, a singer is aware of sensations in bony structures of the head that are quite different from those of imbalanced phonation. Once an association with ideal sound has been established, these proprioceptive sensations become dependable indicators of tonal balance.

Invention of physiology and acoustics is not tenable in respectable pedagogy. Maribeth Bunch, in *Dynamics of the Singing Voice* (1982, Springer-Verlag), quotes research and pedagogic sources, including Negus, Russell, Vennard, Blanton, and Bigg. All prove that the sinuses of the skull "play little or no part in the vocal resonance that is actually perceived by an audience" (p. 97). Herself a singer, Bunch wisely appends that, because of one's own proprioceptive responses, "many teachers are thus misled into giving the various sinus cavities of the head undue credit for resonance." This does not preclude the fact that singers often feel sympathetic vibratory responses in one or more areas of the body. On the other hand, there are fine singers who are unaware of such sensation. The registering of sympathetic vibration is highly individual and can be experienced only personally. It should not be imposed on another person.

EAR-CUPPING AS AN ACOUSTIC DEVICE

QUESTION
Why do some singers cup a hand behind the ear? Is there an acoustic reason?

COMMENT
A hand placed behind or above an ear produces a false impression of the true nature of the spectral balance. Both males and females hear themselves better when cupping the ear (many of the guilty are males), but the sound continues to lack acoustic strength in the very region of the spectrum the singer wrongly surmises is being reinforced.

A simple experiment may help to explain. Energetically speak a phrase without cupping the ears; repeat the phrase while cupping them. You will notice that even in dynamic speech, brilliance and intensity seem to increase when the ears are cupped. Singers who feel the necessity to cup the ear generally suffer from dull production. They instinctively feel the need for brightening the sound and for reducing weightiness. Sometimes, when the habit of ear-cupping is questioned, the singer reports that the voice sounds bigger, louder, better, and that singing feels easier when an ear is cupped. Curving a hand behind the ear increases perception of acoustic strength in the upper portion of the spectrum—that is, in the area of the singer's formant, around 3K (3000 Hz) for the male, with a similar awareness occurring for the female at 4K (4000 Hz). (See figure 4.3.) The singer gets an impression that the sound is brighter, louder, and more resonant than what actually is heard by the listener.

A similar effect can be achieved by singing into the corner of an uncarpeted room in close contact with bare walls, or in a shower enclosure, especially if the walls and the floor are metal or tiled. Acoustic return to the ear is heightened, especially with regard to overtones that lodge in the upper regions of the spectrum. (This is why singing in the shower encourages the hobbyist performer.)

If a singer is accustomed to hearing sound rebound from the walls of an enclosed concert hall, singing on an outdoor stage that lacks an acoustic shell becomes difficult. Both the shell and the cupped ear enhance acoustic return. In immense halls like auditoriums and stadiums (horrible places, acoustically), where slight amplification of sound is in general use, if the amplification equipment fails, the return of sound to its producer is unfavorably reduced. Hoping to "project" better, the performer may disadvantageously alter vocal production in hope of achieving better feedback.

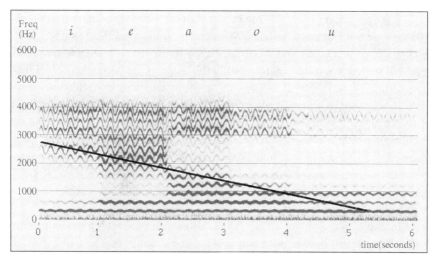

FIGURE 4.3. Spectrogram of a twenty-two-year-old lyric soprano singing an /i–e–ɑ–o–u/ sequence on E♭₄. Time is represented by the lower horizontal axis of the graph; the left-hand axis represents frequency in Hz. The first formant appears at the bottom of the graph. The diagonal line beginning at the left in the middle of the graph (diagonal vowel sequential) shows stepwise descent of the second formant, which together with the first formant is largely responsible for vowel definition. The third formant occupies the upper regions of the graph, with strong acoustic response registered between 3000 and 4000 Hz. Pitch excursion of the vibrato is indicated by the wavy lines of the harmonic partials. (From Vocal Arts Center, Oberlin Conservatory.)

Can ear-cupping ever be a useful device? If, during ear-cupping, the singer is able to sort out factors that contribute to differences in tonal shadings, it might be. Mostly, ear-cupping serves as a traitorous friend. The teacher should take pedagogic advantage of the situation when a student habitually places a hand behind the ear, cups the hand around it, or makes a complete hand shell over the ear. Offer some comment such as "You sense the need for more upper partials in the sound, but what you do with your hand doesn't yield the results you want. Fortunately, there are some specific ways by which you *can* add acoustic strength to that part of your spectrum, increasing resonance, intensity and carrying power, and permitting ease of production." An explanation of the chiaroscuro (light/dark tone that balances depth and brilliance), and how to achieve it, should follow.

Exercises that increase the strength of the third, fourth, and fifth formants need to be routined. Nasal continuants that increase awareness of energy levels in the upper region of the spectrum can be separately drilled, then used as pilot consonants for subsequent vowels. Because the lateral (front) vowel series is stronger in upper partials than is the rounded (back) vowel series, lateral-to-rounded vowel progressions may prove helpful. Despite vowel change, the goal is to ensure uniform acoustic balance between the lower and the upper portions of the spectrum. (See figure 4.3.)

It goes without saying that the proper phonetic postures which permit intelligible vowel tracking must pertain. Zygomatic-arch elevation (achieved naturally through a pleasant expression) will dramatically strengthen overtones of the upper region of the spectrum by slightly altering the shape of the buccopharyngeal resonator tract. These learnable adjustments assist in achieving desirable tonal balance. In all cases, sessions dealing with important differences in timbre should be recorded, preferably by video camera, so that changes can later be recalled through both audio and visual records. If proper acoustic balance has been achieved, the singer will note how cupping the ear gives an impression of excessive tonal brightness. Optimum resonance balance is now understood, and the need to readjust tone perception by a false acoustic aid will be forsaken. The ear-cupping habit will be broken.

In any event, a singer cannot use false acoustic-enhancing maneuvers in public. Were a performer to put a hand behind an ear while singing a love duet, it would seem to the audience that the singer was either suffering a hearing loss or searching for ways to protect ears from a colleague's excessively high decibel level. Even in singing the final climactic unison High C in act 1 of *La bohème* (offstage and unseen), through ear-cupping Rodolfo will not be increasing his dynamic level beyond that of Mimì. If she follows suit, each may think he or she is achieving greater brilliance or higher decibels than is the actual case, or that they dislike one another's sound. They may also be contributing to their mutual tonal detriment. Ear-cupping is evidence that the singer's own musicianly ear is aware of resonance imbalances. When those imbalances are corrected, ear-cupping will be happily discarded.

FORMANT INFORMATION. WHY?

QUESTION
Why should a voice teacher need to learn about formants or ever speak of them to a student? I haven't the slightest interest. What student or teacher even thinks in terms of formants during the course of a lesson? There are plenty of practical ways to address an overly dull sound or an overly bright sound without having to resort to scientific terminology that is probably confusing or off-putting to a student. I find this to be completely unnecessary!

COMMENT
Of course there are plenty of ways to attempt explanations of desirable chiaroscuro balance in the singing voice. Many are illusory descriptions applied

to measurable acoustic events. In some traditional quarters cut off from current pedagogic thought, there remains a prevalent assumption that singers are incapable of understanding the components of voice production. The teacher's job then becomes a mystical search to describe those functions. What are the "practical ways" the questioner raises? "Frontal placement," "billowing, rosy clouds," "bubbling fountains," "the mask," "up-and-over," "projection," "head voice," or other imprecise terminology? Any student with enough intelligence to learn to read music and to be admitted to a school of music or a conservatory, and who has sufficient discipline can very quickly understand what the term "formant" means.

A formant is an area of acoustic strength that results from the cumulative distribution of upper partials (also known as harmonics or overtones). A formant results from the acoustic multiple of the fundamental pitch that originates at the level of the larynx, in response to shapes of the resonator tract, thereby producing regions of prominent acoustic energy distribution. (See figure 4.3.) Surely, anyone engaged in the teaching of singing can understand these concepts as readily as freshman students, who have no problem understanding the principle. Dodging specific information should be abandoned. Information will enhance, not detract from, one's ability as a teacher or singer.

MAINTAINING THE MALE 3K (3000 HZ) FACTOR IN BACK VOWELS

QUESTION

In keeping acoustic strength in the 3K area (singer's formant) in all parts of the scale as the male sings the back vowels, are you modifying the vocal tract, adding more breath energy, or doing something else?

COMMENT

In the elite, trained singing voice, during progression from lateral to rounded vowels, the vowel-defining areas of the spectra (chiefly, first and second formants) alter, but the singer's formant, composed of the third, fourth, and fifth formants, remains. In speech, the back vowels demonstrate a loss of acoustic energy in this 3K region, as is apparent in a spoken sequence of front to back vowels. (See figure 4.3.) No matter what the vowel or the tessitura, the singer's formant ought to be present. To achieve this, the shape of the buccopharyngeal resonator (mouth/pharynx) must match what is "said" by the larynx. In order to retain linguistic clarity, each vowel requires proper tracking on the part of the filtering resonator tube (pharynx and mouth). With male singers, the acoustic strength of the 3000 Hz (3K) region can be lost, particularly in upper range, through excessive modification of the back vowels formed by mouth shapes inappropriate to vowel tracking. What is popularly termed "ring," "ping," or "focus" is lost.

In tracking vowels for singing, even while producing vocal-tract shapes that accord with a particular vowel, the ear must hold to a tonal concept that calls for the subtle balancing of the harmonic integers (overtones) of the fundamental. Especially in the *secondo passaggio* region, this may require adjustment of a back vowel toward a front vowel or, conversely, of a front vowel toward a back or neutral vowel, but in either situation, an increase in breath energy is necessary. Discovering the balance that retains the singer's formant at all times is a primary pedagogic aim. The result is the *voce completa* (complete voice) of the chiaroscuro ideal. Although the mouth undergoes a rounding process (*aggiustamento*) in back-vowel formations, increased buccal opening and rounding ought not to be so great as to lose the inherent acoustic strength of each vowel. Vowel integrity must remain, despite modification, in all regions of the scale.

Proper vowel modification requires that while the mouth opens more for the rounded vowels, the zygomatic muscles do not drop from their slightly raised posture. Preference given to the mouth as a resonator (as in back, or rounded, vowels) increases the acoustic strength of lower harmonic partials. Preference given the pharynx as a resonator (as in front, or lateral, vowels) encourages greater acoustic strength in the higher formants that contribute to the 3000 Hz factor in the male voice, and to the related 4000 Hz phenomenon in the female. A pleasant facial expression—a slight elevation of the zygomatic muscles—will retain the acoustic benefits of the lateral vowel series; lowering the jaw augments the first and second formants so necessary to the definition of rounded, or back, vowels. These elements must be kept in balance as the scale ascends and as the vowel is modified. *Aggiustamento* (articulatory adjustment) includes analogous increases in breath energy.

It is often helpful to preface a rounded vowel with a lateral one (as simple as momentarily replacing "Ah!" by the syllable "Yah!") with its initial /i/ sound. Or insert any vowel from the front vowel series as a pilot device for the introduction of a back vowel, then return to the vowel's initial formation. Pilot consonants serve the same purpose. (See Using Pilot Consonants for Adjusting the Resonator Tract.)

Sound, sensation, and physical appearance that accompany these modifications become indelibly imprinted on the subconscious of a skilled singer. Above all, the musicianly ear must hold to an established concept of balanced tone. The ear conceives balanced tone; what the ear conceives, the body delivers.

MAINTAINING THE FIRST FORMANT (THE *OSCURO* FACTOR) IN FEMALE HIGH RANGE

QUESTION
What can help sopranos and mezzo-sopranos in upper range to preserve the depth of sound you have called the first formant, so that timbre is not shrill or thin?

COMMENT

The historic concept of the chiaroscuro tone can be verified by modern real-time spectral analysis. In untrained singers, the highest notes of the female voice often show distortion (a preponderance of upper partials), whereas in premier female artists the *oscuro* (dark) aspect of the chiaroscuro (dark/light) tone never diminishes. In fact, among prominent female artists, when they are singing in upper range, the first formant and the fundamental are often enhanced and exhibit increased acoustic energy in the lower portion of the spectrum. Why should this be the case? In ascending pitch, the trained singer's jaw drops just enough to avoid the conjoining of high pitch and lateral vowel. She must not hang the jaw in static position. Rather, as the jaw lowers, the singer should keep the elevation of the zygomatic fascia, which is accomplished by a pleasant facial expression.

Assume that at relatively high pitch levels, young Mary sequentially calls out the names of good friends: "Jean, Jim, Jane, Jen, Jan, John, Joan, June!" As she calls each name, her mouth changes shape to accommodate the sequence of shifting vowels, some lateral and some rounded. She would not willingly confuse the identities of friends by holding to one immobile buccopharyngeal posture; she automatically adjusts her mouth and vocal tract to permit vowel intelligibility. (John should not answer when she is looking for Jane.) Holding the mouth in an unmodified lateral position while singing in upper range will forfeit the first formant, produce an overly bright, thin tone, and destroy diction. Conversely, too large a buccal opening will produce disequilibrium among overtones.

In some less than efficient voice pedagogies, vowel differentiation and phonetic phenomena have unfortunately become dissociated. It is disturbing to read published pedagogic literature that advocates drastic jaw-dropping as a means to increase the first formant. Vowel integrity can be successfully maintained in upper range at the same time that the first formant—that is, the "velvet," the "richness" of the voice—is strengthened.

Rule: If, as the mouth opens naturally with rising pitch and amplitude, the integrity of the vowel is retained, the first formant will grow in strength and there will be no loss of upper harmonic partials ("ring," "ping"). Resonance balance will pertain throughout the scale.

FALLING BACK ON THE VOWEL /ɑ/

QUESTION

Why do so many singers complain that the vowel /ɑ/, as in "ah," falls back?

COMMENT

In normal speech, during a progression from front to back vowels, the perception of the pitch center lowers, as is apparent in the spoken vowel pattern

/i–e–ɑ–o–u/. Unless a conscious attempt is made to enforce constancy of pitch level, a downward acoustic curve occurs. A spectrum will display a loss of upper harmonic partials. Migration of acoustic strength in the second formant has been termed the diagonal vowel sequence. The vowel-defining second formant, which together with the first formant largely identifies the vowel, demonstrates a downward stepwise progression, indicated by the descending diagonal line of figure 4.3.

In most phonetic systems the vowel /ɑ/ is considered the first of the back vowel series (in some others, the first of the neutral vowel series); the loss of upper partials becomes particularly apparent when /ɑ/ follows a front vowel, such as /i/ or /e/. Says the singer, "My Ah falls back." Many of the exercises in systematic-technique systems are aimed at maintaining presence of the singer's formant, regardless of vowel sequencing. When the singer learns to retain the third, fourth, and fifth formants, regardless of progressing from lateral to rounded vowels, no vowel will "fall back." How is this favorable condition accomplished? By keeping a sufficient level of upper harmonic overtones in /ɑ/, the first vowel of the back-vowel series to be carried over into the subsequent rounded vowels. (See Keeping Uniformity of Timbre throughout the Changing Vowel Spectrum; and Maintaining the Male 3K (3000Hz Factor in Back Vowels.) Patterns that make use of lateral (front) pilot vowels before the vowel /ɑ/ are particularly useful.

DEALING WITH THE VOWEL /u/

QUESTION
How can one brighten an /u/ vowel that often is too dark? It always seems to fall out of the resonance.

COMMENT
This is a common concern for singers and teachers. As one proceeds from front to back vowels, the spectra undergo significant changes. In the perception of many singers, the first vowel to "fall back" is /ɑ/ because it is the primary vowel of the back-vowel series. (See Falling Back on the Vowel /ɑ/.) Subsequent vowels of the back-vowel series, such as /ɔ/ /o/ /ʊ/ /u/, heighten that impression. During normal speech and in unskillful singing, back-vowel production typically brings a loss of upper partials. For that reason, the most egregious culprit in upper resonance energy reduction is the final member of the back-vowel series, the vowel /u/. In speech, it tends to sound darker or duller than do front vowels, and lower in pitch than even neighboring back vowels.

Any tendency to pucker the mouth into a small, rounded opening for the production of /u/ removes overtone activity. The upper lip should not be pulled downward, covering the upper teeth, because the zygomatic muscles would then be lowered toward the grimacing posture. (Persimmon-eating, with its effects on the lips, is not advantageous.) This gesture alters both internal and external shapes of the resonators.

Several simple devices are useful in correcting the problem of "falling back" on /u/. The English syllable "you," with its /i/ and /u/ components, can be treated as a diphthong. Because the most lateral vowel /i/ is naturally strong in upper partials, it serves admirably as a quickly occurring pilot phoneme to the back vowel /u/. Practice "You–you–you–you–You" in a quickly descending 5–4–3–2–1 pattern. Sing the pattern again on the single syllable of "you," retaining appropriate mouth and lip postures. Then discard the introductory yodh (y) and sing only the vowel /u/, retaining the same configuration of lips and facial muscles.

Another aid is to preface the /i/ and the /u/ with the nasal continuant /n/, as in the word "knew" (/n–i–u/). (Avoid mispronouncing "knew" as "gnu" (/nu/), the large antelope loping across the South African terrain.) This conglomerate syllable combines a nasal continuant with the front vowel /i/, the two phonemes working together as lead-ins to the back vowel /u/. Singing a series of the word "knew" on a descending intervallic pattern is often remarkably helpful in locating a balanced /u/. Finally, the phrase "I knew you" combines front-vowel and consonant phonemes that influence the final /u/ to modify its baneful ways. The phrase should be sung on a single pitch, taken as far upward as comfortable, then on a 5–3–1 pattern in easy range. Because these pilot phonemes incite greater acoustic activity in the region of the singer's formant, they help keep the subsequent /u/ from falling out of the resonance.

USING THE *GOOD* VOWEL /ʊ/

QUESTION

A number of times you used the open /ʊ/ vowel around the upper female *passaggio,* and even more frequently at the *secondo passaggio* of the male, with baritones around $E\flat_4$ or E_4, heavier tenor voices at about $F\sharp_4$ and G_4, and sopranos around $F\sharp_5$ and G_5. You also went a tone or two above those changing points, still using /ʊ/. Since /ʊ/ tends to reduce upper partials, isn't there a danger of darkening the pitches of that region too much, causing the early heavy cover you speak against?

COMMENT

What vowels should be chosen to help gain smooth transition through upper-middle to upper range is dependent on the singer in question. As noted elsewhere, if the vowel is excessively modified (too covered), it is wise to make an approach from a neighboring lateral vowel that will heighten acoustic strength in the upper areas of the spectrum. In the master-class situations cited, several singers re-tained unmodified vowels (too open) that did not sufficiently alter the excessive brilliance that comes from conjoining a front vowel with mounting pitch. Resort-ing to the open /ʊ/ as a practice device is then a wise choice. It is radical enough to turn *voce aperta* timbre into *voce chiusa* quality without being so extreme as the use of /u/, a related close vowel. (See Dealing with the Vowel /u/.)

In cases where transition from the *zona di passaggio* to higher pitches pro-duces a timbre too strong in upper harmonics for acceptance by the sophisticated ear, use the positive word "good." The open /ʊ/ of this common word not only strengthens the lower harmonics of the spectrum, but has positive psychological connotations as well. Before using /ʊ/ on a 1–3–5–3–1 motif in the passage zone

and above, have the student speak the phrase "Look at the good book," observing lip and jaw shapes in a hand mirror. Then the same rounding of the lips, no more and no less, pertains when singing the word "good." Finally, one goes directly from the vowel /ʊ/ to a neighboring vowel, listening for good resonance balances among them. There must be an equalized match of timbre throughout the chang-ing vowel spectrum: lateral vowels should not stick out as brighter; rounded vow-els must not sound darker. Recall again that lateral mouth postures uniformly raise all formants, while buccal rounding lowers them.

USING PHONETIC /œ/ AND /ø/ MIXTURES AS TRANSITION VOWELS

QUESTION
In two cases where male singers seemed to have "woofy" timbres on back vowels, you suggested prefacing those vowels with what you called mixed vowels. Much improvement was made. I'd like to know more about the nature of mixed vowels: what they are, and how you make use of them.

COMMENT
The phoneme /œ/, as in the French words *coeur* and *fleur,* and the German *Köpfe* and *möchte,* combines front- and back-vowel phonetic aspects: the tongue is in the /ɛ/ position, and the mouth and jaw in the position of /ɔ/. As a result, some of the acoustic strength from both the back- and the front-vowel series is incorpo-rated within this mixed vowel. The front (lateral) vowels, it will be recalled, tend to heighten acoustic strength in the upper regions of the spectrum, paralleling overtones that make up the singer's formant, while the back (rounded) vowels favor lower harmonic elements.

When a singer has difficulty transitioning from vowels of the lateral series to those of the rounded series, prefacing the back vowel with the phoneme /œ/ often brings remarkable results. Choose a sustained pitch at the point in the liter-

FIGURE 4.4. "ma soeur je confie." (From "Avant de quitter ces lieux," in C. Gounod, *Faust*.)

ature where the singer has produced what you describe as "woofy" timbre. Briefly sustain a syllable containing the mixed vowel /œ/ as in *coeur*, then, without pause, follow it with a rounded vowel from the back-vowel series.

Consider one of the cases to which you refer. In Valentin's *ma soeur je confie* passage—$E\flat_4$–F_4–G_4—when the singer is moving from $E\flat_4$ through F_4, the syllable *ma* (/ɑ/) heads toward G_4. This fine baritone began to cover excessively. He experienced considerable throat tension, and exhibited the opaque quality you termed "woofy." We asked him first to sing the $E\flat_4$–F_4–G_4 passage entirely on the mixed vowel /œ/. (See figure 4.4.) Then to begin each note of that passage on /œ/, moving immediately to an /ɑ/. Inasmuch as part of the whole high-lying sequence is built on the /œ/ vowel, we asked him to momentarily substitute the word *soeur* for the original text of the entire phase. Subsequently we returned to the $E\flat_4$–F_4–G_4 passage's true text, which he then sang without loss of upper partials, retaining the "ring," the "ping," the "focus" of the singer's formant. Because appropriate modification was reestablished, harmonic balances were improved and throat tension was eliminated.

Another mixed vowel, the /ø/, is formed by keeping the tongue in the position of /e/ while mouth and jaw assume an /o/ position. This vowel is found in the model words *bleu* (French) and *schön* (German). The mixed vowel /ø/ can be used to achieve results similar to those of the more open mixed /œ/, particularly when the subsequent vowel is either an open /ʊ/ or a close /u/. In so doing, the singer takes advantage of acoustic properties of both front- and back-vowel formations.

USING /æ/ AS A PEDAGOGIC ASSIST IN RESONANCE BALANCING

QUESTION
When inducing a lighthearted moment, you had one singer with little resonance in his middle and upper range speak the crazy-sounding phrase "That bad cat has mad black rats" (I wrote it down!), in order to help find the /ɑ/ vowel you wanted. You used it as a prefacing sound for moving into high-tessitura back vowels that had a dull quality. It certainly brought results. Tell more about its use.

COMMENT

With the vowel /ɑ/, which in most phonetic systems is described as the first of the back-vowel series, the mouth assumes its most open vowel-defining position. In the remainder of the back vowel series /ɔ/–/o/–/ʊ/–u/, the lips are incrementally rounded. Singers often complain that in an /i- e ɑ o u/ sequence, the back vowels "fall back." (See Falling Back on the Vowel /ɑ/.) The vowel /æ/ in "cat," while a member of the front vowel series, is a near neighbor of the vowel /ɑ/. In enunciating "That-fat-bad-cat-has-mad-black-rats," the mouth, jaw, and tongue positions on the vowel /æ/ are not far removed from those of the vowel /ɑ/. In moving from the front vowel /æ/ to the back vowel /ɑ/, there is but slight alteration in the body of the tongue, and relatively little change occurs in the shape of the lips and the position of the jaw. Since the phrase is whimsical, in fact quite ridiculous, it invariably induces an ironic smile, ensuring that the zygomatic fascia and the jaw have not been lowered excessively. Then use /æ/ as a pilot vowel to back vowels in order to adjust the resonance balance.

A related procedure is to alternate /e/ and /ɔ/, as in the spoken phrase "They thought they saw—They thought they saw God." (North American singers produce the word God with an /ɑ/ vowel; the rest of the English-speaking community prefers something close to the British "hot,") as in /ɒ/. Transfer the phrase at once to a pattern on the consecutive intervals of a third, 1–3–2–4–3–5–4–2–1, in moderate range and at easy rhythmic pace. The intent of this vowel sequence is not theologic indoctrination but phonetic differentiation. It is constructed so that both the voiced /ð/ and the unvoiced /θ/ consonants preface the vowels. Consonants /ð/ and /θ/ yield the most forward tongue locations in languages of the Western world. Then drop the consonants and sing an /e–ɔ–e–ɔ–e–ɔ–e/ sequence of vowels on 1–3–2–4–3–5–4–2–1 and 3–1–5–3–8–5–3–5–1 patterns. Introduce alternately a vowel from the lateral series and a vowel from the rounded series. Using an /e/ to /ɔ/ progression, revisit spots in the song or aria literature where the back vowels tend to become muddy.

L'IMPOSTO

QUESTION

Some bel canto writers mention l'imposto when discussing the attack of the sound. What exactly does the term mean?

COMMENT

Impostare means to start or to initiate. *L'impostazione della voce* and the related *l'imposto* refer to the manner by which the singing timbre is initiated and perpetuated throughout a phrase. *Imposto* embodies immediate sympathetic resonance sensations resulting from the unity of tonal balance, centered intonation, and vibrancy. (See Sympathetic Vibration.) The term is sometimes too narrowly tied to another traditional voice pedagogy English-language expression: voice placement. (See Forward Placement.) *L'impostazione della voce,* however, does not simply describe resonance balances but encompasses all aspects of the appoggio system. Mastery of the onset assures that airflow and vocal-fold adduction are exact coordinates. By remaining *appoggiato, l'imposto* is assured. (See Appoggio versus Belly Breathing, and Routining the Onset.) Because the expression "place the tone" is encumbered with so many dubious connotations, it might be well to replace it with *l'imposto,* which denotes completeness of resonance balancing.

Current voice research continues to examine prephonatory tuning as practiced by highly trained performers. When breath and resonation are coordinated actions, pitch targeting and exactitude of spectral balance immediately occur. Fine singing depends on an awareness of *l'impostazione della voce.* Untrained singers do not enjoy similar directness in producing the onset, nor do they establish the fine resonance balances effected by *l'impostazione della voce.*

FORWARD PLACEMENT

QUESTION
I've heard many teachers talk about placing the tone forward or in the masque. But a number of respected scientific authors seem opposed to forward placement. Since we have not heard you request any singer to place the tone forward or in the masque, does that mean you are opposed to forward placement? Do you never ask the student to place the tone in the masque?

COMMENT
Much subjective terminology directed to resonance perception is less than utilitarian, because perception of sensation is such a highly individual matter. "Forward placement" is one such term. Sympathetic vibration during singing varies greatly from person to person; to expect everyone to experience the same thing is unwise. (See Sympathetic Vibration.)

It is not possible to literally place tone. Yet sensations for some singers are registered in specific parts of the body, one being the region called the mask, or masque. However, similar mask sensations can be generated by a variety of physical means, some desirable, some not. Certain forms of sympathetic vibration in the mask actually are the product of undesirable timbres. Problems often are exacerbated when a singer is told to place tone. Responses to tone-placement requests frequently generate unwanted by-noises, nasality, pharyngeal distortion, localized control, and breathy timbre. After a tone that exhibits ideal resonance balance has been identified, it is then appropriate to ask the singer to describe the recognizable differences among the several kinds of sensation experienced, including their location.

Significantly, improved sound often emerges when attempts at forward tone placement are abandoned. The teacher may hear from the student "But now I'm not putting it anywhere!" Yet the resonance balance shows remarkable improvement. The best way to build on a singer's proprioceptive response to sympathetic vibration is to avoid confusing the sensation of tone with its actual source. Many problems that continue to plague even advanced singers stem from previous attempts to put tone in some precise spot or slot. Sound does not work that way.

There are many ways to discover identifiable sensations without inventing either acoustics or physiology. Do not ask any student to place tone forward, back, down, under, up, over, or up and over, because such actions are not possible. Instead, make certain that buccopharyngeal resonator shapes properly match laryngeal configurations. As students systematically work through resonance balancing exercises, they discover their own resonance sensations. If a singer feels the tone is now "forward," excellent! I personally have a great deal of vibratory sensation in the frontal regions of my face, but not as a result of trying to put tone there. The singer will develop his or her own imagery after experiencing the presence of sympathetic vibration that results from efficient resonance balancing.

TENOR AND BARITONE RESONANCES

QUESTION
Because the natural pitch and the range of the voice are higher, does a tenor have to introduce more upper partials into his voice than a baritone does? And does the baritone have to produce stronger low overtones in his voice than the tenor? Do you use different techniques in teaching the two male categories? (I am a female singer and teacher, teaching several good male voices. I am not always certain about where to draw the line on this issue.)

COMMENT
Comparable registration events occur in males whether they have high or low voices. In male voices, the *primo passaggio* marks the pivotal point between the speech-inflection range and the call range of the speaking voice. For example, the lyric tenor and the lyric baritone have their respective *primo passaggio* events approximately a minor or major third apart, the lyric tenor's occurring at D_4, and

the lyric baritone's at B$_3$. A more dramatic tenor will experience his *primo passaggio* slightly lower than will the lyric tenor. Similar relationships pertain to positions of the *primo passaggio* of the lyric baritone and that of the more dramatic baritone. Tenors should not be admonished to produce brighter sound by increasing the intensity of upper harmonic partials. Nor must the baritone reduce higher overtones in favor of low harmonic partials. The chiaroscuro (light/dark) timbre of the classic international school demands balance among the prominent areas of acoustic strength, the fundamental and the first, third, fourth, and fifth formants. Every vocal instrument has its own individual quality, but all timbres must adhere to the chiaroscuro principle. (See Chiaroscuro.)

Techniques that try to increase the strength of the first formant in the male low voice often suggest that a baritone's larynx be placed in a lower position than that appropriate to a tenor larynx. Bass-baritones and low basses are falsely advised to attempt an even lower laryngeal position. Low male voices that follow that advice get a manufactured pharyngeal edge to the tone, and they tend to develop wobbly vibrato rates. (See Making Space in the Throat?) In that same pedagogic orientation, it is suggested that the tenor, in order to increase upper partials, sing with a higher laryngeal posture (sword-swallowing position) than should the baritone. High male voices then acquire a thin, reedy timbre and a fast vibrato, often coupled with nasality, producing buffoesque sonority. Spectrographic analysis of premier male singers confirms that specific balances among the formants are characteristic of the resonant voice, regardless of category. Top male singing artists avoid noise elements that are nonintegers of the fundamental frequency. Acceptable timbre will display predictable relationships among the first, second, third, fourth, and fifth formants, without by-noises.

The nature of the instrument itself need not be altered to produce advantageous harmonic integration. Desirable tonal balances exist when freedom of breath application, unhampered laryngeal response, and resonator configurations are in accord with each other. Tenors will sound like tenors and baritones like baritones when natural resonance balancing pertains. False manipulation of a voice to augment or diminish these balances does not produce a commendable outcome.

UNA BOCCA RACCOLTA

QUESTION
What do you mean when you advise "raccogliere la bocca?" You also say "sing with una bocca raccolta." You translated them, but I need to hear it again. Are there not some comparable English pedagogic phrases you could use instead of these Italian expressions?

COMMENT

The questioner refers to my personal preference for historic, traditional expressions now in international use. The vocabulary of musical terms is often expressed in Italian. It seems not amiss to retain that usage for professional singers and teachers of all national backgrounds. *Raccogliere la bocca* literally translates as "to collect the mouth," a rather colorless phrase in English that does not encompass the term's complete significance, which is the avoidance of jaw-wagging or excessive jaw-dropping. The expression is a close relative of *si canta come si parla,* and stands in stark contrast to the techniques of some national schools (and their mid-twentieth-century North American imitators) that espouse lowered-jaw techniques as a means to improve voice resonance. The natural processes of vowel and consonantal definition are inherent components of the historic *raccogliere la bocca* concept. Forsaking flawed jaw activities through the substitution of the *una bocca raccolta* principle restores harmonic balance, especially when singing in the speech-inflection range. (See *Si Canta come Si Parla; Chi Pronuncia Bene Canta Bene;* The Idiot Jaw; and Three Fingers in the Mouth.)

SI CANTA COME SI PARLA; CHI PRONUNCIA BENE CANTA BENE

QUESTION

You use several Italian expressions that seem to base the singing voice on the speaking voice. Can you please define them again?

COMMENT

There are two phrases stemming from eighteenth-century Italian pedagogic tradition which stress that singing and speaking make use of the same mechanical processes. In a nutshell, they present a major principle regarding adjustments of the resonator tract (the buccopharyngeal chamber). *Si canta come si parla* means "one sings the way one speaks." *Chi pronuncia bene canta bene* translates as "who enunciates well, sings well." Their wisdom and beauty lie in their simplicity and directness, circumventing unnatural adjustments of the vocal tract in singing, most specifically in the speech-inflection range. Of course, modifications of this principle occur when a singer goes beyond the speech-inflection range.

THE IDIOT JAW

QUESTION

What do you think of the so-called idiot-jaw position for singing? It has been recommended to me as a way of opening the throat while keeping the same quality throughout all vowels in all ranges.

COMMENT

Idiocy is not normally an ingredient of the singer's psyche. Unless cast as idiots, singers should not choose to look idiotic (!). It is difficult to appear romantic or happy while mimicking idiocy. Opening the mouth by dropping the jaw has no relationship to opening the throat. Indeed, pharyngeal space is reduced. The pharynx can be expanded when the mouth is closed. Holding the jaw in a lowered position produces uniform vowel and timbre distortions. (See *Una Bocca Raccolta*, and Pulling Down on the Jaw.) The pedagogic admonition to hold the buccal cavity in the position of idiocy is in conflict with acoustic phonetics and the physiology of phonation. Doesn't it seem a bit idiotic to purposely violate those principles?

THREE FINGERS IN THE MOUTH

QUESTION

I am an adult who sings in a civic chorus. Our director tells us we should make a perpendicular shield of the three middle fingers of the hand, then place them between our upper and lower teeth. This is to open the throat and increase its space so the tone can come out better. I can't seem to get the hang of it, and it feels very uncomfortable. Any comments?

COMMENT

Your question invites a number of comments, some of which will best remain unexpressed.

Comment must be made concerning how one can or cannot open the throat. The very term "throat" is often indiscriminately used to refer to both the pharynx and the larynx, and is too imprecise to be of pedagogic value. The pharynx extends from the base of the skull to the sixth cervical vertebra, with pharyngeal dimensions determined by the structure of the individual. The pharynx consists of three parts:

1. Nasopharynx, lying above the lower border of the soft palate
2. Oropharynx, located between the soft palate and the upper region of the epiglottis, and opening out into the buccal cavity (the mouth) through the palatoglossal arches (velar region)
3. Laryngopharynx, extending from the top of the epiglottis to the bottom of the cricoid cartilage (the lower border of the voice box).

The posterior larynx projects into the laryngopharynx. (See figure 4.1.) Because the events of singing are more demanding, requiring deeper inhalation, greater energy, and further laryngeal depression, there is a corresponding increase in pharyngeal space. However, given the complex construction of the pharynx, any conscious attempt by a singer to open the throat locally, or to produce space within the larynx itself, is a questionable exercise (see figure 4.1).

Inserting the width of three perpendicular fingers between the upper and lower teeth in a mouth of any size, in the hope of opening the throat, will produce extreme jaw lowering but will not be in line with what is known about normal acoustic function. (Considering the size of many mouths, even inserting two joined fingers could be something of a stretch.) The vowel /i/ ("ee"), with its lateral mouth position, induces greater pharyngeal space than does the vowel /ɑ/ ("ah"), at which the mouth assumes its most open position in speech. Forcefully dropping the jaw from the temporomandibular joint does not produce more space in either the pharynx or the larynx; dropping the mandible actually narrows pharyngeal space and forces the submandibular musculature to press downward on the larynx.

Indeed, in uproarious laughter, the mouth cavity and the vocal tract are both enlarged, the fascia of the cheek region (mask) is elevated, the velum is raised, and the pharyngeal wall is expanded. In such a natural event, the jaw lowers considerably. But it does not drop out of its temporomandibular socket, which is what happens when three fingers force the mouth open.

There is no phonatory task in speech (in any language) that requires the extent of jaw lowering perpetrated by the three-finger-insertion method. Similar buccal positioning occurs only during strenuous regurgitation, permitting the bolus (substance about to be rejected by the digestive system) to be expelled from the esophagus. Regurgitation involves a correspondingly unfavorable rearrangement of pharyngeal space, and shuts off the phonatory mechanism. The more one assumes the buccopharyngeal vomiting posture, the more one diminishes the space of the pharynx (the throat).

What lies behind a pedagogic admonition (occasionally still encountered in some voice studios and among a segment of choral conductors) to place the jaw in such a distended posture? Can it really be intended as a basic position for singing? Can some limited use of this maneuver serve therapeutically? As a compensatory device to avoid jaw clenching (a condition far less common among singers than is frequently thought), there might be some momentary benefit in such overcompensation; but the probability of inducing other problems outweighs its usefulness.

The technique is reminiscent of the admonition to place a fist in the mouth in order to find optimum space for the singing voice, which produces similar results. Another detrimental device is the placing of corks at the molars in order to keep the jaw open. None of these have any place in the voice studio, even as temporary measures. They invite distortion and malfunction.

There is the occasional student who lacks jaw flexibility and holds to a tight and narrow mandibular occlusion. Working to relax jaw rigidity is essential. The answer is not to place the jaw in a distended or dropped position, but to use vowel sequences that are in accord with normal tongue and jaw postures. A dependable pedagogic rubric: "There is no fixated resonator position for speech or song." Have the singer place a hand, palm down, directly beneath the chin while speaking or singing. Note the small extent of jaw motion that ensues. Hanging the jaw in the posture of regurgitation, as with three fingers in the mouth, has no relationship to the changing acoustic events of phonation. (See *Una Bocca Raccolta;* The Idiot Jaw; Relaxing the Tight Jaw; and Pulling Down on the Jaw.)

KNÖDEL

QUESTION
What is a *Knödel?* Is it desirable or undesirable?

COMMENT
Knödel describes a throaty sound, as though a dumpling were caught in the throat. It results from spreading the pharyngeal wall and depressing the base of the tongue. *Knödel* is advocated as a timbre enhancement in some old-fashioned segments of the German school. Among well-informed German teachers it is strenuously avoided, the term being used pejoratively. *Knödel* can be produced with both high and low laryngeal positions. It is not the result of an open throat. (See Submandibular Muscles.)

PULLING DOWN ON THE JAW

QUESTION
I just saw an ad for a choral music camp showing young people pulling forcefully downward on their jaws with their hands while singing. Well?

COMMENT
Pulling down on the jaw to ensure that it drops as far as possible is part of a recognizable voice pedagogy system that advocates reduction or elimination of upper partials that ought to be present during solo singing. This pedagogic orientation makes the assumption that increasing room in the mouth enlarges the throat. Dropping the jaw produces radical changes among relationships of the formants, in both low and high registers, causing a reduction in the harmonics essential to balanced voice timbre. Excessive jaw-dropping upsets natural phonetic processes and uniformly produces dull voice timbre. Vibrancy is measurably reduced, and vocal brilliance is eliminated, regardless of the voice's intrinsic beauty. The aim of the vocally naïve choral conductor is that no individual voice should be permitted to alter ensemble uniformity in regard to tone and vibrancy.

Questionable is the notion that the aesthetic aims of a particular choral conductor should take preference over efficient vocal function. Such a mandibular posture induces undesirable tensions in the submandibular region (muscles located below the jaw), inhibits normal velar elevation, and drastically distorts voice timbre. (See Submandibular Muscles.) This outdated, mid-twentieth-century choral technique may achieve the disembodied timbre a particular conductor considers appropriate to the literature he or she selects for performance, but it is destructive, and ought to be discarded. Should students and their teachers respond favorably to the ad? No, not if it represents the kind of instruction the student would receive there. (See *Una Bocca Raccolta;* The Idiot Jaw; and Three Fingers in the Mouth.)

RELAXING THE TIGHT JAW

QUESTION
Can you suggest exercises and vocalises for a student who sings with a tight jaw?

COMMENT
Jaw tension can occur from two opposing errors: (1) clenching the jaw and (2) hanging the jaw. There are standard exercises for reducing either type of jaw tension, based in part on the Froeschels/Brodnitz relaxation method. With lips apart, simulate a circular chewing motion for twenty or thirty seconds. Next, with lips closed, hum a few pitches, at the same time moving the jaw back and forth in a gentle chewing motion. Imagine chewing a large wad of gum on either side of the mouth. Now, still using the lateral jaw movements experienced during chewing, sing a short phrase in comfortable range. (Some momentary diction distortion unavoidably takes place.) Use a mirror to note the looseness of the jaw as it retains its slightly circular motion. Follow this by singing the same phrase without the chewing motions. Then introduce longer sung phrases, alternating chewing motions with normal articulation postures. Notice that the action is more lateral than perpendicular.

Next, move the jaw rapidly back and forth while speaking a single sustained vowel. Wiggle the jaw sidewise for a moment or two, then stop moving it while sustaining the vowel. Do this with various vowels. Sing the passage that had induced a tight jaw, first while simulating small chewing motions, then without them. Use of a hand mirror is vital in bringing awareness of freely functioning jaw mobility. The answer to a tense jaw is not to drop it, or to force it downward, but to allow it to resume its natural phonetic postures. Some teachers who themselves have been taught to hang the jaw assume that a singer who does not do so has a tight jaw. (Of course, during speaking and singing, the jaw is not shifted from one side to another. This exercise is solely a practice maneuver.)

Individual facial construction determines the degree of buccal aperture in speaking and singing. People should not be expected to look alike with regard to the extent of mouth opening. In a singer with small mouth-and-jaw construction, it is easy to falsely assume that the jaw is not sufficiently lowered. A return to speech postures will indicate what the jaw should be doing over a large part of the singing range. In ascending pitch, the mouth opens additionally, but the jaw is not hung. (See Mouth Shapes in High Piano and Forte.)

TMJ AND THE SINGING VOICE

QUESTION

While working on *Chansons de Ronsard* by Milhaud, I suddenly got a bad case of TMJ. Do you think this was caused by singing too long in a high tessitura, or was it because in trying hard to relax my jaw for high notes, I was dropping it too low?

COMMENT

Elimination of jaw and tongue tensions (closely related) are among the most frequent questions posed by singers and teachers. A singer who hears clicking or popping sounds when closing the mouth or dropping the jaw is suffering from TMJ (temporomandibular joint dysfunction, also termed TJS [temporomandibular joint syndrome]). TMJ may have its origin in congenital physical structure. Head, neck, and shoulder injuries may also be responsible. Although there is not complete medical agreement on the contributing factors, poor posture, with lack of head, neck, and torso alignment, is generally conceded to be one of them. It is highly probable that tensions of the tongue and the jaw—the scourge of many singers—are among the chief TMJ conspirators. TMJ can be induced by forcing the mandible to assume positions not meant for continuous phonatory activity.

The jaw can be lowered in more than one way. For example, although the mouth is widely opened in hilarious laughter, the jaw drops but does not unhinge, whereas in a fully distended yawn it does. (See Three Fingers in the Mouth.) A mandible dropped from its socket is not relaxed—it is undergoing distortion. The incidence of TMJ syndrome is markedly higher among singers who perpetually hang the jaw in order to relax it, or in the hope of introducing additional depth or roundness by strengthening the first formant. Many recover when proper phonetic postures are reestablished. It is interesting to note that for the above questioner, the onset of what she considered to be TMJ came after singing relatively high-lying passages for extended periods of time, with a consciously dropped jaw.

Several current writers advocate enhancing the first formant through jaw-dropping. A valuable adage of the historic international school is that one assumes speech postures in the speech-inflection range (*si canta come si parla*). In upper range, the mouth opens more but the integrity of the vowel, determined by postures of jaw, lips, tongue, velum, and larynx, is maintained. The jaw must be permitted mobility, allowing flexible adjustments for rapid phonemic and pitch variations, not retained in low or distended positions. (See *Si Canta come Si Parla; Una Bocca Raccolta;* The Idiot Jaw; Pulling Down on the Jaw; and Relaxing the Tight Jaw.)

Perhaps the singer needs to make certain that she remains in the noble, axial posture, and that she retains vowel integrity when performing in upper range. If the problem continues, she should, of course, get medical advice.

SUBMANDIBULAR MUSCLES

QUESTION
Should the muscles of the submandibular region always remain soft during singing, or can there be some noticeable outward expansion in that part of the neck? Or is it possible that enlargement in this area is actually a manifestation of tongue tension, to be treated as such?

COMMENT
This question is directly related to concepts of how one "opens the throat." In some techniques of singing, expanding the submandibular musculature (located immediately below the jaw and above the hyoid bone—an area sometimes referred to as the submandibular or digastric triangle) is mistakenly considered to produce an open throat. In this pedagogic practice, the teacher places the student's fingers on teacher's own neck, just below the jaw and above the larynx, then demonstrates what is assumed to be spreading of the pharyngeal wall. The student tries to emulate similar external movements in the throat. This leads to timbre described in the literature of voice pedagogy as *ingolato, engorgé, Knödel,* or *pharyngeal.* (See *Knödel.*) Such activity does not open the throat; it produces tensions among muscle groups located between the mandible and the hyoid bone, including the mylohyoid, geniohyoid, stylohyoid, hyoglossus, and digastric muscles, and causes strain in the tongue and the muscle systems lodging above the larynx. It places the pharyngeal constrictors in positions unrelated to freedom in singing. (See figure 1.4.) The hyoglossis ascends from the hyoid bone to the sides of the tongue; the "loop muscle"—the digastric—is attached to the hyoid bone, from which the larynx is suspended by the thyrohyoid membrane. Efforts to spread the pharyngeal wall by outward movement of the submandibular musculature do not produce an open throat. It is unnecessary to expand the front or sides of the neck to improve either speech or song. Firmly place the index finger and the thumb on alternate sides of the thyroid cartilage of the larynx while speaking or singing a sequence of vowels, as in /i–e–a–o–u/. There is noticeable, limited movement as

the external musculature differentiates the vowels, but there is no sustained outward distension of the throat wall.

A corrective prescription for problems of pharyngeal spreading is to close the lips, to place the tongue apex between the upper and lower teeth, and to gently but rapidly move the jaw back and forth while humming. At the same time, with the fingers check the region below the jaw to see that it remains soft. The same submandibular relaxation should occur equally in speaking and in singing. (See Relaxing the Tight Jaw.)

MOUTH SHAPES IN HIGH PIANO AND FORTE

QUESTION
What should be the shape of the mouth for singing vowels in high, sustained range? Are those shapes different at piano and forte passages?

COMMENT
Vowel definition must always be recognizable, yet vowel modification remains quintessential to upper-range singing. As pitch ascends, the mouth gradually opens (that is, the mandible lowers). However, integrity of the vowel must be preserved. The primary mouth shape for each vowel survives, but the jaw opens slightly wider as the pitch elevates. Extent of buccal aperture in high range must match both the phonetic demands of each vowel and the pitch being sung. Increased intensity also commonly contributes to an additional degree of mouth opening. It should be recalled that there is no single ideal position for the mouth in singing; vowel, tessitura, and dynamic intensity are the determinants. (See *Una Bocca Raccolta.*)

SFOGATO TIMBRE

QUESTION
What is meant by *sfogato* quality?

COMMENT
The literal translation of the verb *sfogare* is to give vent to, to pour forth, to flow, to let loose. *Voce sfogata* refers to timbre produced with freedom and passion. Music reference sources contradict each other in defining the term *sfogato*. A popular music dictionary offers "to sing lightly and airily," and mystifyingly continues, "Soprano *sfogato,* a high soprano voice." The *New Grove Dictionary* mentions two famous and contrasting examples: in Chopin's Barcarolle, *dolce*

sfogato occurs as an expression mark over a delicate filigree passage, while in Liszt's Hungarian Rhapsody no. 14, *ff sfogato con bravura* indicates a bombastic passage.

Some American commentators on vocal matters have interpreted *sfogato* to mean "smoky," perhaps mistaking *foga* (ardor, verve, impetuousness) for a cognate of the English word "fog." Several sources use the term to identify a quality they believe characteristic of African-American female voices. In male voices, the term is sometimes used to describe excessive *copertura,* or covering, at high levels of emotional energy. Sometimes even a slightly husky-sounding or low speaking voice, particularly among females, will be described as showing *sfogato* timbre. A remarkable number of Italian males have similar raspy speech characteristics. Spectral analysis indicates that in some cases, comparable noise elements may be present in a dramatic singing voice.

For Italian commentators, *voce sfogata* generally describes a production that is warmer and more emotive and passionate than the norm. Contrary to one definition cited above, *voce sfogata* does not refer to light voices. In spectral terms, *una voce sfogata* is strong in lower formants that accent the velvety character of the chiaroscuro tonal ideal, producing what some listeners perceive as a sensuous, richer sound. I personally avoid using *sfogata* as a descriptive term.

USING THE ZYGOMATIC MUSCLES

QUESTION
How do you raise the zygomatic muscles without looking wide-eyed? How do you do it without outright smiling? Don't you have to widen the nostrils or wrinkle the nose in order to raise the zygomatic muscles?

COMMENT
Encircling the mouth is the orbicularis oris, a muscle that is made up of several strata of fibers, some deriving from facial muscles that insert into the lips, others from the lip fibers themselves. There are a number of muscles that converge on the two angles of the mouth. Mouth and lip postures are partly determined by the alliance of these muscle groups. Among important facial muscles are the levators and the depressor muscles that elevate and depress the lips and mouth. Of additional importance for singers are the zygomaticus minor, the zygomaticus major, and the risorious muscles. This commingled musculature assists in changing facial expression, and in shaping the lips and the mouth cavity. The minor zygomatic muscle is a paired muscle that rises from the lateral surface of the cheekbone, passing downward and inserting into muscles of the upper lip. It can elevate the

upper lip, and assists in producing the characteristic nasolabial furrow above the center of the upper lip at the base of the nose.

Coming from the zygomatic arch, the zygomaticus major is a paired muscle that inserts into the angles of the mouth. It blends with fibers of the levator anguli oris, the orbicularis oris, and the depressor anguli oris. It draws the angles of the mouth upward and, as in full laughter, laterally. Its participation in facial expression is determined by the emotion to be expressed. The minor and major zygomatic muscles (assisted by the levator muscles) can raise the fascia between the lips and the maxilla (area between lips and cheeks), much as when a fragrance is slowly inhaled through the nose, producing a pleasant facial expression, but not a full-blown smile. Narrowly separated from several other levator muscles of the lips, the zygomatics can remain elevated even during expressions of contempt or disdain, independent of a smile or a grimace.

Raising the zygomatic area for singing need not provoke widening of the eyes, furrowing of the brow, dilating of the nostrils, wrinkling of the nose, or laughter, actions caused by other muscles, including the risorius, the smiling muscle. When a pleasant expression (not a smile) accompanies complete inspiration, prior to velopharyngeal closure, the velum rises slightly, changing the shape of the resonator tract in the velopharyngeal area. This slight elevation of the zygomatic arch is commonly observed among major singing artists who adhere to the international school of resonance balancing.

In addition, elevation of the zygomatics can produce expressions that induce psychological states of ease and comfort. Wrinkling the brow and the nose, or flaring the nostrils, does not. As Jussi Bjoerling once advised this author, "Never drop the cheek area, regardless of the meaning of the text." (See Elevating the Fascia of the Cheek Region.)

ELEVATING THE FASCIA OF THE CHEEK REGION

QUESTION

During the master classes, there certainly is a remarkable improvement in tone when singers who drop their jaws switch to a pleasant look on the face. In the process, the skin over the cheek region seems to rise. You have mentioned that when the jaw is dropped excessively, the soft palate tends to lower, while in laughter it elevates. As I understand the issue, when the cheek area seems slightly raised, the soft palate assumes the higher position where it belongs for all nonnasals. If the velopharyngeal port is already properly closed on nonnasal sounds, why is it the case that the slight upward lift to the face seems to improve quality, producing a more balanced resonance?

COMMENT

Requesting slight elevation of the region called the masque is a recurrent theme in voice pedagogy. Early treatises stress the importance of assuming a pleasant facial expression. The old Italian adage "inhale as though smelling the fragrance of a rose" clearly has to do with elevated zygomatic muscles and a raised velum. Since the palate cannot be raised beyond the physical confines of pharyngeal structure, it is counterproductive to request a singer to locally raise the palate or to consciously hold it high. When a deep, silent breath is taken through the nose ("smelling the fragrant rose"), the soft palate elevates *before* closure of the velopharyngeal port occurs. Subsequent closure of the port ensues as a non-nasal is articulated. The soft palate remains well elevated for all phonemes except the nasals.

Because the entire vocal tract is relatively compact, any change among its components (lips, tongue, jaw, velum, and larynx) has a direct effect on resonance balance. The improvement the questioner heard is dependent on the symbiotic action among these components. Having the zygomatic muscles follow patterns associated with pleasant facial expressions achieves an uncontrived adjustment of the entire buccopharyngeal cavity. It avoids attempts to make space where it is not possible to do so.

FAUCIAL ARCH

QUESTION

What is the faucial arch and what has it to do with the singing voice?

COMMENT

The term "fauces" refers to the narrow passage from the mouth to the pharynx (sometimes called the isthmus of the fauces) that is situated between the velum and the posterior portion of the tongue; the fauces are bordered by the soft palate, the palatine arches, and the base of the tongue. Two muscular folds, the pillars of the fauces, lie on either side of the passage. It is generally conceded that the spatial dimensions of the fauces contribute to resonance factors of the singing voice, and although I am unaware of any hard data that support those assumptions, the notion appears to be a logical hypothesis. As in laughter, so in singing, the faucial arch elevates; the velum and the uvula move backward and upward, providing more space in the oropharynx. (When the zygomatic muscles are raised during deep inhalation, the fauces elevate as well.) When the jaw is dropped, the fauces, the velum, and the uvula tend to lower. (See Velum Lowering; Elevating the Fascia of the Cheek Region.)

UPPER-LIP TENSION

QUESTION
Some of us have been taught that in order to help focus tone, the upper lip should be lowered so that the upper teeth are not visible. You seem to object to that. Why?

COMMENT
During speech, lip postures vary from person to person. If the upper teeth are visible in speaking, they should be visible in singing. For both speaking and singing, the shape of the vocal tract is in constant flux, there being no one ideal position of the mouth or the lips for either. Pulling downward on the upper lip alters the shape of the articulation system. It affects buccopharyngeal space, reverses the role of the zygomatic muscles, and darkens the tone. There are indeed cases when a singer who remains in an exaggerated smile position, particularly in upper range, suffers from bright, edgy timbre, a problem for which solutions must be found. However, pulling the upper lip down to cover the upper teeth as compensation or as an antidote should be avoided. It destroys the chiaroscuro relationship among the harmonic partials. It also looks quite weird.

DIRECTING ATTENTION TO THE TONGUE

QUESTION
I am curious as to why you sometimes have students look in a hand mirror at positions and movements of the tongue. Doesn't that make a singer aware of the mechanical action of the tongue instead of concentrating on artistry?

COMMENT
Artistry will be difficult to achieve if function is disrupted. Freedom of the vocal tract is essential to resonant tone. The tongue is the chief vector for making changes within the vocal tract, occupying the mouth and part of the pharynx. With the hyoid bone and the larynx, the tongue forms an anatomical unit. (See figure 4.1.) The tongue is the main articulatory organ, and if it lacks freedom, the entire resonator tract is upset, which affects both timbre and enunciation. Whatever positioning the tongue assumes has a direct effect on the larynx. Many tension problems in the singing voice are related to a malfunctioning tongue. Indeed, the tongue is among the three chief culprits of tension in singing, others being the jaw and the neck. If the tongue is not a problem, there is no need to draw attention to it. But to ignore faulty tongue action is to be irresponsible.

The apex of the tongue belongs in contact with the inner surface of the lower front teeth, where it lodges when one says "Um-hm!" This is the case for all vowels and for the majority of both voiced and unvoiced consonants in Western languages. For production of several consonantal phonemes, the apex of the tongue ascends to the alveolar ridge, directly behind the upper front teeth. The tongue occasionally assumes other postures within the vocal tract for defining a few voiced and unvoiced consonants. But for something like 70 percent of the time, in the languages of classical voice literature, the tongue apex remains in contact with the inner surface of the lower front teeth. When the tongue apex is placed in unnatural positions during phonation, the entire body of the tongue tenses. Singers should not be taught to place their tongues in nonphonetic positions. Common tongue problems in singing are the following:

1. Curling the apex of the tongue slightly upward toward the hard palate in a retroflex position
2. Placing the tongue apex in a high retroflex location, creating a double buccal chamber
3. Pulling the tongue back from its normal contact with the inner surface of the lower front teeth
4. Placing the tongue below the gum ridge of the lower front teeth
5. Elevating the sides of the tongue against the upper molars (exaggerated /i/ position) regardless of vowel definition
6. Raising or lowering one side of the tongue independently of the other
7. Grooving the tongue as a uniform position for singing, regardless of vowel definition
8. Depressing the base of the tongue in an exaggerated /ɔ/ position, and keeping it there for all phonemes.

Tongue rigidity causes transition sounds that negate good vowel definition. When these disruptions are corrected, natural physiologic and acoustic functions tend to fall into place. Use pilot consonants such as /v/, /f/, /b/, /p/, /k/, /g/, /s/, /z/ to properly position the tongue apex where it must remain for all subsequent vowels. (See Voiced and Nonvoiced Consonant Pairs; Anticipatory Consonants; and Using Pilot Consonants for Adjusting the Resonator Tract.)

The student must become aware of mechanical aberrations of the tongue in order to correct them. Taming an unruly tongue should be a major pedagogic aim. The hand mirror is the best feedback mechanism for corrective assistance.

LEARNED, HABITUAL, OR NATURAL TONGUE POSITIONS?

QUESTION

A young baritone performed the Count's aria from *Le nozze di Figaro* with a fair amount of skill. Despite a rather good performance, you told him he at times held his tongue in a retroflex position, which you called inefficient, and you had him work with a hand mirror to correct it. Isn't it possible that what you termed a retroflex tongue was natural for that singer? It seemed to give his sound a certain depth and maturity. When his tongue was located where you wanted it, I admit that his sound became more lyrical.

COMMENT

A constant reflex location is not a natural, permanent phonetic position for any tongue. Tongue positions in singing can be classified as learned, habitual, or natural, the last being in accordance with the vowel and consonant formations of well-executed speech. It is easy for a singer to mistake what is habitual for what is natural. This young baritone had become accustomed to positioning his tongue in a retroflex manner.

Occasionally one encounters a singer, generally a low-voiced male, who has been taught to hold the tongue in a retroflex position because it darkens timbre by lowering the base of the tongue and depressing the larynx. The depth you noted was the outcome of pharyngeal spreading and of erroneous elongation of the resonator tube. This technique had become a compensatory habit. When he no longer pulled his tongue back in the retroflex posture, the sound lost its manufactured, throaty character and achieved chiaroscuro balance. It was also remarked, by a large number of listeners, that the problem of occasional pitch vagaries was corrected, and diction and the agility factor immediately got better. Above all, as the singer himself noted, the fatigue element was taken away. Timbre falsification was removed by eliminating improper tongue behavior. (See Directing Attention to the Tongue; Retroflex Tongue.)

TONGUE-POINT TRILL

QUESTION

What, exactly, is the tongue-point trill? How is it done? What is its usefulness in teaching?

COMMENT

The tongue-point trill is an extended rolled or doubled /r/, executed by short, quick fluttering of the tongue apex at the alveolar ridge (the gum region immediately behind the upper front teeth). Its duration is dependent on dramatic or emotional surroundings. The sustained rolled /r/ is typically heard in a child's imitation of motor noises, as in B*rrrr*M! B*rrrr*M! B*rrrr*M! European singers often find the double /r/ easy to execute, whereas North American singers, accustomed to the so-called retroflex, the Midwestern /r/, may need to learn how to do it. (See Learning to Flip and to Roll the /r/ Phoneme.)

The base of the tongue is attached to the hyoid bone, from which the larynx is suspended by a membrane. Without instrumentation, it is not possible to see the base of the tongue, but the apex of the tongue remains visible to the naked eye. When the tongue is rapidly trilling in the region of the alveolar ridge it cannot be held rigid in its body or at its base. This ensures that no tongue tensions affect the larynx or inhibit the changing shapes of the vocal tract. Tongue trilling can be a liberating device. Extended over short melodic patterns, the tongue-point trill alerts the singer to sturdy appoggio engagement. While rolling a sustained /r/ at a relatively high dynamic level, place the hands at the sides of the body just below the rib cage, to feel the contact among the abdominal muscles. It is quickly apparent that the tongue-point trill can spur good breath management. A useful exercise is composed of a three-part rapid pitch sequence on the rolled /r/ in comfortable midrange:

1. Sing a *gruppetto* of uninterrupted sixteenth notes on a 5−6−7−8 tongue-trill pattern, in easy range, retaining a fermata on the sustained 8

2. Sing the same pattern, concluding with a vowel on the fermata note of 8

3. Sing the same 5−6−7−8 pattern, followed by a vowel on the fermata note of 8, which now forms the first note of the descending arpeggio 8−5−3−1

4. Onset the vowel at 8 without the rolled /r/, and complete the descending arpeggio.

LIP TRILLING

QUESTION

During this course, you have never once mentioned the lip trill. Several of my students encountered this thing at a major summer music program, and they are driving me bananas by lip trilling in the hallways, in the studio, and probably everywhere else. I have had much success as a teacher for many years, and this seems to me to be a new and very uncalled-for gimmick. Does it have any real value?

COMMENT

At least in part, I tend to agree with the spirit of your reaction. The lip trill (also lip flutter) has become a ubiquitous cure-all fetish in some segments of American voice pedagogy. It is true that during its execution, a reduced stream of air vibrates the vocal folds and the external lips. It has been suggested that because of resistance to exiting air at the fluttering lips, the vocal folds themselves come together at a lower closure rate. That may be possible, but does it follow that the same action is transferable to the phonetic tasks of singing?

Beyond providing certain psychological benefits, it is doubtful that the lip trill is as significant as some of its advocates believe. Lip trilling is claimed to be beneficial for keeping the lips and the jaw relaxed. But in point of fact, the lips and jaw in normal phonation are flexible, not tensed. As you read this, are your lips or jaw tensed? Read a sentence or two aloud. Are your lips and jaw tensed? Of course not! On a more positive note, the lip trill does involve the respiratory muscles in much the same way as the tongue-point trill, thereby increasing appoggio awareness. It also may have some as yet unproved influence on resonator and laryngeal adjustments, but my own investigations do not support that.

I tend to downplay the current lip-trilling craze, in part, no doubt, because I think it a mistake to give a minor device the major role it has assumed in some current pedagogy circles. A real danger is that it may become a weak surrogate for technical maneuvers that prove far more productive. Precious lesson and practice time can probably be put to better use.

EXTERNAL-FRAME SUPPORT AND THE TREMBLING JAW AND TONGUE

QUESTION

What is your opinion about a trembling or wagging jaw and tongue, particularly in soprano upper range? What causes this, and how can it be eliminated?

COMMENT

Shaking jaws and trembling tongues are matters for concern. Tightening of the submandibular (below the jaw) musculature can produce high levels of tension in the jaw, the tongue, and the larynx. (See Submandibular Muscles.) The body's natural response to muscle tension may cause shaking of chin, tongue, neck, and head. This trembling rejoinder to tension resembles what happens in the arm musculature when one vigorously pushes against a resisting object: the arm muscles begin to tremble. For example, if your car gets stuck in a snowdrift, and you and your friends try to push it out, as muscle effort is measurably increased, the arms begin to shake in a rhythmic cycle-per-second sequence, because such shaking relieves the potentially destructive strain placed on muscle tissue. As you and your friends vigorously push your imprisoned automobile, a trembling ballet of heads, necks, torsos, and legs may transpire. In short, a protective response to muscle tension is transferred to all parts of the body. A wagging jaw can similarly result from excess tension and a lack of external frame support. (See *Appoggio della Nucca*.)

Another cause of jaw trembling comes from the downward dragging of the platysma muscle, the grimacing muscle that covers the lower jaw and part of the neck; it pulls down the lips and the jaw. This tendency is reversed when the zygo-matic muscles (cheek area) are elevated, as in a pleasant facial expression. (See Elevating the Fascia of the Cheek Region.) Conscious pharyngeal distention is a companion culprit of the trembling jaw and chin. Intentional spreading of the pha-ryngeal wall encourages jaw displacement. (See Submandibular Muscles.) This action is often accompanied by retention of a laryngeal position that resembles the beneficial temporary yawn, but that plays no role during sustained phonation. With conscious pharyngeal enlargement, as in induced yawning, there is little hope of relieving the shaking jaw. Slow or rapid vibrato rates, depressed larynx, and pha-ryngeal distention contribute to oscillating jaws and tongues. (See Making Space in the Throat.) For correction of abnormal pharyngeal distention, have the singer place the fingers lightly over the muscles below the chin, just above the laryngeal prominence, and speak a phrase from a song text. Then sing the same phrase with no greater involvement of the submandibular muscles than took place during the spoken segment.

It is not solely from faulty technical premises that some slight trembling activity may be seen in jaw and tongue. The tongue is a complex muscle bundle, the only muscle group in both genders anchored at one end while free to move at the other. The larynx is suspended from the hyoid bone by the hyothyroid mem-brane (also known as the thyrohyoid membrane, because its origin and insertions are equally mobile), and together with the position of the larynx, is a chief agent for producing change in the shape of the vocal tract. The larynx/hyoid bone/tongue complex functions as an anatomical unit. (See Directing Attention to the Tongue.) Tiny movements of tongue and jaw can be the normal consequence of the vibrato, which serves as a relaxant principle. Vibrato motion is not restricted to the intrinsic muscles of the larynx. Fiberoptic observation reveals synergistic motions of the pharyngeal wall, the epiglottis, and the base of the tongue. As has been noted, the tongue floor and the jaw musculature are closely related. For that reason, external movement generated by the vibrato is transferred to the body of the tongue through the tongue's attachment to the hyoid bone, and to the sub-mandibular muscle system. (See Free-Swinging Vibrancy, and Identifying and Steadying the Vibrato Rate.)

The first step in the correction of problematic trembling or wagging of tongue and jaw lies in heightening a singer's awareness of its presence and extent. Sev-eral separately employed devices may help establish proper external-frame sup-port, correcting elevated head and larynx postures that lead to oscillatory motions of tongue and jaw:

1. Looking straight ahead, clasp the hands well forward on the top of the head, being certain that the head is neither elevated nor lowered, and that the chin and head do not bob up and down with changing pitch; sing passages from the literature where shaking has occurred.

2. Remaining axial, place the palm of one hand on the occipital bone at the posterior of the head. This self-monitoring device assists in recognizing any tendency to move the head upward or forward during intervallic leaping.

3. Place the little fingers at each temporomandibular joint (the jaw hinge sagittal to the ear), the remaining fingers and thumbs resting at the mastoid bone (located just behind the ear), to make certain that the axial posture of the head and torso is maintained during singing.

4. Remaining in the noble posture, cross the arms over the upper chest, taking care not to move the shoulders forward. One hand lightly cups the chin to ensure that the mandible does not drop beyond the requirements of vowel, tessitura, and amplitude. Make certain the chin does not jut forward or move upward.

5. Place the back of one hand just under the chin to recognize, minimize, and stabilize jaw movement.

Another corrective device for excessive oscillatory movements of the jaw and tongue is momentarily to sing a sustained pitch while rapidly moving the lips and jaw in small lateral movements. Such mobility will lessen pharyngeal spreading and correct jaw tension. (See Relaxing the Tight Jaw.)

Most teachers of singing agree that jaw trembling is more prevalent among female singers than among males. An explanation lies in gender differences in physical structures. The comparatively small larynges of many sopranos are less firmly anchored in the neck scaffolding than are the larger larynges of most males. (Slight tongue and jaw trembling may also be more visible among *leggiero* tenors than is the case with robust tenor, baritone, or bass voices.) Minute trembling of the tongue and jaw, so slight as to go largely undetected by the naked eye, but observable when magnified by the relentless, zooming camera lens, can be detected in all vibrant phonation. As the scale ascends, a number of premier female singers show an almost imperceptible movement of tongue and jaw. Yet when this activity greatly increases in the region of the *secondo passaggio,* laryngeal stability has not been sufficient to support rising pitch and a commensurate increase in breath energy.

If tensions are present because of slack external-frame function of the neck, the singer must be brought back to a noble posture, imagining the ears are lined up with the spine, the back of the neck long, the front of the neck short. At the same time, the anterior-lateral abdominal wall must remain in the inspiratory position, in response to airflow increases demanded by ascending pitch or increasing intensity. The teacher must differentiate between the very slight oscillatory movements of tongue, jaw, and neck—the natural outcome of the vibrato phenomenon—and the presence of tension. Slight vibratory motion may be transferred from the larynx to the tongue or jaw without vitiating good timbre. Habitual shaking is indicative of technical deficiencies.

BACK TONGUE TENSION

QUESTION
What are some good exercises to loosen or relax tension in the back of the tongue?

COMMENT
Numerous muscles compose the bundle called the tongue. Tension in any part of the tongue is not confined to a particular region, such as front, midportion, or base; it is experienced throughout the entire organ. Both front and back regions of the tongue have great mobility, which is essential to definition of lateral and rounded vowels, and for structuring consonants. When in the acoustic-at-rest position, the tongue feels loose and relaxed. The tongue apex normally remains in contact with the inner surface of the lower front teeth for all vowels and for numerous consonants. It rises to the alveolar ridge only for certain consonants, and it occasionally assumes transitional locations for yet other consonant formations. (See Directing Attention to the Tongue, and Learned, Habitual, or Natural Tongue Positions?) Tension results when the tongue is not in accord with the rest of the vocal tract that produces phonetic formation—that is, when the tongue is not permitted to move to the normal postures of speech production. The tongue does not know where to go if the cavities of the jaw and the mouth are fixated in one hypothetically ideal position for singing. It then behaves a bit the way it does in the dentist's chair!

Allowing the lips, jaw, and tongue to follow patterns of spoken enunciation will cure most problems of tongue tension. Speak a phrase while retaining its rhythmic values; then sing it on a single pitch in lower-middle range with the same patterns of phonetic articulation as occur in speech. As pitch ascends, the mouth opens conformably, but relative relationships among phonetic shapes remain. (See *Si Canta come Si Parla.*)

Several specific exercises are useful in reestablishing phonetic mobility during singing. Have the singer sustain an affirmative spoken "Hm!" at comfortable pitch and dynamic levels. Draw attention to the contact of the tongue apex with the inner surface of the lower front teeth. While executing a vowel sequence, such as /i–e–ɑ–o–u/, quickly move the apex of the tongue in small back-and-forth motions against the inner surface of the lower front teeth. While sustaining the tone, stop the lateral movement of the tongue apex. The acoustic-at-rest posture of the tongue is reestablished, eliminating tension in the tongue musculature. Return to musical phrases, insisting that the tongue retain this freedom.

RETROFLEX TONGUE

QUESTION

I see some famous singers pull their tongues back, especially on high notes. At difficult spots, others look like they are raising the tip of the tongue toward the hard palate. I assume these are technical mistakes, because I hear unfavorable changes in the quality of the sound, yet these people continue to have successful singing careers. Why do they do those things?

COMMENT

There is not, nor has there ever been, a perfect singer (forgive me, Jussi!). The questioner is right that neither a retroflex tongue position (the tongue apex pulled back into the buccal cavity) nor an elevated tongue apex can offer advantageous positions for elite singing. She is also correct that there are some noted singers who occasionally display those faults. (Males seem more afflicted than females.) In an ascending scale, or on specific pitches, even a major artist may have technical problems caused by mismanagement of the tongue. There is no doubt that a singer will sound better when tensions that stem from maladjusted lingual positions are eliminated. Certainly, greater technical security and timbre consistency ensue.

Tongue postures largely determine clean vowel definition. The apex of the tongue remains in contact with the inner surface of the lower front teeth. For the production of lateral (or front) vowels the anterior portion of the tongue is elevated, increasing space in the pharynx; the contribution of the mouth cavity as a resonator is diminished. Conversely, the back vowels require a lower tongue position in the forward part of the buccal cavity, and an elevated position in the posterior. The resonating room of the vocal tract extends from the internal vocal lips (vocal folds) to the external facial lips. (See figure 4.1.) What the tongue does within that chamber largely determines language intelligibility and voice timbre. Singers eventually put aside concern for the innumerable configurations of which the vocal tract is capable, but any habitual, pejorative, nonfunctional tongue alterations must be addressed.

In speech (particularly that of North America), vowels experience a high incidence of rapid diphthongization with fluid transition sounds, one vowel migrating quickly in the direction of another. On-glides (a change in shape and timbre of the vowel as it approaches an oncoming consonant) and off-glides (the continuing influence of a departed consonant on a forthcoming phoneme) occur with great frequency during speech, but are destructive elements in diction and timbre consistency for cultivated singing.

A recitation of the alphabet, in any of the European languages that chiefly are used for singing the elite vocal literature, reveals that all vowels are formed with the apex of the tongue at this acoustic-at-rest posture. It is to be heard when a speaker "thinks aloud," as in "*uh*—yes!," or when producing an affirmative "*m-Hm!*" Many consonantal phonemes are formed at the same tongue-point location. Voiced and unvoiced pairs such as /b-p/, /v-f/, /g-k/, and /z-s/ serve as guiding pilots for subsequent vowels. (See Appendix III.) Particularly efficacious is the use of the voiced consonant /v/, as in /vɑ-ve-vɑ-ve-vɑ/. To make the point, I like to use the passionate Italian expressions "Va via!," "Viva la vita!," and "Viva la verità!," both spoken and sung. While using the hand mirror to observe tongue maneuvers, the singer should make certain that in singing each subsequent vowel, the apex of the tongue does not pull away from the initial /v/ location, despite movement of the tongue body for vowel definition.

Some idiosyncratic vocal pedagogies sanction placing the tongue in unnatural locations. To increase the strength of the first formant, one prominent twentieth-century pedagogue recommended placing the apex of the tongue below the roots of the lower front teeth, thereby depressing the tongue apex while elevating the midportion of the tongue, to increase frontal mouth resonance. In actuality, such a position closes off part of the resonance potential of the buccal cavity and changes the shape of the entire buccopharyngeal resonator. It does not create more space, but rearranges it in a less efficient manner. Another current pedagogy endorses retaining the /i/ position of the tongue (high frontal elevation) for all vowels in order to heighten upper harmonic partials that display acoustic strength in the region of the third formant. Still another source believes that if the tongue is curled slightly backward and upward toward the hard palate, two buccal chambers are created (double-buccal resonator theory), resulting in twice as much mouth resonance as would occur from a single buccal chamber! These theories ignore a basic rule for achieving resonance balancing in the singing voice: *it is not the absolute dimension of either chief resonator of the vocal tract (mouth or pharynx) that produces an ideal resonance balance, but the manner in which they are conjoined.* This acoustic rule demands that for each vowel, the vocal tract ought to match the laryngeally generated source of the sound. Because they do not correspond to recognizable vowel definitions, nonphonetic shapes of the vocal tract produce timbre distortions.

Tensions in the tongue can easily be transferred to the larynx. Recall that the tongue is attached to the hyoid bone, from which the larynx is suspended. For freedom in singing, it is essential that nonphonetic tongue positions and retroflex tongue postures be avoided. (See Back Tongue Tension.)

STRUCTURE OF THE NOSE

QUESTION

Does the size and shape of the nose affect the resonance of the singing voice?

COMMENT

That either the size or the shape of the nose significantly determines quality of the singing voice is not a supportable conviction. If there are impediments to free aeration of the nasal passages—from a deviated septum, polyps, or cartilaginous spurs—vocal timbre may be distorted during the production of nasals, as also happens in some forms of a head cold. Of importance for the singing voice is the unimpeded ability of the nares (nostrils) to permit free inhalation, and the ready emission of airflow for the production of nasal continuants and the French and Portuguese nasal vowels. It is the nasal cavity, not the external structure of the nose, that resonates—and then, only during the production of nasals. The natural height or breadth of the bridge of a healthy nose has nothing to do with resonance.

External cartilage that forms the bridge of the nose serves to protect the eyes from intrusive foreign objects. The cartilaginous external nose responds to sympathetic vibration, as do the bony structures of the skull, but it is not a resonator. Proprioceptive awareness of sympathetic vibration in the facial region, including cartilaginous parts of the nose, varies from individual to individual, dependent in part on overall skull structure. Many outstanding singers feel little or no vibratory sensation in any part of the skull, while others do. The height or breadth of the forehead, the size of the cranium, the prominence of the occipital bone, the dimensions of the mandible, and the length and height of the nose bridge do not determine resonance. Contemporary speculation that a large nose ought to give an indication of greater resonance is not surprising, inasmuch as that notion was generally held by some teachers of the eighteenth and nineteenth centuries, who refused to accept singers who lacked large noses. (This tenor would have been totally out of luck!).

Vibratory sensation in the cartilaginous structure of the nose is strongly marked during the singing of nasal continuants. Nasals induce acoustic energy in the spectral region associated with the singer's formant, often eliciting a common error: trying to increase the strength of the third formant by resorting to nasality. Much regional American speech is characterized by a high degree of nasality, with sound partially emitted through the nose on nonnasals (low velar posture). This unpleasant condition becomes exacerbated when the student is told to "feel the resonance" in the nose. (See Dreadful Speaking Voices.)

One of the most pernicious influences on twentieth-century French vocal pedagogy was the way in which Jean de Rezski's statement "Resonance is a question of the nose" came to be interpreted. Despite what may have been De Rezski's original intent, several generations of French singers and teachers literally followed the suggestion that nasality equates with resonance. They attempted to "place the tone in the nose," even in the nonnasals. (With regard to its nonnasal phonemes, the French language is no more "nasal" than others. It just happens to have a quite high incidence of nasal vowels, as does Portuguese.)

The nose is a distinguishing part of facial geography, and it is of importance in defining planes and contours of the face. A nose can be charmingly petite, or rival in size that of Cyrano de Bergerac or of the proboscis monkey, yet be equally adequate to the functional purposes of the singing voice. The size of the nose is not an indication of resonance enhancement for any species of animal. (See Correcting Nasality; Duration of Sung French Nasals.)

FLARING THE NOSTRILS AND WRINKLING THE FOREHEAD

QUESTION
A quite well known vocal coach told me that I should flare my nostrils to give more resonance space to the voice. What about that?

RELATED QUESTION
The choral conductor at my university says that by raising the eyebrows and spreading the nostrils, I will open my throat and increase resonance. Is this true?

ANOTHER RELATED QUESTION
You seem to want a singer, while keeping a quiet forehead, to have a lift in the cheek region. Isn't it a normal reaction to crease the forehead muscles when you try to raise the cheek muscles? How could these two actions be separated during singing?

COMMENT
It is not possible for wrinkling the forehead and flaring the nostrils to produce more favorable spatial arrangements at the laryngeal level. A corrugated forehead is an enhancement neither to physical beauty nor to resonance balancing. (See The Scotch Tape Threat.) As with any distracting maneuver, attention directed to some extraneous event may occasionally offer momentary compensatory results, but one might just as well wiggle the ears or elevate the big toe as distracting devices. Intentional nostril spreaders and forehead wrinklers adhere to pedagogies built on gimmickry, not on efficient function. The question itself raises eyebrows and furrowed brows among informed teachers and singers who find it difficult to believe that such admonitions can be seriously offered the student.

Some teachers and choral conductors believe that flaring the nostrils produces sensations in the mask area and contributes to "forward placement." Others feel it produces a sense of openness. The admonition is a psychological crutch lacking actual acoustic value. As with all compensatory physical devices, nostril flaring gives with one hand what it takes away with the other. The nares (nostrils) and the nasal cavities properly are involved as resonators only in the production of nasal continuants and in French and Portuguese nasal vowels. (I am unfamiliar with Asian languages, but my ear hears a fair degree of nasality in some speakers.) Neither the external construction of the nose nor the degree to which the nostrils may be widened or narrowed at their anterior aperture, has anything to do with efficiency as respiratory channels. The nasal cavities are not conjoined with the laryngeal/buccopharyngeal resonator system for phonation except in nasal phonemes.

Consider the structure of the nares (nostrils). The nares angle backward from their external origins at the front of the face and open internally into the nasopharynx. Wrinkling the nose or distending the nares does not improve spatial arrangements between nose and pharynx, nor do they open the throat, despite the fact that dilated nostrils are often conjoined with sensations of distention in the submandibular musculature. Spreading or wiggling the nostrils produces a distinctly unaesthetic appearance. The habit may be appropriate to the nibbling rabbit, but not to the communicating singer.

Pursuit of a feeling of openness in the nares has been taken so far as to suggest that before a performance, Q Tips soaked in alcohol be inserted into the nostrils and moved backward toward the nasopharynx (which actually has a drying effect.) Equally pernicious is reliance on vasoconstrictor sprays to produce increased room in healthy noses. Flaring of the nostrils often accompanies heavy physical activity, as in strenuous lifting or pulling; wrinkling the forehead registers concern and perplexity; raising the eyebrows furrows the forehead, and transfers tension to the mastoid region. None of these have a place in communicative singing. In normal interplay, a pleasant expression on the face does not include furrowing the forehead. Nor is wrinkling the forehead common to agreeable social interchanges, whereas maintaining a pleasant facial expression is. Indeed, a pleasant face and a furrowed brow serve opposing psychological and physiological purposes. The corrugated forehead indicates worry or fear, not well-being. During singing, if the one function cannot take place without the other, faulty tone-placement theories are the cause.

Nasality, when occurring in nonnasal phonemes, places the velum in unfavorable positions, upsetting relationships among components of the vocal tract. It also introduces unwanted noise in the spectrum. Nostril-flaring brings tension to the face and inhibits the natural registration of emotion. In forced inhalation through the nose, or in labored breathing, the nostrils flare, but nostril-flaring has no positive role in singing. (See Structure of the Nose, and Correcting Nasality.) Nasality as a transition sound—on-glides and off-glides—in subsequent vowels still plagues some classically trained vocalists. (See Nasal Continuants and Non-

Nasal Consonants.) Nasal quality plays an important stylistic role in pop vocal idioms.

THE SCOTCH TAPE THREAT

QUESTION
You joked about the Scotch Tape threat, but you didn't demonstrate it. Why would you ever want to place a piece of Scotch Tape across a singer's forehead?

COMMENT
The Scotch Tape threat is spoken of partly in jest, yet placing a bit of flexible tape directly across the forehead can prove a helpful studio device for alerting persons who habitually raise the eyebrows and wrinkle the brow when singing. The threat should be delivered in a spirit of fun, and the tape, if used, is only a temporary reminder. Brow-wrinkling can transfer tension to the mastoid area, with direct effect on the external-frame musculature of the back of the neck. Its presence also makes the singer look worried and tense. (See Flaring the Nostrils and Wrinkling the Forehead.)

If you or your students are brow wrinklers, try placing a two-inch piece of Scotch Tape laterally across the forehead during a lesson or practice session. Every time the eyebrows rise or the brow is wrinkled, the Scotch Tape band will bring about awareness of those events. With this simple procedure, the forehead wrinkler and eyebrow raiser can be broken of those bad habits very quickly. Don't forget to remove the Scotch Tape when the lesson is over!

MAKING SPACE IN THE THROAT?

QUESTION
I studied with several teachers who told me that in singing, the throat should be enlarged beyond what happens in speaking. I was taught at various times to feel I had an egg, a grapefruit, a dumpling, or a banana in my throat. I have also been told to hold my throat in the yawn position, because that will make more space for vocal resonance. (I spent years and large sums of money on those lessons, by the way.) You seem to be advocating a disturbingly different system called "vowel tracking." I take it you don't want singers to enlarge the throat to improve resonance. How, then, does a singer get additional resonance for singing if throat space is not greater than it is in speaking?

COMMENT

You have become a student of comparative voice pedagogy! Certain late nineteenth-century and early twentieth-century pedagogies, by using the subjective language you mention, advocated localized enlargement of pharyngeal space, resulting in a timbre known as *Knödel* (dumpling). (See *Knödel.*) The early Italian international school remained on a different path, suggesting that when in the speech range, one tends to sing as one speaks. Breath energy is increased, and vowels are modified as the voice moves to higher pitches. This historic approach corresponds to the contemporary phonetic doctrine of vowel tracking, in which a match occurs between what the larynx is saying and how the resonator tract above the larynx responds to that sound generating source.

Persons who attempt to make space locally in the throat do not achieve more space, but simply rearrange the components of the vocal tract, mostly in disregard of the laws of acoustics. Recall the rule that it is not the shape of either the pharynx or the mouth—chief resonators of the voice—that stimulates a good resonance balance; it is the nature of the shifting relationships among them. Trying to hold the throat in some one ideal position for singing is a bit like holding the leg in one position while trying to walk. Both in speech and in song, there must be constant flexibility during articulation. Only as the vibrator (larynx) and the resonator (mouth and pharynx) are allowed to respond freely to each other can balanced resonance happen. Tension can never result in freedom. Pharyngeal-wall spreading is pharyngeal-wall tensing. (See The Idiot Jaw, and Three Fingers in the Mouth.)

With a silent, complete breath intake, the larynx descends slightly; it remains there throughout subsequent phrases and during breath renewal between phrases. Through this process, natural pharyngeal spaciousness is attained without allusions to eggs, grapefruit, dumplings, or bananas. Whether in speech or in song, the spatial arrangements of the pharynx and the mouth follow the phonetic requirements of linguistic communication. Direct eggs, grapefruit, dumplings, and bananas to the esophagus, not to the larynx.

THROAT SENSATION DURING SINGING

QUESTION

During singing, how much sensation should I feel in my throat?

COMMENT

Sensation anywhere in the body during singing is such an individual matter that to attempt a single comprehensive assessment may be deceptive. That is why placement language is dangerous. In speaking, most of us experience no awareness of sympathetic vibration in the throat, yet if asked to think about it, we probably can identify some. When a singer goes from speech to song on the same note in the speech range, he or she may notice a slight increase in sympathetic vibration in the pharynx and at the front wall of the neck in the laryngeal region. Close observation of fine international artists reveals an almost imperceptible movement in the voice box related to the cycles-per-second vibrato rate. This is the case with one of today's reigning tenors, who has long been at the apex of the performance world, as he sings a high B or C. His larynx and the front of his neck visibly exhibit a slight oscillation, yet the tone is glorious. He well illustrates the point that increased breath energy required at high fundamental frequency demands a commensurate laryngeal involvement. Even proper laryngeal resistance to flowing air may produce small, externally visible vibratory movements. Despite firm laryngeal anchorage, superficial oscillatory movement from the vibrato can be conveyed to surfaces of the neck and tongue. A singer may or may not be conscious of them.

For both male and female voices, during dramatic singing in upper voice, slight visible vibratory motion in the laryngeal area may increase. With females it is occasionally conveyed from the laryngeal region to the tongue, neck, and jaw, because vibrato is not simply a function of the larynx. During the execution of vibrato, periodic oscillatory movements, comfirmable by fiberoptic observation, are transferred to the tongue, the epiglottis, and the pharyngeal wall. These movements, no matter how minimal, may be transmitted to the external musculature of the neck. (See Free-swinging Vibrancy.)

More vibratory sensation will be surfacely apparent in thin, long-necked singers (both male and female) than in short-necked singers who have more deeply embedded, hidden laryngeal prominences. Therefore, a limited sympathetic vibratory action, discernible on the neck surface, is not necessarily problematic. However, a shaking neck, together with a wagging jaw and a waving tongue, is an entirely different matter. They are indicative of faults that originate in poor breath management or structural support. Noticeable perturbation during singing, whatever its source, is generally attributable to slack coordination among contributive muscle groups. (See External-Frame Support and the Trembling Jaw and Tongue.)

Yet another point regarding throat sensation should be raised. When a non-vibrant singer first discovers vibrancy, he or she may become conscious of new responses in the throat and neck regions, described by some singers as "a buzz." Because such vibratory sensations go beyond those of speech, the singer may worry that they are being produced through tension. Quite the contrary—they may be the consequence of the desirable relaxant principle coupled with energy that characterizes the vibrato phenomenon. Most skillful singers have become so accustomed to sympathetic vibratory sensation that they no longer take notice, unless attention is drawn to it. There is no need to be concerned about subtle vibratory sensations in the throat, so long as they are not induced by malfunction. These favorable comments regarding consciousness of minimal sensations in the laryngeal region should not be construed as an endorsement of induced, localized sensation.

NASAL CONTINUANTS AND NONNASAL CONSONANTS

IPA SYMBOLS FOR CONSONANTS

QUESTION

Do you make as much use of the IPA symbols for consonants as you do for vowels?

COMMENT

Precise consonant symbols are equally necessary for achieving phonatory accuracy in the singing voice. How a singer handles voiced and unvoiced consonant phonemes helps determine the success of phrase direction and legato line. The consonant is as important as the vowel. Appendix III illustrates IPA symbols for most of them, with model words in several languages. In my teaching I draw particular attention to the need for skillful handling, in every musical phrase, of anticipatory consonants, single consonants, doubled consonants—both voiced and unvoiced—and the retention of their phonetic values. Relationships among properly articulated vowels and consonants are the very substance of good vocalism. Diction is not something that is added on as an overlay to voice technique; it is one of its chief determinants.

CORRECTING NASALITY

QUESTION
You reported an incident about a teacher hoping for tenure who didn't
know how to correct nasality in one of her students. You described a
lot of placement language she used as she tried to correct the problem,
apparently without success. What *should* she have done?

COMMENT

She should have known the cause of nasality and how to eliminate it. Instead, she invented imaginative locations in various parts of the head where the tone was to be sent. Had she known that nasality is caused by a falling velum, producing an open velopharyngeal port during production of nonnasals, she could readily have offered suggestions for a solution. (See Structure of the Nose.) Nonnasal quality demands velopharyngeal closure; nasality results from insufficient closure of the velopharyngeal port. A teacher of singing should have such minimal anatomical information at hand.

As a check for the elimination of unwitting nasality, tightly occlude the nostrils with the fingers, then sing nonnasal vowels and pitch consonants. Sustaining the same note, release the fingers. (Of course, the nares must not be closed off during production of the nasals themselves.) This stratagem, in use for nearly four centuries, alerts the singer to the differences in sound and sensation between the two timbres. Its use often brings about an immediate solution to hypernasality. The singer must recognize and memorize the marked differences in sound and sensation.

VELUM LOWERING

QUESTION
I have been taught that the soft palate must stay in a low position for
almost all of the singing range, only lifting upward on high notes. True?

COMMENT

Not true. The velum is lowered during speaking or singing only for the formation of nasal consonants. If velopharyngeal closure is lacking during nonnasals, undesirable nasality intrudes. Although this closure is present in all good nonnasal phonation, in upper range the fauces elevate even more, with the soft palate following suit, just as happens in high-pitched laughter. Regardless of range, if your velum stays low, sound will be nasal. That the soft palate should hang low for most singing is not a supportable tenet. Your question offers an opportunity for some tangential comment regarding the issue of velopharyngeal-port closure. There is nearly universal agreement among phoneticians, speech therapists, and teachers of singing that nasality (also known as "nasalance"), apart from intended, intermittent nasal phonemes, is unacceptable timbre. A fair degree of confusion exists, however, as to how such closure of the port is accomplished, and as to what language should be used to induce closure. This stems from a singer's individual perception of space in the velar area. When the velum hangs low, as in /ŋ/ of the word "su*ng*," the impression is that the posterior part of the mouth has been closed off. When the syllable "sung" is followed without pause by a vowel, an increase of space in that area is experienced. (See Nasals Followed by Vowels.) Requesting a singer to locally lift the velum is not productive. To suggest the velum be held low during nonnasals is contrary to the laws of acoustics.

NASALS FOLLOWED BY VOWELS

QUESTION

A recent article in a major professional voice journal proposed the discontinuance of warm-up exercises that use nasal consonants followed by back vowels, as in the syllable "maw," because it would force singers to begin phonation in one velar posture to be immediately followed by another. Yet, I see that you purposely juxtapose nasal continuants and vowel sounds. Would you respond to these conflicting ideas?

COMMENT

Natural linguistic patterns require the juxtaposition of all possible spoken phonetic combinations, as occurs with poetic texts set to music. How could one sing something like Purcell's "Man, man, man is for the woman made—And the woman for the man" without encountering the natural process of alternation between nasals and nonnasals? Try this fun weather report: "The month of May may be warm in Miami; more moisture may modestly modify numerous normal conditions in March." How could we remove the nasals or eliminate subsequent vowels in speaking, or sing such phrases, and remain intelligible? The flexible velum quickly rises and lowers during the production of language sounds, all of which are completely singable.

In fact, a major device for the elimination of unintended nasality is to sustain the final /ŋ/ phoneme of a word such as "su*ng*." Without pause, suddenly conclude its lingering nasality with a vowel. The velopharyngeal port is open during the nasal; the velum rises and closes off the port for the elimination of nasality as soon as the vowel appears. In this exercise, most singers feel an immediate velar shifting from open to closed nasal port. By occluding the nostrils at the conclusion of the nasal, variances in timbre and sensation can readily be identified. Proof is given that no sound is emitted through the nose on the nonnasal vowel. (See Correcting Nasality.) Because there is less space in the oropharynx when the velum hangs low, and more space when the velum rises to close off the velopharyngeal port, most singers actually feel a greater sense of openness when the port is properly closed. (See Velum Lowering.)

Nasals are prominently used in all pedagogy systems. The nasal continuants, because of the nature of their spectral balance, favorably adjust the resonator tract and induce a greater awareness of muscle responses in the abdominal wall. Humming amounts to singing a vowel with the mouth closed. A slowly executed portamento on /m/ at a fairly high dynamic level makes this fact particularly apparent. It is baffling to suggest, as reported by the questioner, that normal combinations of phonemes and other phonatory events should be avoided in technical training and performance!

DURATION OF SUNG FRENCH NASALS

QUESTION
Could you expand on your remarks about delaying the onset of nasality in sustained syllables when singing French nasal vowels?

COMMENT
It is current practice among major French singers, as well as with prominent native French singing teachers, to delay introduction of nasality into a sustained nasal syllable until near its completion. In a phrase such as "Mon enfant, ma soeur, songe à la douceur," from Duparc's "L'invitation au voyage," because of the brief duration of the syllable "mon," the nasal is naturally introduced early into the syllable, just as one would in speech. But nasality of the longer syllables "-fant" and "songe" is delayed until near termination. On the climactic "en-sem-ble," the quickly occurring syllable "en-" is immediately nasalized, as it would be in speech, but on the long syllable "-sem-" on high G, nasality is deferred until near completion of the note. (See figure 5.1.)

To immediately introduce nasality into notes of long duration produces a kind of parodistic honking, a common fault of English-speaking singers when singing the classic French *mélodie*. It is to be avoided just as much as the mistaken habit of carrying French nasals over into nonnasal syllables. As Gérard Souzay once asked me, "Why do many Americans think they have to do 150 percent nasality on nasal syllables, bringing them early, when a later and very small percentage of nasality will do?"

FIGURE 5.1. "Mon enfant, ma soeur, songe à la douceur." (From H. Duparc, *L'invitation au voyage*.)

VOICED AND NONVOICED CONSONANT PAIRS

QUESTION

What is meant by voiced and unvoiced consonants?

COMMENT

The articulation postures of the vocal tract are identical for each voiced/
unvoiced consonant pair. Similar tongue and lip positions pertain to each. Voiced
consonants are produced by the adduction (coming together) of the vocal folds in
resistance to expiratory airflow. (See figures 3.2 and 3.3.) Unvoiced consonants are
phonetically formed in the same locations as their voiced counterparts, but with an
open (abducted) glottis that permits laryngeally unobstructed airflow, avoiding the
vocal-fold approximation that produces pitch. The tongue is a highly mobile muscle
group. Most consonants are classifiable by the tongue's articulatory patterns within
the several regions of the mouth cavity. These include the teeth (dental); the upper-
gum ridge (alveolar); the forward portion of the hard palate (prepalatal); the highest portion of the palate (medial-palatal); the junction of the hard and soft palates
(postpalatal); and the region of the velum (velar). A few examples are /t-d/, /k-g/,
and /f-v/. A list of voiceless and voiced consonants, with model words that illustrate them, is found in Appendix III. Used as pilot consonants, these phonemes af-
ford some pedagogic possibilities. (See Anticipatory Consonants; Consonants as
Assists in Creating Legato; Using Pilot Consonants for Adjusting the Resonator
Tract.)

USING PILOT CONSONANTS FOR ADJUSTING
THE RESONATOR TRACT

QUESTION

A number of times you demonstrated inserting a consonant in front of a
word that starts with a vowel, particularly at phrase beginnings. Then the

singer went back to the original word without the inserted consonant. It seemed helpful, but why?

COMMENT

Suppose that at the moment of onset, a singer pulls the tongue away from contact with the inner surface of the lower front teeth—the acoustic position for all vowels and for a number of consonants as well. (For IPA symbols for consonants, see appendix III.) The labiodental consonants /v/ and /f/ relocate the apex of the tongue to its proper acoustic formation. With the forthcoming vowel, the tongue apex remains in contact with the lower front teeth while the body of the tongue alters, providing buccal positions that permit good vowel tracking. Similar maneuvers can be effectively accomplished by using the consonant pairs /b-p/ and /s-z/. Because the consonants /k/ and /g/ occlude the velopharyngeal passage by stopping the flow of air into the buccal and nasal cavities, they also encourage precise onset of a subsequent vowel. Executing a vigorously hummed portamento on /m/, with the hands placed at the sides of the body just below the rib cage, yields awareness of firm contact among muscles of the abdominal wall that produce the appoggio. As mentioned elsewhere, the nasals /m/, /n/, /ɲ/, and /ŋ/ serve as pilot resonance-balancing devices. Phrases such as "ogni uomo" and "ogni ignudo," sung on small intervallic patterns, alternate nasals with both front and back vowels. Followed by a vowel, /ŋ/ directs attention to the shift from a low to a high velar posture. (See Nasals Followed by Vowels.) The rolled phoneme /r/ of the tongue-point trill releases tension throughout the body of the tongue, and also brings awareness of appoggio contact. (See Tongue-Point Trill, and Learning to Flip and Roll the /r/ Phoneme.)

Teacher and singer diagnose the cause of a troublesome onset (often unsuitable tongue postures), then choose the appropriate consonant to assist in correcting the fault. Ultimately, the consonant is dropped and the original syllable is sung.

ANTICIPATORY CONSONANTS

QUESTION

What, exactly, is meant by anticipatory consonants? What are they, and how are they used?

COMMENT

Because they have pitch, voiced consonants can be vocalized over varying lengths of time; contrariwise, unvoiced consonants can have some continuance, but lack pitch. How voiced and unvoiced consonants are handled has a direct effect on legato, word inflection, phrase shape, dynamic intensity and control, and, most important, interpretation. Understanding the nature of consonant formation and the importance of consonants plays a major role in constructing a skillful performance palette.

Single German consonants that introduce nouns and verbs often require special consideration (in this regard, the lesser grammatical parts of speech usually are not as important as nouns and verbs). The single consonants /l/ (*Liebe*), /m/ (*Mut*), /n/ (*Nacht*), /z/ (*Seele*), and /v/ (*Wonne*) frequently have strong dramatic emphasis, requiring longer duration in singing than in spoken German. (See Consonant Doubling.)

It is, of course, not only pitch consonants that have duration. Both German and English nonpitch consonants are essential to diction and line, and play a role in sophisticated interpretation. In German, the fricative /f/ usually requires emphasis, as in *Fahren, Fürst, Vater,* and *Vogel.* The aspirant /h/, as in *Hause, Herr, Himmel,* and *Hof,* takes on importance. The initial velar/lingual stop /k/, as in *kalt, keiner, Kind,* and *Kunde,* is more marked in German than in English. The plosive /p/ of *Paar, Peter,* and *Post* generally receives more definition than in English-language words.

The German /ʃ/ (sh!), as in *Schatz, Schimmer,* or *Schönheit,* is frequently met in the poetry of the lied, often in conjunction with other consonants: *Schlummer, Schmerz, Sprache, Sprödigkeit, Stadt, Sterne, Stimme, Stolz, Strom, Stunde,* and *schweigen.* Other examples of unvoiced consonantal clustering in German are *Pfarrer, Pferd, Pfeife, Pfeffer, Pflanz,* and *Pflege.* In words such as, *Qual, Quark, Quatsch,* and *Quelle,* the unvoiced and voiced consonants /k/ and /v/ also are joined. Poets often play on their cumulative emotive value within a verse. A complete listing of German consonantal clusterings, and their enhancement of poetic expression, would require a treatise in its own right.

In English words such as "star," "still," and "storm," depending on the degree of drama represented, the sibilant /s/ also may need to be slightly emphasized, but much less so than in German words that begin with the /ʃ/-laut. By contrast with those of English and German, the French and Italian initial consonants usually are given quick, precise enunciation. However, doubled consonants, as in bri*cc*one, ma*mm*a, tu*tt*o, and piani*ss*imo, require sustaining. (See Consonant Doubling.)

The technique of anticipatory consonants applies largely to initial unvoiced phonemes. They ought to occur rhythmically in advance of harmonic phrase movement, so as not to reduce the continuity of vocalized sound. This means that the subsequent vowel can then be given the full duration of the indicated note value, and that the duration of the pitch will not be diminished because of the time it takes to enunciate a nonpitch consonant. For example, in singing German, one anticipates the nonpitch consonants of syllables such as *Stille* in advance of the vowel, so that the vowel may enjoy full phonatory presence (this technique extends to all of the nonvoiced consonants indicated above.) In a word such as *Tränen,* which combines an unvoiced and a voiced consonant, /t/ is the quickly executed anticipatory consonant. By the technique of consonant anticipation, the singer synchronizes a forthcoming vowel with the arrival of the underlying instrumental or keyboard chord. Dietrich Fischer-Dieskau, exemplary practitioner of the anticipatory German consonant, has made this diction technique an earmark of his subtle lied artistry.

The technique of the anticipatory consonant ensures that vowels arrive accurately without disrupting rhythmic or harmonic continuity. If not incorporated into the sung line, voiced consonants can disturb the continuity of tone, and work against a flowing legato.

Regardless of the ethnic or national origin of the singer, excellence in diction and enunciation are to a large extent dependent on the principle of anticipatory consonants. Nicolai Gedda is a prime example of an international artist who sings beautifully in languages not natively his. Like Fischer-Dieskau, he makes much use of the anticipatory consonant. A list of current singing artists who have mastered this technique would include most of today's great performers.

CONSONANT DOUBLING

QUESTION
When should consonants be doubled in singing foreign languages?

COMMENT
In German and in Italian double consonants take up a small but important percentage of phonation time allotted to a sung syllable, as for example, double /n/ in German Männer and in Italian Giovanni. Syntactic doubling in sung Italian also produces elongated consonants. (See Syntactic Doubling in Italian for a fuller account.) To prevent doubled German and Italian voiced consonants from interrupting the legato line, they must always be sung at the same dynamic level as the neighboring vowel. With the unvoiced doubled consonant, the singer must not fall into the vicious habit of decrescendoing a vowel as it approaches the stopped consonant, a habit which is a major detriment to legato singing.

CONSONANTS AS ASSISTS IN CREATING LEGATO

QUESTION
To have understandable diction, consonants have to be strong. When you lay such importance on making the vowels long, isn't there a danger that diction will become unintelligible?

COMMENT

The consonant is not the natural enemy of the vowel. A quickly occurring consonant need not interrupt the legato any more than a twig cast upon a flowing mountain stream impedes the current. The consonant becomes culprit only when it encourages the vowel to fall victim to transition sounds in which the tongue forgoes its proper location, gliding onward toward an early introduction of the subsequent consonant. Each consonant must be rendered as cleanly as every vowel. Crisp, clean consonants are essential to linguistic clarity. Nonetheless, excessive lingering over the pitch consonants in unimportant words labors the line, while exaggerated unvoiced consonants interrupt vocal sound. Percussive singing based on exaggerated consonant definition does not enhance comprehension; it produces boiler-room diction, with plosives resembling exploding steam valves.

The singer must be on guard against inadvertently doubling a single consonant, which may change a word's meaning. "Wohne" must not sound like "Wonne." "Caro mio ben" becomes a quite unromantic expression when the performer sings "Carro mio ben!" (See Anticipatory Consonants; Consonant Doubling.)

ICH AND *ACH*

QUESTION

On recordings, I hear certain well-known German singers pronounce the final consonants of words like *ich* and *ach* differently than do some other native German singers. One noted American coach I worked with in a master class insisted that *ich* should be sung "ish." You illustrated that sound by distinctly pronouncing the initial "H" (/h/) of the name Hugh. By the way, the same coach told me that there is no real difference between the endings of *ich* and *ach* in sung German. My native German professor insists on two distinctly different sounds. Who's right?

COMMENT

When listening to recorded performances of lieder, it is sometimes hard to distinguish nonvoiced consonant subtleties. It is also true that some native German singers show better enunciation than others, just as is the case among native English-language singers. Regional speech is as endemic to Germans and Austrians (not to mention the Swiss) as to their North American, British, and Southern Hemisphere counterparts. Each of these frequently occurring nonpitch German consonants is identified by a unique symbol: "ich-laut" /ç/ and "ach-laut" /x/. The first is formed by air friction occurring in the region of the hard palate (hence Hugh!); the second, by velar friction. The two phonemes should never be confused in sung German. Trust your German professor. (Consult *Siebs Deutsche Ausprache* as the ultimate authority on German pronunciation.)

LEARNING TO FLIP AND TO ROLL THE /r/ PHONEME

QUESTION

I have students who have a hard time getting away from the American /r/ when they sing English. It turns into even more of a problem for them when singing in foreign languages. There also are some students who seem unable to roll an /r/. Do you know of some helpful exercises?

COMMENT

The single-flip /r/ and the consonant /d/ are both formed with a quick tongue tap at the alveolar ridge. Choose word combinations—one in English, the other in Italian—that contain these consonants, as in the English/Italian word pair "body/Bari." In "Take my body to Bari," the /d/ of body and the /r/ of Bari share close formation. Try alternating another set of syllables, "Ma-dia, Ma-ria," insisting that the singly flipped /r/ mirror the location of a light /d/. Practice will produce nearly identical sounds, pointing up differences between the dialectical American retroflex /r/ and the lightly flipped /r/. The retroflex "American r" should be restricted to pop-voice idioms.

Several exercises correct a sluggish tongue that finds difficulty in flipping an /r/. Rapidly say "pot-a-tea" several times, then quickly juxtapose it with the Italian "parti." Although there are some subtle phonetic differences between them, by alternating the two phrases as swiftly as possible, the tongue will be influenced to accomplish the flipped version of the phoneme /r/ in "parti." Similarly, rapid repetitions of "put-it-out" (purraut) are of assistance for the rolled /r/. Over a period of weeks, daily persistent practice of these simple phrases will probably make the rolled /r/ possible. Don't give up too quickly.

THE PHENOMENON OF VIBRATO

FREE-SWINGING VIBRANCY

QUESTION

You have several times told singers to allow a full-swinging vibrato. You told them it would happen if they didn't try to control the tone so much, or to hold back breath on long phrases. What do you mean by the term "full-swinging"?

COMMENT

Professional vocalism is characterized by a vibrato rate that is neither too narrow nor too wide in its pitch excursion. Sometimes singers, in the hope of avoiding oscillatory timbre (the dreaded wobble), are hesitant to let the full extent of pitch variance occur. They need to be reminded that full vibrancy, the source of normal vibrato, cannot result if pitch variation is restricted. Fiberoptic studies reveal that not only the vocal folds oscillate during vibrato; motion takes place in the pharyngeal wall, the epiglottis, and, to some extent, the base of the tongue. This motion is a major component of the relaxation process that comes from coordinating breath energy with vocal-fold responses, and is essential to professional vocalism. Vibrato is generally assumed to result from neuromuscular excitation of the laryngeal mechanism; yet despite frequent subjection to analysis, the precise source of the phenomenon of vibrato remains elusive. Vibrato lies in the necessity for periodic muscle relaxation during heavy-duty activity. The parameters of vibrato include pitch excursion (oscillation), the temporal rate (cycles per second), and amplitude variance. Some singers cite a further parameter, completeness of resonant timbre. Despite the small oscillatory motions of intralaryngeal areas, during vibrato the basic position of the larynx remains relatively stable (unless a singer suffers from wobble or tremolo). When vibrato is permitted to take full-swinging pitch excursion, it actually acts as a centering intonation device. Fully vibrant tone is squarely on pitch. Vibrato is essential to elite singing. It is an important element of resonant timbre, and should not be removed from the voice, except for an occasional coloristic effect.

IDENTIFYING AND STEADYING VIBRATO RATE

QUESTION
How do you manage to get a vibrato, and how do you steady it?

COMMENT
A consistent vibrato can be achieved only when airflow is evenly regulated and vocal-fold closure is sufficient. As with many problems of the singing voice, faulty breath management may be the cause of nonvibrancy. Sometimes a young singer has been advised that he or she is suffering from excessive vibrato, when the problem has to do with inequality of the cps (cycles-per-second) rate, not with the concept of vibrancy itself. As a corrective move, retain the inhalatory abdominal-wall position throughout an upward vigorous glissando, adding an emotional content as though suppressing high-pitched laughter. Next, if you are willing to be a bit foolish, play the childish game of "I am a ghost!" with "scary" vibrancy as you glissando up and down. Notice the almost imperceptible pulsing in the abdomen, while at the same time appoggio contact is retained. These maneuvers will help to induce vibrato and steady its cycle-per-second rate. Some singers find success in imagining a rapidly low-bouncing ball while singing a single pitch. Do not become discouraged if results are not immediate; repeated attempts generally produce an awareness of abdominal breath management that steadies the vibrato rate. Alternating neighboring pitches—beginning slowly, then gradually increasing velocity—may prove fruitful, although I have not generally found it so.

COLORATURA AND VIBRATO

QUESTION
I have heard people talk about matching coloratura passages to the vibrato. I'm not sure what this means or how to do it.

RELATED QUESTION
Does it make sense to try to coordinate the per-second vibrato rate
with the number of notes in a run? I found that suggestion in [a
highly respected technique manual].

COMMENT
You are correct that an influential published pedagogic source maintains that
if a singer who has a 6.0 per second vibrato rate sings a rapidly moving melisma,
the vibrato must be eliminated, because there is not time for each note of the passage to accommodate the excursions of the vibrato rate. This hypothesis assumes
that vibrato is perceived as a pitch variant, when in fact vibrato is discerned as a
vocal timbre evenly distributed over the group of notes that make up the melismatic passage. Removing the vibrato for velocity passages, or attempting to syn-
chronize its occurrence with changes of pitch, negates the resonance balance. Basic
timbre can be retained regardless of the rapidity of moving passages.

TRILL

QUESTION
You advised to be on guard against practicing the trill too much. What are
the consequences of overdoing trill work? Can everyone be taught to trill?
How does the trill differ from vibrato?

COMMENT
Some singers consider the trill to be simply an agitated vibrato. Although
clearly related to the vibrato phenomenon, the trill represents an even greater degree of laryngeal movement. As part of the inducement of pitch variation, trilling,
unlike vibrato, depends on rapid oscillation of the voice box by quick, small perpendicular motions. The slight and speedy upward and downward laryngeal
movement that produces trill may be externally observable in the front of the neck.
This is not true of vibrato, or if so, to a far lesser degree. (See Free-Swinging Vibrancy; Identifying and Steadying Vibrato Rate.) When trill is first attempted, inducing the larynx to slightly shake up and down may give the impression that all
control has been lost. Therein lies its pedagogic value. Through conscious letting-
go in the laryngeal region, trill often frees the singer from trying to localize control over laryngeal function.
Assuming the teacher can trill, he or she should begin by trilling on a pitch
in easy range. Invite the student to join in. (Apart from hearing and seeing a demonstration of trilling, learning to trill is difficult.) The imitative process may bring
about an actual trill. If, following numerous attempts over a period of time, no results emerge, try associating trilling with kinesthetic movement, such as playing a

half-note trill on the pianoforte while imitating the pitch change and the physical action with the voice. Or with the index and middle finger on a solid surface, imitate a minor-second keyboard trill, simultaneously attempting a vocal trill. None of these devices is sure-fire, but all may be worth a try.

Some coaches go so far as to suggest a slight up-and-down head shake, perhaps in literal imitation of the oft-told incident of young Cotogni shaking his leg to induce trilling. This is problematic, because although it does initiate rapid laryngeal oscillation (part of the trill syndrome), it becomes difficult to disassociate the trill from excessive physical shaking.

It is largely the coloratura soprano and the coloratura mezzo who encounter trills in their literatures. Because of the freedom it prompts, all categories of voice, assuming a thorough technical foundation, should practice some trill. Male voices, except for the *tenore leggiero,* are seldom asked for trills in the standard literature. By contrast, some literatures of the eighteenth century require trilling from every voice category.

Learning to trill is generally easiest for females in upper-middle or upper range, and for males in speech range (below the *primo passaggio*). A lesson in trill perfection can be experienced by listening to and watching video clips of Joan Sutherland performances. During trilling, this remarkable artist exhibits externally visible movement in the front regions of the neck. Spectral analysis of her recordings reveals her extraordinary ability to accomplish various levels of nearly simultaneous pitch variation, followed by an immediate return to the basic vibrato pattern. Contemporary performances of fine singers, such as Renée Fleming, show similar patterns.

Why should one limit trilling? Because there may be a danger of becoming so accustomed to the physical motion of the trill that its faster rate and wider pitch excursions inadvertently intermingle with those of the singer's normal vibrancy rate. Unfortunately, some singers suffering from tremolo sound as though they are producing a permanent slow trill. The laryngeal oscillatory movement of the larynx essential to trill must not be mistaken for normal vibrato.

Eventually, the trill must be the result of a musical concept, not a corporeal act. Yet it results from an acquired physical action that almost always requires instruction. In rare cases, usually restricted to sopranos, the trill seems to be immediately possible.

TRILLO

QUESTION

What is *trillo,* and is it the same as trill? Doesn't its use during the Baroque period prove that Baroque music was sung without vibrato, unless an ornament such as the *trillo* was indicated? (I have been told that by an ensemble conductor who considers himself a Baroque expert.)

COMMENT

Robert Donington, in his excellent *A Performer's Guide to Baroque Music* (1973) defines the early Italian Baroque ornament *trillo* as "a tremolo-like pulsation (but not punctuation) on one note, with or without a gradual acceleration of the pulsation if time allows, but never precisely measured nor quite breaking the sound (beware of exaggeration)." This vocal ornament is not to be confused with the classic trill, nor considered as proof that Baroque vocalism was sung with straight-tone timbre except for the occasional *trillo*. Says Donington, "What we should call a normal and moderate vibrato went on inconspicuously all the time in baroque singing and string playing."

VIBRATO IN THE YOUNG SINGER

QUESTION

Is there an age below which a singer is too young to develop a vibrato?

COMMENT

In voices of any age, if sufficient energy and vocal-fold freedom pertain, vibrancy results. Children are often discouraged by their music teachers from singing vibrantly, but if taught to breathe well and to enunciate well, vibrancy will soon be present. There is no reason why a treble voice should not exhibit vibrant timbre. Unfortunately, there are hypotheses that equate vibrancy in a youngster's voice with unnatural, forced production. Because of some conductors' preference for a disembodied, "ethereal" quality of sound, many participants in children's choruses have been taught to remove the natural vibrato.

Children who are allowed to use their voices as solo instruments develop a natural vibrato rate. My own experience as a child who sang with vibrato was that the district music teacher, who periodically visited a number of our local grade schools, totally disapproved of me, although as a boy soprano I was already singing extensively in public. Outside the classroom, I enjoyed great approval; inside, I was a pariah. In my preschool period, my mother, who sang with vibrato, was my first voice teacher, teaching me numerous songs. She and her singer friends became my voice models. It is clear that if a child learns to manage the breath and to enunciate well, vibrancy in the singing voice will result. (See Free-Swinging Vibrancy; Identifying and Steadying Vibrato Rate.)

SPECTROGRAPHIC VIBRATO DISPLAY

QUESTION
Why do the third, fourth, and fifth formants (singer's formant) near the top of the spectrography graph show wider vibrato wiggles in spectral analysis than do the fundamental and the first formant in lower areas? Does the vibrato rate get wider in the accumulating higher overtones?

COMMENT
What may appear to be wider pitch variants in upper partials in spectrographic vibrato display is purely an artifact of the machine. Both the extent of pitch excursion and the rate of the vibrato produced by the fundamental are identical in all overtone components of each phonation.

USING STRAIGHT TONE AS A PEDAGOGIC TOOL

QUESTION
If pitch excursion of the vibrato is too narrow and the temporal rate too fast, producing a tremolo, could straight tone help solve the problem? Could not the straight-tone concept also be useful in achieving better pitch centering for a singer who has too wide a pitch variant and too slow a cps rate?

COMMENT
Good question. In general, compensatory corrections are to be avoided. The vibrato, a relaxant principle, is a major component of well-balanced resonance. (See Free-Swinging Vibrancy; Identifying and Steadying Vibrato Rate.) By removing all vibrato, inexpedient laryngeal changes happen to breath management and to resonance balancing. If vibrancy is removed, the timbre sounds held and lifeless. Many times, a tremolo (offensive speeding up of the vibrancy rate) comes about because a singer assists the vibrato by increasing glottal pressure. I like to suggest, "Don't assist your vibrato; it is already there." Model the two timbres— tremolo and vibrato. It may also be the case that a singer is simply trying too hard to "support the tone." It can be helpful to ask for a slightly straighter tone. In nine cases out of ten, the singer will not really sing a straight sound, but in thinking about removing some of the vibrato, pressure at the glottis may be reduced, resulting in a slower, more acceptable rate.

With regard to the singer who suffers from a slow oscillatory rate (wobble), I have not found the suggestion to sing straight to be useful. The problem in cases of oscillation is not too much energy, but too little. More productive is the use of short, energetic agility motifs that require flexibility and incite greater freedom.

Conclude them with a sustained note, retaining the same energy. Excitation of the fast-moving, short pattern will induce vibrancy on the longer note as well. Resonator-tract distortion from static vocal-tract shaping often contributes to the oscillation problem.

IS THERE A GERMANIC VERSUS AN ITALIANATE VIBRATO RATE?

QUESTION
I am a senior voice performance major at (a major school of music). I have been told that because of the timbre of my voice and the rate of my vibrato, I am probably going to be a German soprano rather than an Italian one. What does that mean? Is there really a German versus an Italian sound based on the vibrato speed?

COMMENT
Timbre variances are geared to aesthetic ideals. Internationally successful singers trained by well-informed German voice teachers do not show a slower and wider vibrato rate than what is considered acceptable in the international performance world. Nor do teachers of the Italian tradition look for a fast vibrato rate. Yet some German-schooled performers do have slower vibrato rates than do singers trained in an Italianate method. This is because of the tendency in some segments of northern and eastern European voice pedagogies to artificially darken the voice, thereby slowing down the vibrato rate through "down-and-out" breath support techniques, immoderate dropping of the jaw, and excessive lowering of the larynx. (See Appoggio versus Belly Breathing [*Bauchaussenstütz*]; Protruding the Stomach Wall.) Overweighted voice production can slow down both the temporal and pitch excursion rates of the vibrato cycle. Because of accumulating air pressure, some Italian-schooled voices tend toward the tremulous.

Physiologically, there is no reason why the larynx of a singer born north of the Alps should produce slower vibrato rates than those of a colleague born south of the Alps. Large, dramatic voices are essential to some German operatic repertoire, but a good singer is not restricted to any one national literature. Although vibrato rates relate somewhat to the size of the performer's instrument, slow vibrato rates are not characteristic of outstanding dramatic singers of any culture or style. In all events, young voices should stay away from attempting heavy vocal literature.

Without knowing the questioner's exact age, it is fair to speculate that her slower vibrato rate has more to do with inadequate breath management and distorted acoustics than with the nature of her instrument. She ought not to settle for an oscillatory sound, but search for a well-balanced timbre to which an even vibrato rate testifies. Based on vibrato rate, no young singer should be told he or she belongs within a particular *Fach* or national style.

REGISTRATION

FACH DESIGNATIONS IN THE YOUNG MALE VOICE

QUESTION

How do we safely determine the *passaggio* points of a young male singer?
Can they change with maturity? If they can shift over time, how reliable is
it to depend on them as early indicators of voice classification?

RELATED QUESTION

What, exactly, should one be listening for in identifying the registration pivotal points of a male voice?

ANOTHER RELATED QUESTION

I think I have a fair handle on female registration. But what do registration events sound like in the male voice? How can you tell when a
passaggio pivotal point has been reached?

YET ANOTHER RELATED QUESTION

Why do you designate the *passaggio* points of male voices over a
wider range than those of female voices? For example, you indicate a
number of specific pitch designations as *passaggi* for the several tenor
categories, and quite a few for baritones and basses. But you show
only a semitone or whole-tone difference among soprano and
mezzo-soprano categories, and only about a half-step difference between the mezzo and the contralto.

COMMENT

Laryngeal changes experienced at puberty are not as decisive for the female as for the male. There is greater diversity of laryngeal size and vocal-tract construction among males. In speech and laughter, females inflect their voices over a wider range, paralleling much of the singing voice. Males speak almost entirely in so-called chest (modal) range. A male is required to sing a large portion of his scale beyond the boundaries of speech range. Range demarcations among male voice categories are more distinct than those of female voices. Some young men, after experiencing puberty, arrive quickly at vocal stability, immediately revealing a category. If the young male singer has had previous solo or choral experiences, he may already have been designated a tenor or a baritone, and be comfortable with that classification. Unfortunately, early determinations sometimes are based on local ensemble needs rather than on physical realities.

In the young or untrained voice, pitches at which the timbre changes are fair indicators of *passaggi* locations. Although it is possible for a young man to mask pivotal pitches by producing unnaturally heavy and falsified timbre, it usually is possible to hear these slight changes, later to be smoothed out by good registration practices. The system for locating registration events is helpful but by no means foolproof, yet probably more reliable than trusting chiefly to a young male's current range capability.

Designation of voice category depends on personal history related to the events of puberty. Some youths experience a gradual transition from treble to adult male timbre, while others undergo sudden voice change. Puberty comes early for some males, and late for others. Rapid transformation from hearing oneself speak as a child can be psychologically traumatic. The male larynx undergoes radical growth during puberty. Like general body height, the thyroid and cricoid cartilages often show a remarkable increase in size, so that the laryngeal prominence may become a new physical landmark. The vocal folds grow correspondingly. In general, the taller the individual and the more prominent the larynx, the lower the speaking voice. Yet it is not out of the question for a tall, thin-necked young man with protruding laryngeal prominence to fit into one of the tenor categories. Although physical attributes at times are indicative of *Fach,* it is unwise to base early classification on physical appearances. Some baritone and tenor body builds are similar; others, diverse.

An indication of a young man's probable category can be hinted at by noting where certain events of his speaking voice occur. Have him inflect his spoken voice upward in a glissando as high as comfortable, with energized phrases such as "Well?" "Hi!" and "How are you?" Use these and other short speech patterns that rise to the highest speech-inflection range. Note at what pitch timbre lightens or terminates before the young man has to resort to outright calling. Next, have him lightly sing an upward-moving passage in a "marking voice." At reaching the termination point of the speaking range, the young untrained singer may involuntarily raise his head and larynx. Timbre becomes thinner, indicating that the young man has reached his first registration pivotal point. By placing a hand on his chest while speaking, he feels sympathetic vibration (leading to the false notion that the chest is a major resonator). As he inflects his voice upward, vibration seems to leave the chest. This change in sympathetic vibration happens in the region of the first *passaggio* (registration pivotal point).

For the potential baritone, this event may reveal itself at $B_3/B\flat_3$. If the young man is a potential tenor, at $C\sharp_4/D_4$ or even $D\sharp_4/E_4$. Subsequently, have him softly sing a nine-note major scale in $B\flat$ major, beginning at $B\flat_2$, ascending to C_4, and returning to the initial pitch. Again, determine at what pitch the timbre began to lighten. Another plan consists of lightly humming a rapid ascending and descending glissando phrase. In the early-teen voice, a change in timbre will probably occur near the *primo passaggio,* suggesting eventual *Fach* determination. A lyric baritone may experience this slight change at B_3; a more dramatic baritone, at $B\flat_3$; a bass-baritone, at A_3. When the change in timbre, or a shift to falsetto production, is necessary at C_4, depending on voice timbre and in part on physical build, the singer may eventually have to choose between training as a baritone or as a tenor. Indications of lighter timbre occurring on $C\sharp_4$ detail a fairly robust tenor instrument; on D_4, a lyric tenor; on $E\flat_4$, a *leggiero;* on E_4, a *tenorino.*

The second registration terminal point (*secondo passaggio*) occurs roughly a major fourth above that of the first (*primo passaggio*): for the lyric baritone, at E_4; a somewhat heavier baritone, at $E\flat_4$; for the bass-baritone, at D_4. For tenors, the *secondo passaggio* for the potentially heavier tenor voice occurs around $F\sharp_4$; for the lyric, at G_4; for the *leggiero,* at A_4. The region between the *primo* and *secondo passaggi* is designated as the passage zone (*zona di passaggio*). When normal speech extends to a point in the ascending scale where additional energy is required (as in calling), a young, untrained singer has an urge to elevate the chin and larynx. For singing, he needs to avoid the call of the voice as he enters the *zona di passaggio* (*voce mista*) and the area above (*voce di testa*). He does so by adhering to the *aggiustamento* principle of vowel modification and increasing breath energy.

Light tenor voices that very early leave no doubt as to category manage the *zona di passaggio* with relative ease and are not numbered among the questionable cases which concern the high school choral conductor or the private voice instructor. Perhaps the major mistake in determining male *Fach* designations too early happens when a young potential tenor of sizable voice exhibits good low notes but has difficulty in freely negotiating pitches in upper-middle and upper ranges. Detailed technical work through the *zona di passaggio* lies in the future. He should not be expected to immediately manage a high baritone or tenor tessitura. At this moment in his vocal instruction, freedom in middle range is the pedagogic aim.

In the period immediately following the change of voice, a youngster may be able to growl impressively at the lowest end of the speech-inflection range. This phenomenon is generally restricted to an individual who has undergone extensive laryngeal growth over a period of a few months. A young male may revel in the suddenly deep sound of his instrument, and augment it through laryngeal depression. Proudly, he may even request to be placed in the bass section of the choir. Delight in making new, impressive low notes may cause him to mask his true registration pivotal points. Early low-pitch capability has led to some professional tenors having been told as teenagers that they were basses.

It may take many examinations of the protocols suggested above before teacher and student can successfully determine at what point in the scale speech inflection tends to terminate. Both teacher and youngster need to be aware of the relationship of the speaking voice to the singing voice, and avoid manufacturing sounds imitative of mature voices.

When it comes to voice categorization, an early-teen male voice often should remain simply "young male voice." During early development, a male's technical work and solo song repertoire should be largely restricted to medium range. In the twenties, as the vocal instrument matures, there may be some lowering of the *primo passaggio* registration event, but seldom by more than a half-tone. A change of *Fach* is not obligatory, but may indicate that the singer is now ready to move on to more dramatic literature.

The male singer who continues to perform into his later years may notice changes in the *passaggio* area that require modified repertoire choices or even downward transposition of the literature. Yet many older males retain their initial *passaggio* locations, with little or no range loss.

EVALUATING *FACH* CHANGE FROM BARITONE TO TENOR

QUESTION

How do you advise a baritone who is thinking of becoming a tenor? If the change of category is going to be ok, how quickly can it happen?

COMMENT

Extending from *tenorino* through *basso profondo,* there are many subcategories of the male singing voice, in some ways analogous to female designations that extend from soubrette coloratura through dramatic contralto. Male voice categories are even more clearly delineated by the nature of registration events. (See *Fach* Designations in the Young Male.) Questions regarding male *Fach* designation largely pertain to the overlapping of tenor and lyric-baritone operatic categories. There are circumstances in which sizable baritone and tenor instruments can temporarily sing successfully in nearly identical ranges. One has only to think of the numerous opera duets in which the tessitura of baritone and tenor are paralleled, sometimes even in thematic imitation, both voices able to display their corresponding timbres for emotive purposes in similar range. Some few males are faced with a genuine choice of category. Based on training, they could go either the tenor or the baritone route. Determining pivotal registration points should be a deciding factor.

A number of premier operatic tenors have been confronted with "Are you sure you are not really a baritone?" An equal number of performing lyric baritones have faced the query "Are you sure you are not really a tenor?" Such quizzing may reveal more about a questioner's cultural and pedagogic orientations than knowledge of the individual singer's endowment. Why, for example, should there be such an overabundance of French lyric baritones and an equal profusion of Italian spinto tenors? The frequent Italian tendency to increase air compression through excessive breath pressure, and the French inclination to resist the necessary degree of breath energy, may in part explain the otherwise inexplicable Italian tenor/ French baritone ratio. Some teachers demand dark quality from any sizable male voice, together with premature heavy cover (*Deckung*). (See Early Covering in the Young Male Voice.) These adjustments produce slower vibrato rates, inhibit upper-range extension, and mask registration events. National tonal aesthetic preferences may adversely affect accurate determination of *Fach* designation.

The decision as to whether the singer should become a tenor or a baritone is not affirmed only by the comparative size of the larynx. Although it is generally the case that the larger the laryngeal construction, the lower the pitch level, there are some tenors who have larger larynges than their baritone counterparts (similar relationships exist among sopranos and mezzo-sopranos.) Nor is range extension itself the final determinant in establishing male voice categories. Many fine baritones eventually have a ringing high A, B♭, B, or even High C. Some designated tenors easily negotiate low A♭, G, or even lower pitches. It is not range extension but voice timbre—the peculiar combining of physical and psychological factors—that determines the final classification of a voice.

If a young singer cannot readily negotiate the *zona di passaggio* (for the lyric tenor, D_4 to G_4; for the lyric baritone, B_3 to E_4), it is tempting to assume that another voice classification is in order. It must not follow that because freedom in the passage zone is not early achieved, a lower voice category is indicated. However, if over a period of time, and with extensive attention given to stabilizing the *zona di passaggio,* the area remains effortful, a reassessment of *Fach* designation may be in order. Final *Fach* determination must be based on the degree of skill established in the upper range (above the *secondo passaggio*).

A shift in voice category beyond one's late twenties is seldom a wise move. In a mature singer, the change from baritone to tenor generally cannot be facilitated in less than eighteen months to two years of daily intensive work, and only if the singer already enjoys good breath-management skills and laryngeal freedom, and has a hold on resonance balancing. Yet in rare cases, the change of *Fach* can occur rapidly.

Although occasional, sudden upper-range breakthroughs are possible, range extension for most males takes place in a half-step-by-half-step, week-by-week, month-by-month process. Not to be overlooked is the singer's self-image. Personal esteem and confidence may play as much of a role as physiology does. Some potential tenors who continue to sing as baritones have not recognized their true category because they hesitate to risk the necessary energy it takes to secure the legitimate upper range of the professional tenor voice. This is equally true of some lyric and dramatic baritones who settle for classification as basses. For the male singer who has struggled unsuccessfully for years to attain tenor status, it may be well to accept that entrance into the tenor kingdom was never in the cards. He should become satisfied with dwelling in less rarefied realms where, in any event, most male singers are quite content to function. There are also males who very much want to sing the literature of the high-lying baritone *Fach,* having fallen in love with its many appealing arias, who must finally learn that singing the often less romantic bass-baritone roles is really proper homeland.

In all cases, the factor of age must be a primary consideration. Premature classification of a young singer's voice is counterproductive, and may lead to years of frustration. Early technical concern should be directed to coordinating the motor, the vibrator, and the resonator, not to the determination of *Fach.* When production becomes free, the voice tends to reveal its proper category.

CHEST VOICE IN THE LOW-VOICED MALE

QUESTION
In [a highly respected source on voice technique and physical function] I read that basses and baritones carry the chest voice up to E_4 or F_4, at which point they go into head voice for the few remaining high notes. It states that tenors sing in a light chest voice up to about F_4, or $F\#_4$, then pass into head voice to high A_4. All notes above that are in a pure or reinforced falsetto. What is your opinion?

COMMENT
Habitual male speech extends upward to the area of the *primo passaggio,* the point at which a male must begin using "the call" of the voice when speaking. The male middle range (*zona di passaggio*) stretches to approximately a fourth above this termination of the speech range, arriving at the *secondo passaggio.* Upper-range expansion lies above the *secondo passaggio.* Middle and upper ranges require greater energy. Where these pivotal points occur marks a major determinant of voice categorization. (See *Fach* Designations in the Young Male Voice.)

To assert that all males sing in chest voice throughout most of their negotiable ranges, with tenors adding on something called "head" or "reinforced falsetto" in upper range, is to misunderstand the principles of voice registration and the differences among male larynges. Similar registration events appertain to all; they simply happen at different degrees in the mounting scale. (See Energy Levels in Tenor and Baritone Voices.) In general, the longer the vocal folds and the larger the larynx, the lower the pivotal registration points in the scale and the lower the voice category. Were males to use solely the quality traditionally called "chest," they would be shouting through much of their middle and upper ranges; were tenors to use a reinforced falsetto, they would be producing a sound appropriate only to the operatic countertenor. I am not in agreement with the source you cite, with which I am familiar.

TENSION BUILDUP DURING SOPRANO HIGH-LYING PHRASES

QUESTION

I am unable to stop tension that often builds up when I sing long, sustained high passages, as with Sophie's "und weiss nur eins" from the *Rosenkavalier* final trio, where the pitches jump from Ab_5 to high B within one long, high-lying phrase. As the phrase goes on, either I become strident or the tone just begins to diminish, which is not my aim! Sometimes I experience unpleasant sensations at the front of the neck, or even in the larynx, and I feel at the very end of my breath before getting to the phrase finish.

COMMENT

The singer's age and vocal category are not indicated, but only a technically secure soprano of vocal maturity ought to be tackling Sophie's demands. Her cumulative long phrases are typical of Strauss. The cited passage follows a long series of strenuous phrases, and the role is demanding for even the most skilled singer.

Let us assume that the singer is technically stable, perhaps preparing the role for a stage appearance. Almost any professional singer will admit that somewhere in nearly every long opera role, there are one or two passages that feel vocally ungrateful. Such challenges must be identified, tackled, and licked. Repeating the demanding aria or troublesome passage over and over again is not the best way to solve the problem. Try breaking the difficult phrase into brief segments: F_5 to Ab_5, G_5 to Bb_5, then the single note B_5. At each release, insert an additional onset or two at the terminated pitch, with silent breath renewals between the segments. Every note must be fully vibrant in order to ensure completeness of timbre in later moving from one note to the next.

Next, remove the inserted onset; combine the first two bars of the passage into a single unit. Follow it by silent, quick breath renewal, then sing the next two bars. Producing these phrase segments with vibrancy, each followed by an inserted, refreshing, silent breath renewal, should alleviate the phrase's fierceness. Finally,

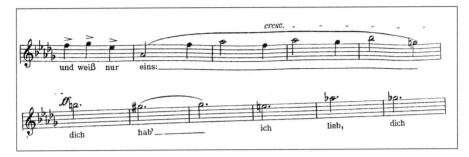

FIGURE 7.1. "und weiss nur eins: dich hab' ich lieb." (From R. Strauss, *Der Rosenkavalier.*)

sing the complete original phrase. This plan can be applied to any arduous phrase several times per day in short practice sessions. Over a period of several weeks, it will no doubt become easier. Then reincorporate the phrase or phrases into the whole musical fabric.

It probably is not simply an isolated phrase or two that contributes to the tension buildup, but the sum of the many sustained phrases that precede it. Earlier phrases may require similar detached treatment. Sophie is concluding a prolonged, strenuous ensemble. Whenever a particular spot in an aria or a song becomes problematic, the singer should begin with a phrase or two just before the troublesome place, take it apart, work the detailed segments, and then sing the entire phrase. Gradually add additional phrases.

The singer mentions that her tone turns strident, indicating that vowels may not be properly tracked or modified. Her mouth must be appropriately opened to accommodate the tessitura of the passage in question, with vowel integrity maintained by avoiding excessive modification or too high a dynamic level. She should check with the hand mirror to be certain that the tongue remains in contact with the inner surface of the lower front teeth, and that the fascia of the zygomatic region does not fall. (See Elevating the Fascia of the Cheek Region.) Keep in mind that the whole ensemble is sung only once in actual performance, so don't overdo repetition of it in the practice studio.

Reference to unpleasant sensations in the front of the throat and larynx could indicate insufficient external-frame support. Recall that the front of the neck should feet short; the back of the neck, long. (See Always Noble and Axial?) Good luck!

NARROWING AT THE *PASSAGGIO*

QUESTION
I am a female teacher. What is physically happening at the *passaggio* when male singers say they feel a narrowing there? Is this good or bad? If good, should it be taught to singers who lack that feeling, and how do you induce it?

I have tried using a registration chart included in a standard pedagogy text that tells males at exactly what point in the scale they
should shift one vowel to a neighboring one, that is, modify it. Some
vowels get broader; some, narrower. The chart is placed above the
keyboard and indicates at what note these registration modifications
should occur. Do you recommend its use?

COMMENT

As males enter the *zona di passaggio* and pass above it, no single experience
regarding vowel modification and adjustments of breath management can be uniformly expected. Many fine male singers have no sense of narrowing at the *passaggio* region. But it is common for an untrained or less than skillful singer to
express concern regarding changes in sensation as the *secondo passaggio* is approached. When first properly modifying the vowel, a male singer may get the impression that the sound has become more compact, narrower. *Voce aperta,* as its
name implies, feels "open," whereas *voce chiusa* is perceived as more concentrated, focused, "closed." These expressions do not refer to conscious maneuver-
ing of the larynx or vocal tract, but to measurable acoustic factors that ensure good
vowel tracking and desirable modification. (See *Voce Aperta* and *Voce Chiusa.*)
Because each voice is unique, it is not possible to establish a uniform standard for
the modification of every vowel in an ascending scale.

I find the generic vowel-modification chart to be unnecessarily restrictive
and too general. Establishing individual timbre consistency in the passage zone
and upper range constitutes a major part of male professional voice training. Although there is the general rule that vowel modification occurs in the passage zone
and above, no two singers handle it completely alike. Vowel modification is a sophisticated technique that must be tailored to each individual voice. Its application
is perhaps the most subtle of all technical matters.

I would never request a sensation of narrowing at the *passaggio,* nor would
I advise use of the predetermined chart for directing the ear to vowel modification.
If, in achieving an even scale, the singer experiences a narrowing sensation in
the *zona di passaggio,* well and good, but the teacher should not try to induce that
perception.

DEVELOPING UPPER RANGE

QUESTION

I have a very weak upper voice. Should I just keep banging away in
upper register until top tones come? Should I try screaming up there
"like a Neapolitan fishwife," as I was advised to do by [noted teacher]
in a seminar dealing with pop style? I was kind of afraid to try that.

COMMENT

It is tempting to respond that there is something fishy about the suggestion that you should scream like a Neapolitan fishwife. In my opinion, you were wise not to follow that advice. Regardless of gender, it is a mistake to try to develop the upper range in separation from the rest of the instrument, by carrying the chest (call) voice upward. Above all, don't scream. Unless upper-middle voice is relatively stable and freely produced, ventures into upper range are rarely profitable. Occasionally, some sudden excursion into upper range can produce results, but the high range is built gradually on healthy functional responses previously established in middle range. A far better measure than screaming is to engage in hilarious laughter, delivered with abandon. We often laugh in ranges well beyond those encountered in normal speech. Laughter is an unconsciously controlled yet normal function of the voice. On the contrary, the scream occurs at extremely high levels of vocal-fold resistance to airflow, and with excessive damping (See Damping.) Although it is true that breath energy must increase when ascending pitch exceeds the speech range, there is no need to add disproportionate vocal-fold closure such as occurs in screaming.

The person who recommended that you scream has one foot in physiologic verity but the other foot mired in false assumptions regarding vocal-fold closure and airflow pressures. The scream is a product of high-level psychologic and physiologic tensions; laughter is not. Screaming accompanies fear and terror. Phonatory freedom is not present in screaming, whereas freedom is the very essence of high-pitched laughter. In yelling, the vocal folds are elongated for pitch extension; but the ligament edges are forced together with such resistance to airflow that pathologic phonation is the only possible outcome. Screaming is the ultimate form of pressed phonation, attested to by spectral, stroboscopic, and EGG analyses. The questioner should practice flageolet maneuvers. (See Flageolet; Vocal Glissando [Extended Portamento].) Try laughter and siren calls on vowels or on the sustained consonants /v/ and /m/. Begin a systematic, daily routine of *passaggio* exercises. Visit Naples, have a bit of *frutti di mare,* but don't scream, no matter how revered the person who recommends it to you may be!

LOW-RANGE LOSS IN THE FEMALE VOICE
AFTER HIGH-RANGE SINGING

QUESTION

I am a soprano actively engaged in a successful performance career. Sometimes after having sung an entire role, or with an orchestra in something like the Verdi Requiem, my speaking voice is noticeably higher than it was when I began the performance. This also happens at the close of some recital appearances. Then my low voice, even in speaking, becomes less clear. The bottom seems to fall out. What am I doing wrong?

RELATED QUESTION

After I have warmed up a long time, or worked through a couple of arias such as "Caro nome" and "Nun eilt herbei," I can sing C_4 (middle C), D_4, Eb_4, and E_4 only in a chest voice. Mixtures won't work. If I don't go into chest, the sound is very airy and thin. Any explanation?

ANOTHER RELATED QUESTION

Losing a couple of pitches at the bottom of the range after sustained vocalization in the top voice is a common occurrence with me. How can a soprano add notes to her top range without losing quality and volume at the bottom? Sometimes, at the end of a full recital, even my speaking voice is embarrassingly high. What does this mean? Do I need to worry about it?

COMMENT

As pitch ascends, the vocal folds elongate; their mass diminishes, offering greater resistance to airflow than is the case in lower scale regions. No one, male or female, can sustain the highest tessitura for inordinate periods without experiencing some laryngeal fatigue. Much of elite vocal literature, including strenuous arias, hovers in upper-middle voice, not in the stratospheric regions, although there are notable exceptions. High-lying phrases are generally reserved for moments of climactic passion. Part of the reason for the development of *Fach* designations was to make certain that dramatic literature not be demanded of light voices. In attempting to sing ponderous literature, a more lyric voice may suffer fatigue and experience a loss of the first formant upon returning to lower range. (See Air Pressures in High and Low Singing.) No singer should choose an entire program of high-lying literature. Perhaps the questioner is choosing literature that lies too high or is too dramatic for the nature of her instrument.

Establishing ease in upper range depends on establishing a free middle range. Brief agility patterns should first be brought into play. (See Sensation Associated with Melismatic Movement.) No singer, female or male, should thunder away at upper range in hope of securing it. Range extension is a gradual accomplishment. Following a reasonable period of upper-range singing, there should be minimal, if any, loss of quality upon returning to lower voice. If a singer quickly fatigues after moderate high-range exposure, acoustic and physiologic factors may be in conflict.

In an evening of energetic singing, particularly at high tessitura, the vocal folds experience some degree of superficial swelling. On returning to low voice, the somewhat thicker surfaces of the folds respond less well than when stretched in high range. That is the reason why the second questioner must resort almost entirely to chest voice when singing the lowest notes of her range.

Is this bad? Not necessarily. It depends on the degree of vigor necessary to the performance of the task. But a loss of low voice after modest amounts of vocalization in high range may indicate that vocal-fold tension has been excessive.

There is no doubt that the more skillful the singer, the lower the incidence of any aftermath of vocal-fold puffiness following high-tessitura singing. The problem seldom faces low-voiced female singers, who are less frequently requested to maintain high tessitura levels. If incidences are occasional, no permanent damage results. Overnight voice rest reduces modest degrees of performance edema. Recurring bouts of this condition betoken the need for more complete coordination between breath and larynx, most likely calling for reduced energy and less volume.

HOW MUCH FEMALE CHEST IS TOO MUCH?

QUESTION
I am a soprano. I studied and sang a number of years in Germany, where I was taught never to use chest voice. You have displayed spectral analyses applied to recorded performances of a number of premier singers from the past, including Leontyne Price, Eleanor Steber, Mirella Freni, Graziella Sciutti, Shirley Verrett, Risë Stevens, and Blanche Thebom. Some of these performers make drastic quality changes as they enter low range. When they do, they sound to me as though they had suddenly become baritones. They make a mannish sound. Is that healthy vocalism, and is it acceptable practice these days?

COMMENT
"Chest voice" is a valuable timbre coloration that should be available to the accomplished female singer. In classical singing, its use is limited entirely to low range. (See Weak Spots in the Female Scale.) The introduction of chest timbre is common to singers trained in the historic Italian school, but largely shunned among singers who have emerged from the Nordic/Germanic tradition. Even the great Norwegian dramatic soprano, Kirsten Flagstad, made almost no use of chest. Approval or disapproval is largely an aesthetic decision. Most premier female singers, such as those you mention, use chest and chest mixtures as part of the interpretive palette. Marilyn Horne makes stunning use of contrasting registration colors, for example. There is no reason not to engage chest timbre in low voice, since it is essential for emotive purposes in much of the literature. The only danger arises when chest voice is carried into upper range.

EARLY STEPS FOR DEVELOPING FEMALE CHEST VOICE

QUESTION
How do you develop female chest and mixtures in low range?

COMMENT

Brief legato descending patterns, such as $5-4-3-2-1$, should first be sung in low range entirely in head. Begin in the key of B, with $F\sharp_4$ as the starting pitch: $F\sharp_4$, E_4, $D\sharp_4$, $C\sharp_4$, B_3. Sing the passage all in head except for the concluding B_3 in head/chest mixture. Then F♯ and E_4 in head, $D\sharp_4$ in head/chest mixture, $C\sharp_4$ in chest/head mixture, and the concluding B_3 in chest. Next, sing $F\sharp_4$ and E_4 in head, $D\sharp_4$ in chest/head mixture, and $C\sharp_4$ and B_3 in chest. Return to head for the entire pattern. In some cases, early attempts are a bit frustrating, but persistence pays off. Try this exercise in neighboring tonalities, making certain that chest is not carried upward beyond $E\flat_4$ for the soprano, or beyond E_4, for the mezzo-soprano. Light soprano voices may not be able to carry chest up as far as $E\flat_4$, whereas mezzo-sopranos will have little problem in doing so. More advanced low-range register transition drills should be delayed until this principal maneuver produces results. The more dramatic mezzo-soprano may want to begin the pattern at the tonalities of C and C♯.

Another procedure is to use a broken arpeggio on $8-1-8-3-8-5-8$, starting in the tonality of A major. The octave downward leap requires a transition from head to chest timbre; the $C\sharp_4$ third of the scale is sometimes sung in head, sometimes in chest or mixture. At E_4 the fifth of the scale will be in head, as will A_4. Repeat the exercise in neighboring tonalities, adjusting degrees of chest and mixture timbres.

WEAK SPOTS IN THE FEMALE SCALE

QUESTION

When singing a descending pattern, some of the females I teach have a sudden weakness around the octave above middle C [C_5, the pivotal midregister point between upper-middle and lower-middle voice]. Others seem to have a noticeable loss of volume and quality in descending passages, beginning about G above middle C. When they go right into chest from E♭ on down, they are ok. Suggestions?

COMMENT

This is a significant registration question. Bridging lower-middle to upper-middle range, or the reverse, is essential for an evenly balanced descending scale. When an unskillful singer reaches the upper pitch of her habitual speech range, there may be a noticeable timbre change, having to do with vocal ligament/vocalis muscle relationships. Depending on the size of the voice, this probably occurs at C_5 (octave above middle C) or at B_4, a half-step lower. It is the point at which upper-middle and lower-middle subregisters of the long female middle register converge. Soubrettes have little awareness of any change, whereas big lyric or dramatic voices often find those pitches somewhat troublesome. Some female singers describe a midrange hole at this scale point. A mezzo-soprano may experience the same event a half or whole tone lower.

It should be kept in mind that the soprano's middle range is longer than the mezzo's. Because some female singers with sizable instruments rarely speak in upper-middle range, coordinating participating muscle components must be routined for that transition area. Begin with brief descending passages around the *secondo passaggio*, carrying them downward through the pivotal midway point in the long female middle range. Alternately use front and back vowels, making certain that mouth postures appropriately shift to maintain vowel integrity. Subtle adjustments of breath management are highly important in this region of the scale. It may be that your problematic singers are not adjusting breath energy during descending passages. Sometimes there is a tendency to reduce the appoggio too early or, conversely, to retain too high an energy level as the scale descends. In my experience, it is mostly the former.

FLAGEOLET

QUESTION
Do all high sopranos have a flageolet? When singing in the highest upper range, should the flageolet voice produce a quality noticeably different from the rest of the head voice?

RELATED QUESTION
When sopranos first attempt their highest flageolet sounds, the aesthetic result is seldom great. They can make very high vocal sounds that would not be suitable to performance. Exactly why do you advocate daily flageolet practice?

COMMENT
Female flageolet function brings about the fullest elongation of the vocal folds and produces the greatest diminution of the vocal-fold mass. In pitches above C_6 (High C), the folds become thinner, with greater damping, offering more resistance to the exiting air. Inasmuch as this process also happens in the very highest pitches of the female voice, the additional stretching through flageolet practice makes high notes within the standard repertoire more readily negotiable. Daily flageolet practice helps secure the upper range of the female voice. Some few light soprano instruments can produce flageolet as high as C_7, adding freedom to the performable upper range. Flageolet events depend on registration pivotal points of an individual voice.

Almost every female, with the possible exception of the true contralto, can learn to produce sound in flageolet range. For pitches at the outer extremity of the upper range, the vocal folds are fully elongated and heavily damped. A limited anterior portion of the vocal fold is in vibration; the rest, firmly occluded. This produces a quality somewhat different from conventional head voice, being excessively bright and edgy. However, flageolet is simply an extension of head voice. An example of modified flageolet is to be heard in the high-lying staccato passages of the Queen of the Night arias and in most stratospheric coloratura displays. The purpose in practicing flageolet is not to produce a timbre markedly different from head voice, but to receive the benefit of the full extension of the vocal folds so that more generally encountered areas of upper range will become easier of execution.

THE ROLE OF FALSETTO IN THE TENOR VOICE

QUESTION
You appear not to believe, as did one of my former teachers, that the upper range of the tenor voice is produced in falsetto. Despite your negative view on that, do you think falsetto is of any use in training male singers, especially tenors?

COMMENT
The issue of falsetto in the male singing voice is compounded by the fact that the term "falsetto" has had various meanings for different groups of users. Was the *haute-contre* voice of early music and of the French Baroque actually falsetto? Was the upper range of the castrato (unlike the function of the unaltered male) what certain eighteenth-century treatises termed "falsetto"? Does falsetto lie in the midrange between chest and head, as Garcia designated? Is falsetto any vocal quality that is not modal (chest register), as asserted by several modern researchers who seldom work with the premier professional singing voice? Or is falsetto the male imitation of upper-range female voice quality, a sound that can be produced by most males for comic or coloristic effects and serves as the chief register of modern-day operatic countertenors? An understanding of the pitch-changing mechanism may help clarify the issue and determine what the true relationship of falsetto to registration practices ought to be.

For both speaking and singing, the vocal folds are shortest and thickest in low registers. As pitch ascends, the folds elongate and their mass diminishes. Two muscle pairs, pars recta and pars obliqua, lie between the thyroid and the cricoid cartilages. These cricothyroid muscles are both extrinsic and intrinsic laryngeal muscles, originating on the exterior of the cricoid cartilage and having internal insertions on the arytenoid cartilages, to which the vocal folds themselves are attached. (See figure 3.1.) It was formerly thought, and is still incorrectly maintained by some writers, that only the thyroid cartilage is tilted forward and downward as pitch ascends. However, the cricoid cartilage also shares in the movement induced by the cricothyroid muscles. These actions alter the length of the vocal folds and correspondingly change dimensions of the body of the folds. As the fundamental pitch rises, the vocal folds become thinner and tauter. Through this tensing process in high pitches, the vocal folds increase their resistance to airflow.

It is confusing to equate falsetto with all male vocal sound produced above the speech range, and shortsighted to take into account only the elongation process of the vocal folds. This ignores the magnitude of vocal-fold adduction and the synergistic actions of the laryngeal mechanisms that produce precise vocal-fold closure. Although vocal-fold elongation takes place in male falsetto, vocal-fold adduction during falsetto remains slacker and incomplete. The fact that falsetto timbre avoids firm, clean adduction of the vocal folds is verifiable through stroboscopic examination.

Each vocal fold is composed of three closely knit subdivisions: a cover, including the ligament that forms the fold's inner edge; a transition material; and the vocalis muscle that extends inward to the wall of the thyroid cartilage. Approximately one-third of the posterior portion of the vocal fold is attached to the arytenoid cartilages and remains nonvibratory during phonation. Depending on the fundamental being sung, the rest of the vocal fold (the membranous portion) vibrates at varying cycles per second (cps). For example, 440 approximations per second result in A440 Hz (A_4).

The pyramidal arytenoid cartilages, to which the vocal folds are attached at the vocal processes, swivel outward as the glottis opens, then inward as the glottis closes. The cricothyroid muscles are largely responsible for pitch change. While it is the duty of the posterior cricothyroid (sometimes called the posticus) to open the glottis, a muscle group composed of the interarytenoids (transverse and oblique cricoarytenoids and lateral cricoarytenoids) incites glottal closure. Action is not limited to one static open or closed vocal-fold setting; degrees of closure occur. For example, if a speaker begins to phonate in a breathy whisper, gradually introduces tone of more substance, then arrives at well-balanced phonation, he or she has altered relationships among the muscles of the glottal opening/closure system. If the speaker continues to increase the degree of vocal-fold closure and subglottic pressure, thereby squeezing the folds tightly together, pressed phonation results.

Although it is possible to reinforce falsetto timbre, neither the function nor the resultant tone is identical to that of *voce piena in testa* (full head voice). *Voce piena in testa* is essential to the negotiation of the professional male singer's upper range, and it demands full vocal-fold closure. No healthy professional tenor of international standing publicly produces his upper voice in falsetto, except for some rare moment of vocal coloration.

In a not far distant incident, one international tenor when singing at La Scala used falsetto for high-lying bel canto passages. He was met with a chorus of deri-sive shrill whistles. (Pitch designations follow the U.S.A. Standards Association system. See Appendix I.) Reinforced High C ($[C_5]$ or High D♭$[^{D♭}_5]$) in falsetto sim-ply does not exhibit the same quality as do those pitches when produced in *voce piena in testa*. (See figure 3.3. Although the vocal folds are not as firmly occluded in falsetto as in *voce piena in testa*, cultivated falsetto seldom displays such an extensive glottal gap as that indicated by 3.3*e*, which represents a very light, airy falsetto sound.)

It is notable, however, that in some *tenorino* and small *leggiero* instruments, there is less drastic timbre change when going from falsetto to full voice than in sizable voices of potential professional viability. Still, substituting falsetto for full voice in any male category is something of a dodge, an avoidance of the discipline it takes to find true *voce piena in testa*. Reliance on falsetto for high-lying pitches attests to an inability to accomplish a completely balanced vocal scale. The argu-ment is sometimes made that by singing the top voice in falsetto, a young tenor will lose his fear of high notes. On the contrary, it makes him realize that he is avoiding the very energy and resonance levels necessary to accomplish enough vocal-fold closure to produce legitimate upper-range sounds.

What goes for the tenor is equally true of the baritone, the bass-baritone, and the bass. Within the latter two categories, events of registration occur lower in the written musical scale but constitute the same degrees of registration phenomena, adjusted to each individual voice. (See *Fach* Designations in the Young Male Voice.) Low categories of voices seldom have to attempt extremely high range.

Many pop idioms make use of male falsetto. Some remarkably lucrative cur-rent entertainment careers are built on mechanically amplified falsetto singing, just one aspect of a performance package that includes glittering costumes (or remnants of them), an abundance of hair (or total lack of it), conspicuous corpo-real gyrations, spectacular lighting, and fantastically attired, noisy backup bands. Falsetto (the term itself describes removal from timbre reality), while appropriate to some aspects of popular spectacle, does not play a part in elite repertoire, ex-cept as a singular, momentary interpretative departure.

Because of the structural differences between male and female larynges, the male speaks and sings for a greater portion of his ascending scale in what has tra-ditionally been termed chest voice than does the female. Although it is clear that the chest cavity cannot be of resonator significance, there is some fixed resonance in the trachea and bronchi. Sympathetic vibration is conveyed by bony and carti-laginous parts of the sternum and rib cage. A hand placed on the sternum of a speaking male will detect sympathetic vibration. As the upper level of the speech range is reached, vibratory rumbling in the chest becomes markedly reduced. As the singer continues into the *zona di passaggio* and approaches the *secondo pas-saggio* (approximately a fourth above the *primo passaggio*), sympathetic vibra-tory sensations seem to move upward into the head, conveyed to various locations by bone conduction. The resulting proprioceptive responses have given rise to the traditional designation of "head voice." (See *Fach* Designations in the Young Male Voice; Chest Voice in the Low-Voiced Male.)

Perhaps the subtlest technical work in the training of the classical (elite) male singer lies in accomplishing proper *aggiustamento* (adjustment) of chest and head sensations in the *zona di passaggio*. Technique systems which suggest that all males suddenly go from modal to falsetto at Eb_4, or E_4 (or even F_4) ignore the most fundamental principle of international historic vocalism. (See Register Separation.) Carrying the call of the voice (that is, the "chest voice") upward through the *zona di passaggio* results in pressed phonation, during which the closure phase of the vibrating vocal folds is too long and the opening phase too brief. When singing the treble-clef notation of 880 Hz, the tenor is singing at 440 Hz (his high A). His vocal folds undergo an opening and closing cycle 440 times per second. In pressed phonation, although the number of vocal-fold approximations remains the same, the closure gesture of each vibratory cycle lasts longer than it should, whereas in breathy production, each closure phase is briefer (or less complete) than it ought to be. In balanced phonation, the degree of vocal-fold closure and opening corresponds precisely to what the pitch desires. Many young males, but also some mature singers, rely on too great an increase in subglottic pressure and on aggressive vocal-fold closure when singing pitches that lie beyond the speech-inflection range. They indulge in pressed phonation, which is described in voice teaching circles as "forcing." Harmonic partials that lie below 2K (2000 Hz) then become dominant and the first formant grows excessively prominent, with loss of acoustic energy (overtones) in the region of 3K (3000 Hz), where the singer's formant is generated. In such cases, falsetto exercises can provide remarkable assistance. Because the vocal folds are not fully occluded in falsetto production, resistance to airflow is slackened. Nevertheless, in falsetto, the vocal-fold elongation necessary for pitch elevation still takes place.

When a male tends to grab at the onset, that is, to rely on heavy vocal-fold adduction, causing excessive resistance of the glottis to the accumulating airflow, momentary substitution of falsetto timbre as a practice device will assist in avoiding the rigid vocal-fold response present in the "call of the voice." A sudden transition, going without pause from falsetto timbre to legitimate full voice, produces a lighter onset, stronger in upper partials, in keeping with the singer's formant. The closure mechanism thereby avoids overactivation, and more appropriately matches the befitting degree of vocal-fold stretching.

Several useful exercises are recommended for developing this coordination. The singer begins with falsetto in the upper regions of the voice on a 5–4–3–2–1 single-vowel pattern, bringing into play the closure mechanism (the return to full voice) on the sustained final prime pitch. For example, a tenor begins in falsetto at high Bb_4 (notated in most scores an octave higher), then continues downward in that timbre on a 5–4–3–2–1 sequence to Eb_4, at which point he shifts from falsetto to *voce piena in testa*. He should learn to alternate two types of timbre: (1) a marked movement from falsetto to *voce piena* and (2) a gradual shift from one timbre to the other. If he does not have easy entrance to falsetto timbre at high B♭$_4$, let him truncate the exercise to a 3–2–1 pattern, beginning on G$_4$. He then follows the same procedure by transitioning from falsetto timbre to *voce piena* (full voice) on the concluding E♭$_4$. This maneuver is to be practiced in several neighboring keys.

One of the most useful practice techniques for avoiding pressed phonation is to move on a single pitch from falsetto to *voce piena in testa*. Try singing the pitch D$_4$ in falsetto, then immediately move into full voice on the same pitch with no pause between the falsetto and full timbres. Gradually introduce higher-lying neighboring pitches. Do this exercise in two ways: (1) make a distinctly audible switch from falsetto timbre to full voice with a noticeable register transition, then (2) gradually switch from falsetto to full voice, avoiding any sudden change of timbre at the moment of transition. Both approaches should be practiced with equal frequency. Proceed with neighboring onsets through the *zona di passaggio*.

An expanded exercise begins falsetto in upper-middle range on a single note, then makes a sudden changeover (complete vocal-fold approximation) to full voice, followed without pause by a descending 8–5–3–1 arpeggio. Replenish the breath, then onset directly on the transitional note at comfortable dynamic level, in full voice. Without interruption, complete the phrase on a downward 8–5–3–1 arpeggio.

To sum up, the purpose of these exercises is not to substitute falsetto for legitimate upper-range *voce piena in testa* during public performance, but to practice reducing excessive pressure by which the vocal folds offer too much resistance to the exiting breath. (See Pressed Phonation.) Moving from falsetto to complete voice helps the young tenor, baritone, or bass (adjusted for characteristic registration pivotal events) to find easier onset in the *zona di passaggio*. In the process, the singer establishes proper resonance balance for achieving free *voce piena in testa* timbre. Though it has pedagogic value, falsetto should never substitute for legitimate solo performance timbre.

IS THERE A FEMALE FALSETTO?

QUESTION

I've heard comments about a female falsetto, but I've never found one. Have you?

COMMENT

It is somewhat illogical to speak of a female falsetto, because the female instrument is incapable of producing a timbre in upper range that is radically differentiated from its *mezza voce* or *voce piena in testa* qualities. The male instrument can do so by the falsetto. Although the female experiences vocal-fold elongation and adduction in upper range as does the male, when her vocal folds are not fully approximated, she merely sounds breathy. While the possibility of male falsetto is largely restricted to sound produced above his *primo passaggio,* the female experiences no comparable function or timbre mutation in any part of her range.

VOCE FINTA

QUESTION
You played spectral analyses of arias sung by wonderful male artists such as Robert Merrill, William Walker, Leonard Warren, Fischer-Dieskau, Dmitri Horostovsky, Jussi Bjoerling, Ferruccio Tagliavini, Richard Tucker, Nicolai Gedda, Luciano Pavarotti, and Placido Domingo. You pointed out that each of these singers on occasion used a rare quality termed *voce finta.* How is it done? Is it something every male can learn to do? I heard it and I loved the effect. Is there a female *voce finta?*

COMMENT
    Voce finta (incorrectly termed *voce di finta* in one major pedagogic encyclopedic source) is best defined as "feigned voice." It happens when a skilled male singer purposely slightly raises the head so as to shorten the vocal tract through intentional laryngeal elevation, simultaneously reducing breath energy and dynamic level. It generally is restricted to midvoice—the *zona di passaggio* region. Carrying *voce finta* upward beyond the *zona di passaggio* is perilous because the removal of support invites cracking.
    In contrast to falsetto production, vocal-fold approximation in *voce finta* is complete. *Voce finta* is an intentionally and momentarily unsupported sound, meant to produce an ethereal or disembodied effect. With added energy and a return of the head, neck, and larynx to the axial, noble position, *voce finta* becomes *voce piena.* *Voce finta* timbre can remain fully vibrant or take on straight-tone character. It is useful as an occasional, subtle coloristic device. Some male lieder singers rely on it to such an extent that it becomes a cloying mannerism, especially when coupled to straight-tone timbre. The only real danger in an inexperienced singer's making use of *voce finta* is that he might become accustomed to using it as a surrogate for true *mezza voce.*
    A female can, of course, remove energy and support from her voice in upper-middle range, but in so doing she mostly sounds like she is distorting tone for an emotive purpose, or is marking. Yet when she introduces this rare vocal coloration, there is a similarity to male *voce finta* quality. She cannot, however, make

a true, comparable timbre alteration. The term *voce finta* is best reserved to describe a male vocal phenomenon.

FALSETTO AND AIRFLOW

QUESTION

Why is it that when working with falsetto exercises to ease onsets in the *passaggio* zone, my male students and I get a rapid escape of air, leaving us quickly winded? We cannot maintain lengthy phrases in falsetto.

COMMENT

Falsetto's unique quality of sound comes from the fact that the vocal folds are less completely occluded than in *voce piena in testa.* That is one of the reasons why, in performance, falsetto should not be substituted for *voce piena* in upper male range. Your experiences verify that falsetto production is not part of the performable male upper range, except for an occasional effect and in its service to the counter-tenor. You should, however, continue with the falsetto-to-full-voice exercises.

By an increase of appoggio activity in reinforced falsetto, a higher degree of vocal-fold approximation and a more complete voice quality are created, as is common with today's dynamic countertenor voices. Still, glottal closure is less constant than in traditional *voce piena.* (See Countertenoring.) One of the advantages of occasionally prefacing onsets with falsetto during technique sessions is that any tendency toward the pressed onset is reduced. When transition to *voce piena* occurs, the onset becomes balanced rather than pressed. (See The Role of Falsetto in the Tenor Voice.) In short, you, your male students, and the rest of us males experience a faster loss of breath when singing falsetto because vocal-fold closure is less complete than in *voce piena in testa.* (See Falsetto and Airflow; More on Falsetto; and Pressed Phonation.)

MORE ON FALSETTO

QUESTION

A revered teacher of singing recently wrote that all great tenors and sopranos, past or present, used or use falsetto in their high ranges. This raises three questions: (1) What does falsetto for the female voice mean, since it can't be made to sound like falsetto in the male voice? (2) How is male falsetto produced? and (3) Is falsetto, as the mentioned teacher states, really normal upper extension of the tenor voice?

COMMENT

In order to understand the reasoning of persons who place such importance on falsetto, let us briefly review a nontraditional hypothesis regarding the number of voice registers that was developed in the second half of the twentieth century. Three registers are identified: vocal fry, modal, and falsetto. Even by this theory, vocal fry, although designated a register, is not considered a usable performance timbre. (See Vocal Fry.) Modal register (roughly the speech-inflection range) is equated with traditional "chest voice," while everything lying above modal is termed falsetto. This usage is not in line with the language of traditional pedagogy, in which the term "falsetto" is reserved to describe the sound imitative of the female voice that most males are capable of making in upper range. (See The Role of Falsetto in the Tenor Voice.) In male falsetto, the degree of glottal closure is less complete than in *voce piena in testa,* which is often called "head voice." Differences in vocal-fold action between falsetto and *voce piena in testa* are fiberoptically verifiable.

The countertenor is, of course, almost entirely a falsettist, except for pitches in his lowest range. He must give special attention to breath control as a means of countering less than optimal glottal closure. (See Countertenoring.) Although a female may be lacking in ideal upper-range vocal-fold approximation, the resulting quality becomes breathy but does not sound as though she has switched to another register, as is true in going from pure falsetto to *voce piena* male production. (See Is There a Female Falsetto?)

Contrary to the statement that great singers always use falsetto in developing upper range, my experience is that most premier singers do not consider falsetto training to be the route to *voce piena in testa.* Jussi Bjoerling, often considered the ultimate tenor technician, told me that he never had practiced, nor would he publicly sing, falsetto. Further, any tenor who resorts to falsetto production in upper range when performing the standard operatic literature will soon learn that it is not acceptable practice. (See Falsetto and Airflow; Pressed Phonation.)

VOCAL GLISSANDO (EXTENDED PORTAMENTO)

QUESTION
You asked for a long siren sound from several female singers. What is its purpose? Should both males and females do it?

COMMENT

In a wide-ranging pitch glide executed from the bottom to the top of the scale by an uninterrupted glissando, then returning to the starting pitch, the vocal folds go through a rapid process of elongation and thinning during the ascending phase, and in the sweeping descent a reverse process takes place. The singer automatically and unconsciously adjusts vocal-fold ligament and vocalis muscle interactions. An extended glissando (rapid portamento) makes a good, quick warm-up exercise, and it assists in register bridging. It also is useful for clearing superficial phlegm. Both males and females should practice this on the /m/ hum and on the sustained /v/ phoneme, which will increase awareness of appoggio activity. Suggest imitating a siren. Both females and males should begin the glissando in low register, the male switching into falsetto for the uppermost regions of the scale.

MEZZA VOCE

QUESTION
Is mezza voce done by mixing breath into regular tone, thereby reducing volume?

COMMENT
Giovanni Lamperti supplied the best advice: singing piano is in all respects the same as singing forte, except it is softer. If breath is added to tone in order to reduce volume, the resonance balance cannot remain of one piece with the timbre of other dynamic levels. In fact, a legitimate mezza voce requires an increase, not a decrease, in appoggio action. An old adage is "While singing piano, support forte." If the rate of exiting breath within a passage is higher than normal during the mezza voce, the singer will lack sufficient breath for completing the phrase. On rare occasions, a breathy quality may answer the need for a particular color, but mezza voce should be developed through disciplined *messa di voce* technical routining, not through breath admixture. (See *Messa di Voce.*)

BELTING

QUESTION
You seem to believe that belting is hard on the female voice. Why?

COMMENT
This is a question I hesitate to answer because I do not teach belting techniques. A number of current teachers believe there are ways to modify the negative effects of belting. I sincerely hope they are right. I suspect my colleagues who teach belting may wish I had excluded the topic from this collection.

Consider for a moment the stretching action experienced by the vocal ligaments (inner edges of the vocal folds) in ascending pitch. In superhigh pitch, vocal-fold fibers have been stretched to their fullest elongation. Tension can continue to be increased, but not vocal-fold length. To request a female singer to carry her chest voice into upper range is to encourage her to hold her vocal folds in a dense configuration while raising pitch, thereby inhibiting normal vocal-fold elongation. As a result, the singer approaches upper range by induced registration malfunction. The larynx is asked to function in an elevated position, so that the ventricular sinuses (spaces between the true and false vocal folds) are narrowed, eliminating a resonance source within the larynx.

The chief singer clientele in more than one metropolitan otolaryngologist's office is the untrained professional singer (a recent category of vocalist!) who characteristically carries chest voice into upper range. Belting carried into the middle and upper regions of the range must surely induce physical conflict. I doubt that this can be done with impunity. A number of teachers who are considered specialists in belting believe that *voce mista* (mixed voice) can be turned into some form of belt. If that is the case, they probably are no longer maintaining true belt quality. I remain unconvinced that unmitigated belting does not take a toll on the singing voice. I speak as a traditionally trained singer and voice teacher whose responsibilities have been restricted almost entirely to classical singing styles. I must also objectively note that some popular belters seem to enjoy long performance careers. Most do not. (See The Broadway Sound.) Are we still friends?

REGISTER SEPARATION

QUESTION
As you deal with registration for the male singer, you do not work on separating the registers by carrying each register function throughout all ranges before balancing them out. Are there reasons why you avoid teaching register separation?

COMMENT
Yes, I believe I have solid reasons for not teaching register separation. The aim of good teaching is to unite registers, not to separate them. Nonetheless, there are a few teachers who claim that the registers of both males and females must be separated before being properly united. Douglas Stanley was an early proponent of the system, which gained considerable vogue during the period before and following World War II. The number of Stanley followers has considerably diminished over the passing decades, partly because of the pejorative experiences encountered by singers who attempted to carry the "heavy mechanism" into upper regions of the scale. There is no physical danger in bringing the "lighter mecha-

nism" downward. In fact, it plays a major role in achieving an even registration throughout the voice. Traditional pedagogies attempt to bridge registers, particularly in middle voice, through the use of both descending and ascending melodic patterns. Most eschew the extreme measure of carrying chest as high as possible (that is, separating the registers). Inasmuch as melodies go upward as well as downward, it is also foolish to maintain that only descending rehearsal patterns should be used.

Given the nature of the pitch-changing mechanism with its subtle balancing between vocal-fold elongation and diminution of vocal-fold mass, holding the mass constant (as in chest voice) while ascending to high pitches invites register violation. No evidence exists that the intrinsic musculature of the larynx is strengthened by register-separation techniques. The proposition is a prime example of the dangers of pseudoscientific voice pedagogy. I want to unite the scale, not divide it into segments.

COUNTERTENORING

QUESTION
Should we traditional voice teachers consider the so-called countertenor voice a useful performance instrument? How should the technical training of a countertenor differ from that of other male singers?

COMMENT
As is well known, in Renaissance polyphony the term "contratenor," or "countertenor," denoted a voice part lying above the tenor line (*contratenor altus*) probably sung by a male with a small and unusually high-pitched voice. In the latter part of the fifteenth century, this singer was known in France as an *haute-contre*. At least by the seventeenth century, the French *haute-contre* was neither a castrato nor a falsettist, as the operatic roles given to him by Lully, Rameau, and their contemporaries attest. In England, as early as the sixteenth century, the contratenor began to be called a countertenor. Later on, the same kind of tenor instrument was dubbed a *tenorino,* a term still applied internationally to a very light tenor voice with facile top.

In England during the early seventeenth century, the term "countertenor" was used to identify a male alto falsettist (not a castrato). By the nineteenth century, it was almost solely the male falsettist who became known as a countertenor. Adult falsettists (that is, countertenors) had long been an important part of the Church of England's venerable choral tradition, reinforcing soprano and alto boy-treble voices in chapel and cathedral choirs, just as they do today. Despite occasional solo lines, few of these singers were notable as solo performers.

It is scarcely an exaggeration to say that Alfred Deller "invented" the modern-day English countertenor in the 1940s by turning what had been an eminent ensemble art into a solo medium. The countertenor role of Oberon in Britten's *A Midsummer Night's Dream* (1960) was written with Deller in mind. The American countertenor Russell Oberlin sang that role in 1961. In 1951, Oberlin had joined Noah Greenberg's newly formed New York Pro Musica group, and through the beauty and fullness of his timbre, and his exceptional musicianship, brought the countertenor voice to prominence in North America, singing the literature of former centuries as well as contemporary works. His timbre was much fuller than what for long had been considered the norm in the British falsetto tradition. Current American countertenor sound also departs from that of the traditional British countertenor, being more closely related to the Russell Oberlin model.

Many musicians began to look to countertenoring as an integral part of a new movement, a revitalization of a style of solo singing with roots in Early Music and Baroque literatures. It was nourished by the growing devotion to performance authenticity (HIP, historically informed performance). This gave rise to two frequent misconceptions concerning the countertenor: (1) that his is the modern equivalent of the castrato voice; (2) that he is the possessor of a rare laryngeal construction unlike that of other males.

There is limited laryngeal correspondence between the castrato voice of the Baroque era and today's countertenor. Castration inhibits bone growth. Boys who were castrated grew to be tall men with oversized chests and small larynges. They had prepubertal larynges located in large male bodies. If contemporaneous reports can be trusted, the castrato had phenomenal breath management skills, a large and often penetrating voice (capable of competing with trumpets). Unless puberty has been arrested, a countertenor does not have the laryngeal construction of a castrato. Although his presence is often a welcome addition to the performance world, the countertenor is not recovering the sounds of the Baroque operatic male solo voice.

Today's solo countertenor is largely a product of the period since the 1940s. It is ingenuous to be astounded by a countertenor's exceptional velocity ability, his subtle dynamic control, and his often three-octave performable range, none of which is normally matched by the traditional male singing voice. Vocal-fold elongation and diminution of the vocal-fold mass in ascending pitch are identically produced in falsetto and in complete male voice, but glottal closure is less complete in falsetto. Yet, increased breath reinforcement of falsetto can bring about a full, dramatic sound. This discussion does not rule out the pedagogic advantages of falsetto as a technical device in male voices. (See The Role of Falsetto in the Tenor Voice; Falsetto and Airflow; and More on Falsetto.)

Should they wish to take that step, a number of baritones and some tenors are potential countertenors. The kind of timbre associated with countertenoring can be available to many trained male vocalists. Almost any accomplished male singer can easily produce quickly running passages and pianissimo dynamic levels in falsetto production that would be much more difficult in *voce piena.* But it takes special skill to incorporate these procedures into a viable performance whole. There are male voices in which the sounds of falsetto are far more beautiful than those of *voce completa.* It is not unusual to encounter a male whose "other" voice, although pleasant, is far less gratifying than his countertenor one.

A number of male singers have wisely chosen to perfect skills that can be acquired when in falsetto register, and shifted into the countertenor category. The impressive part of fine countertenor technique lies in the singer's ability to sing sustained lines and long phrases, because the countertenor must learn to compensate for a normally less firm glottal closure than occurs with his other voice. It is not that he must try to locally control his breath or his vocal folds, but he must be particularly careful to preserve what is popularly termed "support." In an effort to do that, some countertenors reinforce the falsetto sound at constant high energy levels, a practice that could eventually raise health concerns. This means that in the operatic repertoire, the modern countertenor may be singing even more vigorously than his male colleagues. He no longer aims to sound like the countertenor of the British cathedral/chapel tradition. Yet, although he can make just as much noise as his soprano colleagues, he clearly does not sound like them.

Special skills are required of the countertenor, velocity capability being one of them. Above all, as he leaves falsetto range, he must discover how to incorporate the low-range singing voice (related to his speaking range) into the descending scale without a noticeable change of timbre. Most males can carry falsetto production no lower than a few pitches below the *primo passaggio,* at which time there is a noticeable shift in volume and quality. Achieving a seamless descending scale is a major challenge for the countertenor. It takes patience and time to manage. The countertenor can, of course, use his regular speech-level voice for a sudden "chest" effect, much as a mezzo-soprano or contralto does.

One successful practice device is to have the countertenor begin in comfortable upper range with a five-note descending passage in falsetto, then, without pause, sing the same pattern an octave lower in his "other" voice, aiming to equalize the two timbres. Return to singing the two segments in unbroken falsetto.

Yet another vocalise of merit is to begin the uppermost note of the great scale in its two-octave descent, determining at what point bridging between the two registers occurs. Then, small segments of the scale that lie on either side of the bridging point are drilled upward and downward. These exercises should be extended to other descending tonalities. Slow sustained octave leaping from upper to lower pitches, and the reverse process (lower to upper range) also prove useful.

The same skills that pertain to all elite singing can be applied to the training of the countertenor—breath management, agility, vowel definition and modification, the use of consonants to adjust the vocal tract, register equalization, and the *messa di voce*. However, because the modern countertenor's part in solo and operatic literature is a relatively recent phenomenon, there is no great historic solo pedagogic tradition on which to rely. Falsetto references in early treatises chiefly refer to the castrato or to imitation of the female voice. In Australia, England, France, Germany, the Netherlands, New Zealand, North America, and Scandinavia, master-class teachers are increasingly requested to teach countertenors. A number of American schools of music annually audition and admit a few male singers who wish to pursue countertenoring. Many national and international voice competitions are open to countertenors. Countertenors are cast in major opera roles at major houses. Because of current aesthetic demands, the countertenor is here to stay. Some singers can manage well in either voice, but using both techniques for separate public performances often becomes problematic. It is best to make a decision to go one way or the other.

The current generation of countertenors includes Jochen Kowalski (whose Gluck *Orpheo* in East Berlin before the toppling of the Wall remains a never-to-be-forgotten performance), Drew Minter, Brian Asawa, Derek Lee Regin, Jeffrey Gall, and the sensational David Daniels and Bejun Mehta. These fine artists, and a number of emerging others, bring new dimensions to the art of countertenoring. Despite inherent pitfalls, countertenoring is a viable choice for some male singers. Although special attention to particular techniques is necessary in teaching the countertenor, good vocal pedagogy is applicable to all voice categories. No mystery should surround the teaching of the countertenor.

STROHBASS

QUESTION
I've heard of a register called *Strohbass*. Where is it located, and what is its purpose?

COMMENT
Strohbass, also called *Schnarrbass,* is a male voice phenomenon that can be produced well below pitches normally used in traditional singing. By drastically lowering the larynx and expanding the pharyngeal wall, as in a sustained full yawn, the lower section of the vocal tract is widened and the pharyngeal resonator lengthened. This elongated resonator tube produces a voice quality that resembles deep growling.

In Russian Orthodox liturgical literature, *Strohbass* singers were specialists whose contribution was limited to a select number of low pitches. Through vocal-tract alteration, they became specialists in performing low-lying literature. Several touring Russian male choruses were much admired for the sonorous depth produced by their very low basses. It was, however, seldom possible for these low-note specialists to negotiate the rest of the scale with ease. Any male singer can temporarily add several additional pitches to low range by this device.

There is no real danger in an *occasional* use of *Strohbass*. It can momentarily be used with impunity to strengthen a pitch or two at the bottom of a male singer's accessible range, but is not suitable for extended phonation. If, for example, a young baritone can sing standard Mozart arias but has a disappearing A_2 or Ab_2, he can with impunity momentarily depress his larynx for those individual pitches. To retain that laryngeal posture as a general procedure would not permit registration events of the ascending scale to occur naturally. The singer returns to normal production as soon as the problematic low note (or notes) is terminated. Retaining an excessively depressed larynx and an extended pharynx, actions that can scarcely be separated, elicits laryngeal tension.

VOCAL FRY

QUESTION
What is vocal fry? What is it supposed to do? Do you use it yourself and with your students?

COMMENT
The term "vocal fry" is descriptive of the sound it makes: a glottal scrape, rattle, or "click." A sustained phonation in fry can be executed on one breath for a remarkable number of seconds. Because of the characteristic nonperiodicity of vocal-fold vibration it generates, fry can serve a research role in determining formants of the singing voice. When accomplished on one long, sustained breath, it may help to heighten awareness of abdominal-wall stability.

I am unaware of any scientific verification of fry's ability to strengthen the vocal ligament (inner edge of the vocal fold), to extend the range of the voice at both ends of the scale, or to improve agility. In opposition to fry advocates, a number of medical authorities consider fry an unhealthy procedure, because it places unaccustomed activity on the laryngeal mechanism. Fiberoptic observation shows heavy squeezing of the arytenoid cartilages.

Fry sounds like an extended bad onset. It is not necessary to make ugly sounds in order to arrive at aesthetically pleasing ones. Fry has invaded some voice studios along with several other recently advocated maneuvers that easily lead to gimmickry and becomes a substitute for solid, traditional technical work. Instead of experimenting with the hypothetical performance benefits of vocal fry, it is more productive to rely on proven voice maneuvers, such as training the glottis to respond to proper levels of airflow through the balanced onset, thereby achieving vocal-fold flexibility, and increasing stamina for range extension by sostenuto exercises.

BARYTON MARTIN

QUESTION
What is a baryton Martin?

COMMENT
The term "baryton Martin" derives from the proper name of French baritone Jean Blaise (Nicolas) Martin (1768–1837), celebrated for his extensive range. He was reputed to have upper range timbre approaching that of tenors, coupled with sufficient depth to sing roles of the baritone and bass-baritone literatures. His publicly performable scale extended more than two and a half octaves, from $E\flat_2$ to A_4. Whatever the actual sounds produced by Martin, a number of roles sung by the modern-day baryton Martin require vigorous, dramatic singing over a long range. The Muleteer (listed in the score as "baryton Martin") of Ravel's *L'heure espagnole* (1911) is an example. The roles of Escamillo, Pelléas, Il Prologo, and Valentin are sometimes cited as baryton Martin roles, although they lack exceptional low-range extension.

Much of the modern operatic repertoire requires the baritone to display extensive upper-range facility. Indeed, the upper range possibilities of many baritones equal those of their tenor colleagues. In addition, much of the current standard literature for baritone voice, written after the demise of Jean Blaise Martin, came at a time when range expectations for low-voice male categories were expanding. Perhaps Blaise Martin's long range would seem less remarkable to us today.

YOUNG TENORS AND UPPER RANGE

QUESTION
When should a young tenor begin to develop upper voice, and how would you go about initiating that development?

COMMENT
There is the occasional young tenor who early enjoys relative ease of range extension. His is normally a light voice—*tenorino* or *leggiero*—with little awareness of *passaggi* locations. He can respond quickly to exploratory vocalises into

upper range. Larger tenor voices arrive at upper-range ease more gradually. (See *Fach* Designations in the Young Male Voice.)

As with all categories of singer, and young males in particular, freedom in singing must be established within the comfortable lower-middle and upper-middle ranges before serious concentration on high-range extension can begin. If the young tenor has discovered freedom in the *zona di passaggio* (lying most likely between D_4 and G_4), he is ready to explore his upper range. If he grips or tenses in upper-middle voice, falsetto-to-full exercises may be helpful (See The Role of Falsetto in the Tenor Voice).

Development of upper range is generally a gradual process, calling for time and patience. It is traditionally accomplished through half-step sequences, using rapid passages that touch pitches beyond G_4, then quickly descend. When G_4 shows some degree of comfort, the pattern is moved a half-tone upward. Over time, additional semitones are added and upper pitches sustained. Patterns such as $1-3-5-6-5-3-1$ in keys extending from B♭ to E♭ should be added cautiously. Above all, an increase of breath energy and the application of natural vowel modification as the pitch ascends must be carefully undertaken. It is unrealistic to expect a young tenor to find his top voice without addressing these two factors.

LARYNGEAL ELEVATION AND THROAT TENSION AT THE TENOR *SECONDO PASSAGGIO*

QUESTION
I have an undergraduate tenor who has excellent tone until F_4 or F♯$_4$, at which point the muscles of his throat tense and his larynx rises, particularly on the vowel /ɑ/. Is there some specific exercise to help him overcome this serious problem?

COMMENT
No single exercise provides a complete solution. The answer lies in presenting the young tenor with the pedagogic tools for routining a stabilized laryngeal position. In all probability, the reason he has a problem at F_4 and F♯$_4$ is that his larynx begins to elevate at those pitches. He tends to raise the larynx as he approaches his *secondo passaggio,* which probably is located at G_4, because he has not yet learned to coordinate vocal-fold resistance with breath energy. In order to do so, the larynx must remain securely poised between the two strong sternocleidomastoid muscles, which in cooperation with the scaleni, capitis, and trapezius muscles, provide a laryngeal scaffolding known as the external-frame structure of the neck. Together with the nuchal muscles situated at the nape of the neck, this complex of muscles retains the head and neck in a stable relationship. With an in-

crease of breath energy, as the singer passes over the *passaggio* pivotal point, and with proper support from the musculature of the neck, he will gradually gain freer access to upper range. (See *Appoggio della Nucca*; Elevating and Lowering the Larynx; Developing Upper Range; and Young Tenors and Upper Range.)

LARYNGEAL ELEVATION AT THE BARITONE *PRIMO PASSAGGIO*

QUESTION
If a young baritone's larynx leaps up at B_3 or C_4, is it OK to get really direct with him and have him watch his laryngeal action in a mirror? Or is it better not to mention it?

COMMENT
Do follow your inclination to be direct with him. If he is not aware of the physical actions that prohibit him from making smooth transition from lower-middle voice to upper-middle voice, your young baritone will have no ammunition with which to combat the problem. If he observes his larynx in the mirror, or watches a video recording of his singing, he will see what is happening and will be well on the way to correcting his fault. He must be given information as to how the larynx can be stabilized, and his teacher must insist on the necessity to avoid laryngeal dislocation. If his attention is not directed to the laryngeal instability he suffers, his problem will not be solved. (See Elevating and Lowering the Larynx; and Developing Upper Range.)

EARLY COVERING IN THE YOUNG MALE VOICE

QUESTION
How early should covering be introduced in a young male voice? Is there any value in first allowing him to sing openly, then having him later attempt covering? How does covering relate to range extension?

COMMENT
The meaning of the term "covering" should first be considered. Its use is deeply ingrained in the language of voice pedagogy: Italian *copertura*, French *couverture*, German *Deckung*, and English *cover*. Because covering may involve degrees of epiglottic lowering, a physiologic basis for the term exists. The epiglottis is one of three unpaired cartilages of the larynx, the others being the thyroid and cricoid cartilages. (See figure 3.1.) It can act as a protective shield over the larynx

during swallowing, so that food and drink are deflected away from the glottis and trachea. Cancer victims who have had the epiglottis removed must learn special maneuvers to achieve this deflection.

In the progression from front to back vowels in speaking, postures of the tongue alter, and the epiglottis gradually angles over the vocal folds. It is for this reason that the laryngologist, when observing the vocal folds with the laryngeal mirror, pulls the patient's tongue forward, requesting the vowel /i/ ("ee"). If instead of /i/, which elevates the epiglottis, the person being examined says /ɑ/ ("ah"), the epiglottis will lower and the glottis will no longer be visible. Fiberoptic laryngeal examination helps avoid this visibility problem. The extent of epiglottic descent during singing varies remarkably among concepts as to how vowels ought to be altered for ascending pitch. Fiberoptic and stroboscopic observation of larynges reveal that among singers trained in the international *aggiustamento/copertura* approach, there is far less epiglottic lowering than in German *Deckung* and in some related North American practices of cover.

Depending on the degree of phonetic alteration, and on the nature of the voice technique in use, the epiglottis may heavily obscure the larynx during the differentiation of vowels. A number of voice teachers—I am one of them—prefer to substitute the term "vowel modification" for the term "covering," in part to avoid conflict of meaning. Although clearly related, German *Deckung* is not an identical process with Italian *copertura,* French *couverture,* or English "cover." There are also colliding viewpoints as to the meaning of the term itself. In some cases "cover" refers to acoustic elements during vowel progression from /i/ through /u/ (graduated epiglottic lowering), in certain others it involves conscious alteration of the pharyngeal wall and adjustments in laryngeal positioning.

What about having the student first sing an "open" sound before introducing vowel modification? If he is falsely darkening vowels, a request to open them may be in order. But if a singer's ear is taught to conceive the complete complement of lower and higher harmonic partials in all sung quality, acoustic adjustments that are determined by the shapes of the buccopharyngeal resonator tract will naturally avoid both *voce aperta* and excessive covering. (See *Voce Aperta* and *Voce Chiusa.*)

In calling and in singing, the mouth opens somewhat more than in speaking, but vowel integrity remains. If a male encounters Jane at close quarters, he greets her with a spoken "Jane." His mouth cavity assumes the lateral shape and opening appropriate to the vowel /e/. In calling across the street to Jane, he raises the pitch of his voice so that his mouth opens considerably; the vowel /e/ maintains its integrity but begins to modify. If Jane at a distance is in danger, he shouts "Jane!" with his mouth even more widely opened. Although the syllable is additionally modified, Jane is still able to recognize her name. If the caller drops his jaw into the /ɔ/ posture, it will be John, not Jane, who comes running. Similar confusion ensues if Pamina changes the dramatic situation by singing "die Labe" instead of "die Liebe." (See Maintaining the First Formant ... in Female High Range.) If Rinuccio sings "viva la gente nuova e Gianni Sch*a*ccha!" rather than "Gianni Sch*i*cchi!"), in Italy he may be greeted by peals of laughter.

It is instructive to watch the great *Firestone Hour* video performance of Leonard Warren singing the climactic G$_4$ pitches of the final "Largo al factotum" phrase, as he retains complete integrity of each vowel while progressing through the vowel sequence in "della città"! Here is vowel modification without vowel distortion. When singing in the speech range, a well-trained baritone or tenor uses approximately the same buccal and mandibular postures as he does when speaking. As pitch moves upward, breath energy increases and the mouth gradually opens, but vowel definition is not sacrificed.

As soon as some degree of freedom has been achieved in the *zona di passaggio,* the young male singer should be taught to subtly modify the vowels of an ascending scale as it passes through upper-middle and upper ranges. In early phases of voice training, the pedagogic aim should not be to modify the vowel but to achieve an even resonance balance. A coordinated onset with precise airflow coordinated with an appropriate vocal-fold response must first be established in speech range.

It is unwise to assume that a young male will easily negotiate pitches above his *primo passaggio* if problems remain in lower-middle voice. Inasmuch as a large part of the male singing voice is an extension of the speaking range, voice instruction should initially be concentrated in that region. Unlike the occasional female, seldom does the youthful male have sudden breakthroughs into upper range. When freedom to accomplish basic maneuvers of the singing voice has been established in lower and middle voice, gradual extension of the singing range and the need for vowel modification become essential. They go hand in hand.

VOWEL MODIFICATION AT THE MALE *PASSAGGIO*

QUESTION
I am an active operatic baritone. I have a question regarding vowel modification as I sing into the *zona di passaggio* and as tessitura rises above the *secondo passaggio.* When singing high passages on the high vowel /i/, as in German *Liebe* and French *vie,* and the /e/ in German *Seele* and French *beauté,* my mouth opens wider than for lower pitches on those vowels, as I think it is supposed to do. Yet, that seems to put my mouth and jaw closer to the /ɑ/ or /ɔ/ position than to the phonetic shape of either /i/ or /e/. They lose their own distinguishing sounds. Should I try to bring in a little more /e/ or /i/ to balance out the lower-formant strength with that of the upper formants? In short—when I sing the vowels /e/ and /i/ in upper range, how do I modify them without losing their identity? Is

it right thinking to try to reintroduce the actual pure phonetic sounds of those vowels? How can I do this while modifying them when the pitches call for a low jaw posture and an opened mouth? (Sorry this question is so long!)

COMMENT

Lowering the jaw lowers all formants; the lateral front vowels /i/ and /e/ enhance acoustic strength in the upper portion of the spectrum. Were you to keep, in the upper octave, the lateral mouth posture that is appropriate to the lower, you would upset resonance balance and produce overly bright or shrill timbre. In lowering your jaw while formulating a front vowel, you are approaching a back-vowel position, which lowers the intensity of upper harmonic partials. You ask if you should reintroduce the actual phonetic sounds of those vowels. If the apex of the tongue remains in the lateral vowel postures while the jaw lowers, you will have the modification for which you are looking. To a large extent, you have answered your own questions, and very well. Bravo!

EXTENDING THE LOW RANGE IN YOUNG MALE VOICES

QUESTION

How can we teach young basses to extend their very lowest range? Should they feel additional space in the pharynx?

COMMENT

It might be best not to be overly concerned with extending the lowest range of the young bass or baritone until he has reached a certain level of maturity, or at least until the lower-middle and upper-middle parts of his scale have become stabilized. Many young males that were early classified as basses are actually baritones who have not yet learned to extend their voices much beyond the speaking range. Because they have problems negotiating pitches above the *primo passaggio,* a false assumption was made that they are basses. They may then try to add low notes that will never be theirs.

Regardless of age, some successful professional baritones have difficulty singing a sumptuous low A_2 or even Bb_2, while there are tenors who can sing a downward scale with ease, even touching a respectable low G_2 or $F\#_2$. To even things out, a number of premier baritones are able to produce a ringing High C (C_5) that fills some of their tenor peers with envy. It is not the case that a singer develops upper range at the expense of the lower, nor is the reverse true. As freedom increases, range is extended in both directions.

Questionable techniques for securing the low range suggest elongating the vocal tract through laryngeal depression and conscious spreading of the pharynx. Altering the length of the resonator tube by increasing the distance between the vocal folds and the soft palate, and through pharyngeal-wall distention, will produce more depth of quality by strengthening the first formant at the expense of the others. Additional low notes are then available, because the entire vocal tract from the internal lips (the vocal folds) to the external lips has been significantly enlarged and elongated. But there will be inevitable losses in the extent of the upper range, because such a weighty production cannot be carried upward with ease. (See *Strohbass*.)

Almost any young man who has a modest degree of vocal talent can in an instant be made to sound more mature than his years, simply by having him move his larynx downward, and hold it there in a deep-yawn position. A listener, uninformed of the necessity for a technique that encompasses the entire scale, may be astounded by the miraculous, immediate "improvement." Knowledgeable observers will recognize the cavernous color as distorted and manufactured. Carrying that timbre upward requires effort and pushing, so that the singing resembles yelling. All possibility for the young male singer to achieve a unified mounting scale is negated.

The most practical answer to how the lowest part of a young male singing voice can be extended is to suggest that it may best be left to its own maturation. As the instrument finds growth through freedom, in time the low notes will follow. Any pedagogic system that forces maturity into a young male voice by advocating deep laryngeal depression and conscious pharyngeal spreading as standard procedure is to be shunned.

INSERTED /h/ ("HA") IN HIGH-LYING INTERVALLIC TENOR LEAPS

QUESTION
Why do so many professional tenors insert an /h/ ("ha") just before leaping to a high note?

COMMENT
A number of prominent Rodolfos have been known to sing "la spe-*he*-ranza," inserting an /h/ before ascending to High C (C_5), or even to have duple aspirated insertions as in "la-*ha*-spe-*he*-ranza." As the vocal folds elongate in the production of the highest pitches, their resistance to airflow increases. Subglottic pressure inevitably rises with pitch elevation and with increased dynamic intensity (although far less so in the well-trained singer). In a passage such as the *La bohème* phrase, the operatic tenor combines extreme vocal-fold elongation, firm glottal closure,

and probably considerable damping of the ligament (inner edge of the vocal fold), while at the same time increasing appoggio activity, all at a high level of emotional exhilaration. With the inserted /h/, mounting tension is reduced for a split second, because the vocal folds must part to produce it. An /h/ insertion is often part of the singer's unconscious attempt to reduce vocal-fold tension. He instinctively feels that the inserted aspirant allows easier production at the climactic note or notes of the phrase.

An argument could be made that during speech the consonant /h/ allows frequent rapid insertions to be accomplished without apparent loss of air. (Try saying "Happy Harry has huge, heavy hives!") It might seem to follow that the insertion of /h/ would be no more significant in singing than in speech. This assessment discounts the fact that energy levels, including airflow rates, are greatly increased when a tenor sings high-range pitches never encountered in speech. Because the vocal folds are parted and air is expelled at the nonpitch consonant /h/, the breath reservoir is reduced just at that point in the phrase where breath management should be at its most efficient. Resorting to the inserted /h/ may well be an indication that the singer's subglottic pressure has mounted too quickly, and that the extent of vocal-fold closure is approaching pressed phonation.

Considered from a musical standpoint, there is no doubt that a "ha" insertion breaks phrase flow and is stylistically unacceptable. It can become a vicious habit, an unnecessary crutch. Reliance on it probably should be eliminated, even for Rodolfo.

CRACKING IN MALE VOICES

QUESTION
Why is it that advanced male singers who sing really well sometimes crack in upper-middle and upper voice, while, except for beginners, females seldom do?

COMMENT
This question presents an opportunity to address some fundamental differences in the training of female and male voices. In arrival at upper-middle voice, energy levels greatly differ between the genders. A male generally speaks in modal register, traditionally termed "chest voice," over a much longer segment of his negotiable range than does a female. This means that when the male reaches his *primo passaggio,* the pivotal point in the ascending scale that corresponds to the upper extent of his habitual speech range, were he to continue to try to speak, he would need to call or shout. He could manage to use his "call voice" for an addi-

tional brief segment in the ascending scale—roughly the interval of a fourth—but only with great effort and considerable discomfort. He would probably be incapable of shouting beyond that point without subjecting his instrument to serious abuse. (See *Fach* Designations in the Young Male Voice.)

In upper-middle and upper ranges, the young male may fail to coordinate breath and glottal closure in a graduated fashion. During an ascending scale, if he does not increase breath energy at appropriate pitches, or falls short of retaining contact with the surrounding laryngeal external-frame musculature, cracking will occur. The French descriptively call this a *canard* (a duck squawk). Cracking comes not because of too tense a relationship among muscle groups involved in vocal-fold elongation and mass diminution, but because of laxity among intrinsic and extrinsic muscle groups. The mechanism jumps because vocal-fold occlusion and resistance to exiting air are not commensurate with requirements of the mounting scale. Muscle slackness causes the involuntary *canard* in upper-middle and upper-range singing.

On the other hand, harmful, pushed male vocalism typically will not crack. It may be driven, rigid, and lacking in full-swinging vibrancy, but so tightly fixated that the musculature cannot suddenly jump from one adjustment to another. In hope of avoiding cracking, the young male singer is sometimes told to relax, when in point of fact he should be increasing the flexible dynamic muscle equilibrium of his torso, not reducing it. He must stay in a noble, axial position; he must augment the sensation of expansion in the anterior/lateral abdominal wall; he needs to stay near the inspiratory posture. (See Intermittent Cracking on the Male High Note.)

Although the question posed deals only with cracking, or breaking, in the male voice, young, inexperienced female singers are not entirely immune to it in the area of the *secondo passaggio,* particularly at $F\sharp_5$ and G_5. Despite differences in laryngeal construction and registration events, a female also needs to increase energy in the ascending scale, although less than her male colleague must. A wise teacher, reexamining the degrees of energy in play, will recognize that with female voices as well, an increase in energy in and above the *zona di passaggio* may be desirable.

INTERMITTENT CRACKING ON THE MALE HIGH NOTE

QUESTION
I am a baritone in my late twenties and am beginning to have a successful performance career. I've been through several apprentice artist programs, won a couple of high-level contests, covered roles for some fine artists, and have appeared in a number of good secondary roles in regional houses. One thing still holds me back from reaching higher performance goals.

Often when I sing a sustained high G [G$_4$], the start of the note will sound just fine. Then it makes an ugly crackling sound—but it immediately comes back on track. It isn't just a crack and a loss of pitch. This may happen rapidly two or three times on a single sustained high G. It almost never happens on high F♯ [F♯$_4$], and never anywhere else, even in shorter notes above the high G. I don't feel any pain, and it doesn't make me tired or hoarse. I am hesitant to include some of the great arias in my audition program, because no matter how well the rest of the aria goes, when that sizzling noise happens on the top notes, the show is over. I know a couple of other good baritones who from time to time experience the same thing. What could be the cause? How to get rid of it?

COMMENT

As you indicate, you are not alone. Other young baritones have experienced the identical problem, some at G$_4$, some at F♯$_4$ or even F$_4$. Most could vocalize well above G$_4$ on quickly moving passages, but on the sustained high note, the momentary crack-recover/crack-recover syndrome happens, what you have so well described as a sizzling noise.

Proper support of the cartilaginous structures of the larynx secures a balance among the extrinsic and intrinsic muscles attached to them. A popular term for this cartilaginous structure is the voice box. This box must be soundly anchored through firm external-frame support provided by the nuchal muscles (see *Appoggio della Nucca*) and by the strength of the sternocleidomastoids. In-and-out cracking will terminate if laryngeal immovability can be established and maintained. This can be done through a number of compensatory measures that could of themselves become problematic if adopted for more than brief periods. Because of their possible danger, it is with considerable hesitancy that a few exercises are here described. Yet, in a number of hard cases, they have proved enormously effective. So here they are.

The first is an adaptation of the Emil Froeschels pushing exercises, recommended by the legendary Dr. Friedrich S. Brodnitz in his *Vocal Rehabilitation* (1971, pp. 100–101). Brodnitz explains that whenever the arms are involved in heavy work, the glottis closes more firmly. He instructs that the fists be placed on the upper chest, then thrust downward in a firm, elastic stroke, the fists landing in front of the thighs at the completion of the stroke. Then the subject synchronizes the downward thrusting of the fist with spoken phonations, beginning with one of the plosive consonants /p–b–t–d–k–g/ joined to a vowel from the series of cardinal vowels /ɑ–e–i–o–u/. My added suggestion is that these patterns then be sung in comfortable pitches in upper-middle range at a fairly vigorous dynamic level, with the same energetic downward arm thrust, while gradually raising the pitch to higher levels. Then return to the passage that typically exhibits the problem.

A second device is executed as follows. In a well-supported stage voice, re-cite the text to be sung. During this recitation, the instructor should slowly pull steadily down on the singer's wrists with such force that in order to remain erect, the singer has to counter the downward pull by resisting with his nuchal, pectoral, and abdominal musculatures. He should stand totally erect, remaining completely axial, with the back of the neck long, the front of the neck short, the sternum and pectorals positioned relatively high. This produces isometric tension in muscles of the nuchal region and the torso, extending to the abdominal and pelvic regions, and inducing firm glottal closure, yet without audible tension at the laryngeal level as the text is being spoken. The difficult passage is then sung while the teacher and singer repeat the isometric exercise. Then sing the passage with identical torso support, but without other assistance. In many cases, the intermittent cracking on the designated note will be eliminated.

A similar exercise further increases the degree of isometric resistance. Play a tug-of-war with the singer, he and his antagonist each planting a foot forward against the corresponding foot of his opponent, with the body weight on the other leg, fingers of both hands interlocked with those of his combatant partner. As much competitive resistance as possible is exerted. The offending passage is al-ternately spoken at full dynamic level, then energetically sung. As physical energy endures, the sound will probably remain free.

A final alternative corrective device is to have the singer place his elbows in-ward against the sides of the upper torso, arms extended forward, palms up. Load his outstretched hands and forearms with books or other objects that can be held only through an axial posture of the thoracic cage, the spine, and a supportive torso. The singer maintains his noble stance as his arms resist the gravitational downward pull. Again, spoken and sung phrases are alternated.

These exercises induce firm glottal closure and eliminate intermittent crack-ing. They demonstrate that it is possible to both speak and sing with laryngeal freedom while applying a high level of directed isometric energy. Based on this new awareness of contact among muscle groups of the head, neck, and torso, a heightened degree of laryngeal support is discovered and retained when the tech-nical devices are put aside. *They should be used only as a last resort* after long as-sociation with a daily systematic breath-management routine has not alleviated the problem. There is an inherent danger that one or more of these exercises could un-wittingly occasion excessive body tension; they are clearly compensatory maneu-vers intended for seldom employment. However, over several decades, a number of males (tenors as well as baritones) have profited from the rare use of these devices. But it must be kept in mind that they are drastic, temporary measures appropriate only in extreme hardship cases of intermittent upper-range cracking by a mature, advanced student who has already found security in the rest of the voice.

HEALTHY SINGING

THE SINGING ATHLETE

QUESTION

I notice that you put great emphasis on athleticism in singing. You often tell the singer "You are a singing athlete." Isn't there a risk that in following this advice, singing will become too visceral and lose artistic subtlety and poetic nuance? Do you then agree with teachers who have special exercises for developing individual muscles of the laryngeal mechanism? If not, what sort of vocal athleticism do you have in mind?

COMMENT

An Olympic skater or tennis player displays subtlety and poetic nuance as a consequence of disciplined control of motor responses. Unless the physical instrument is adequately developed and trained to meet performance tasks, there is little possibility of producing high-level artistry. Fortunately for the singer, the musculature of the larynx is an anatomical given. Mechanical coordination among the intrinsic muscles of the larynx is not dependent on localized attempts to develop the cricoarytenoid, cricothyroid, or thyroarytenoid muscles through specific maneuvers, as is sometimes claimed. Nor can the vocal ligament and the vocalis muscle undergo development as though they were biceps or pectorals. There is no evidence that vocal fry, lip trills, shouting, or silent, rapid laryngeal oscillations develop the intrinsic musculature of the larynx. (See Lip Trilling; Vocal Fry.) Nor does manually wiggling the larynx from left to right free it for phonatory tasks. Techniques that consciously try to separate the cricoid cartilage from the thyroid cartilage in order to develop the pars recta and pars obliqua cricothyroid muscles are potentially dangerous, particularly when hands-on manipulation of the cartilages is attempted. Muscles that produce changes in the laryngeal region are not subject to voluntary control or to independent action. It simply is not the case that the hyoid bone, which is attached to the base of the tongue, and from which the larynx is suspended by a membrane, has to be "unfrozen," as though some form of ossification had made it immobile. Apart from phonatory acts, it is pointless to try to strengthen intrinsic laryngeal muscle groups.

It is highly doubtful that in order to loosen it, the body of the tongue need be rolled out of the mouth, or the apex of the tongue distended while grimacing. These exercises may be appropriate to trick-or-treating, but not to voice technique. There is no empirical evidence that regurgitation exercises ("vomit the tone") strengthen muscles of the pharynx. Protocols for stretching the pharyngeal wall, for locally raising the soft palate, or for increasing flexibility of the uvula are equally nonproductive. Any action of the larynx and the vocal tract required of a singer is already available to the singer. The larynx is constructed to perform the numerous pyrotechnical tasks of singing. Elite singing is not accomplished through muscle manipulation or by bizarre maneuvers but through skillful coordination, dictated by tonal concepts originating in the mind.

There are, on the other hand, physical activities that can improve external support for the larynx and the breath system. Flabby neck, pectoral, and abdominal muscles are hindrances as much to laryngeal performance as to any energetic activity. Over the course of a long professional singing career, musculatures of the neck, the pectoral region, and the abdominal wall gradually strengthen through being used, but their general tonus can be more quickly acquired through daily physical exercise.

Laryngeal stability is in part dependent on the activity of extrinsic (outer) muscles of the neck that provide external support for the larynx. *Appoggio della nucca* refers to concerted action of muscles originating in the posterior (nuchal) region of the neck, specifically the sternocleidomastoids, the trapezius, the scaleni, and the capitis muscles. (See *Appoggio della Nucca.*) The scaleni muscles have their origins in the mastoid region; two scalenus muscle pairs have insertions on the anterior regions of the first and second ribs. They help position the manubrium of the sternum, which in turn maintains the erect sternal position essential for good rib-cage expansion and for full contraction of the diaphragm upon inhalation. Together with the sternocleidomastoids, the scaleni are auxiliary respiratory muscles. Weak scaleni and sternocleidomastoids do not give the muscle support needed for energetic phonation, especially in the upper-middle and upper ranges. Through suitable muscle strength in the neck region, the external frame of the larynx can offer structural support for the strenuous tasks often encountered in singing.

Several simple neck exercises tend to strengthen these external muscles, but should be avoided by anyone suffering from cervical disc or spine problems. Keeping the sternum and torso axial (that is, without movement of the hips or waist), turn the head quickly but gently to one side until a sense of resistance is felt in the sternocleidomastoid muscle on that side. Then, while maintaining the axial position, with the torso still positioned forward, turn the head in the reverse direction, experiencing similar resistance at the opposite sternocleidomastoid. This exercise ought to be repeated at least a dozen times during a practice period. Its effectiveness is increased if several short, sideward thrusts of the head accompany each stretching maneuver. Following this sequence of head and neck movements, give the head an easy circular roll on the shoulder girdle, to the left, to the right. Then shake head and facial muscles gently back and forth (like a playful dog with a stick). Many persons are aware of a "cracking" sound in the cervical vertebrae as they accomplish these exercises, clear indication that they are sorely needed.

A "flying" exercise, arms extended sideways and upward, rapidly circling first in one direction and then the other, while maintaining a forward torso posture, involves both nuchal and pectoral musculatures. One feels activation of the neck muscles and those of the upper chest. This may be followed by "windmilling," in which the arms are simultaneously and vigorously moved across the body, as sometimes happens during vigorous swimming, first to the left, then to the right, while hips and torso remain frontal. The exercise stimulates muscle groups of the chest wall and abdomen.

Again assuming the noble position, stretch the arms over the head with hands clasped. Leaning backward, move the pelvis as far forward as possible. Now, while silently exhaling, swiftly throw the arms downward in a chopping, log-splitting fashion. Allow the head and neck to hang as low and relaxed as possible. While noiselessly inhaling, return to the upright axial position, suspend the breath a moment, and silently exhale as the log-splitting is repeated. Engage in the action a dozen times. This activates the musculature of the low dorsal region, and reminds us to reestablish quickly the noble, axial position following complete torso collapse. Then, facing directly forward in axial position, move the pelvis and hips from left to right in slow, dancelike, rhythmic movements. Finally, with the body poised on the toes, take small, quick dance steps in place while concentrating on relaxing the arms and legs.

Other exercises that contribute to building structural support for the tasks of classical phonation include pull-ups, push-ups, and sit-ups (crunches are sometimes found preferable). Cautious, sensible amounts of weight lifting, always accomplished with an open glottis while breathing in and out, may also be useful. Voice teachers who oppose weight lifting assume that heavy glottal closure must always pertain. Pressing the glottis closed will be avoided if the respiratory cycle (inspiration and expiration) is accomplished with quiet breathing. A number of supine floor exercises, involving alternate leg movements, arching of the back, and body rocking, also have value. (See Singing in the Supine Position.)

If there is a tendency to undersing, that is, to back away from the physical engagement that singing requires, the singer needs to be reminded that he or she is a vocal athlete. Athleticism is an inherent part of the art of singing. Optimal physical status is as much a plus for singing as for any special athletic activity. The exercises suggested develop both stamina and flexibility for the demands of performance. A few minutes each day should be devoted to them, before warm-up of the singing voice begins, and prior to every lesson, recital, or public performance. A strenuous program of physical fitness need not be undertaken, but a singer ought to be willing to acquire the physical condition requisite to the many tasks of singing. One doesn't learn to sing by building muscles, yet unless the musculature is sufficiently toned to conform to the levels of dynamism that skillful singing demands, the breath/larynx/resonator machine will not reach its fullest potential, nor will interpretive freedom be possible.

INCREASING THE SIZE OF THE VOICE

QUESTION
I frequently have a few students who come to me with a pleasant tone but not much of it. Both they and I want to find a bigger sound. How?

COMMENT
No voice can be made larger than its physical boundaries. Lamentably, however, many voices of strong potential never manage efficient collaboration among breath, larynx, and resonator, so that the voice neither grows nor blossoms. The singer should not strive for a bigger voice but for a complete sound based on proper airflow, acoustic definition, and vocal-fold freedom.

A soubrette voice can carry just as well as a dramatic soprano if it has the proper spectral balance. A *leggiero* tenor can be as audible as the *drammatico*. Gilda can make as much sound as can Rigoletto and the Duke. All are dependent on relationships of the overtone series to the fundamental being sung. There exist vocal Niagaras, but they must never serve as models for others. Their stage colleagues must recognize that fact and not try to compete with these extraordinary forces of nature.

Some voices, sweet in character, will always remain too small to be professionally viable. Trying to inflate them is pointless. Let each instrument sing the literature appropriate to its own level of sound, or find engagement in ensembles and vocal styles where the higher dynamics of solo singing do not have to be met. The teacher's goal is not to enlarge the voice but to free it, so that its full dimension can be heard. When energy is increased independently of decibel level, the voice sounds bigger and fuller. An old rule pertains: Increase energy, not volume.

DREADFUL SPEAKING VOICES

Q<small>UESTION</small>

Many of today's voice students, especially young females, have dreadful speaking voices. (I am a female, by the way.) They are constantly nasal as they speak, let alone when they sing. They seem to equate nasality with charm, or with being sexy. Is this a concern I should be addressing?

C<small>OMMENT</small>

By all means! Most North American singers, both male and female, have regional speech habits that, unless corrected, carry over into singing. The pervasive invasion by television dominates American culture. National soap operas and local "news personalities," with their aim to be folksy and charming, have added to language-enunciation deterioration. The cultivated speaking voice (not to mention the state of grammatical accuracy) has become a thing of the past. Nasality reigns supreme. (See Correcting Nasality.) Colloquial pronunciation is appropriate to pop vocal idioms but proves disastrous for the classical singing voice. The more aware a singer becomes of untidy speech habits, the easier it is to eliminate phonetic distortions from the singing voice. In addition to the prevalence of nasality, defects often consist of transition sounds within single syllables, on-glides and off-glides between vowels and consonants, and the heavy diphthongization of vowels. Enunciation is paramount to voice technique. A clinical voice assessment known as The Rainbow Passage was constructed to serve as a monitoring device of spoken English:

> When sunlight strikes raindrops in the air, they act like a prism and form a rainbow. The rainbow is a division of white light into many beautiful colors. These take the shape of a long, round arch with its path high above and its two ends apparently beyond the horizon. There is according to legend a boiling pot of gold at one end. People look, but no one ever finds it. When a man looks for something beyond his reach, his friends say he is looking for the pot of gold at the end of the rainbow. Throughout the centuries men have explained the rainbow in various ways. Some have accepted it as a miracle without physical explanation. To the Hebrews it was a token that there would be no more universal floods. The Greeks used to imagine that it was a sign from the gods to foretell war or heavy rain.

Have the singer record this passage for direct feedback analysis with the teacher (or speech therapist). Many readers are astounded at the distortions such a recorded reading reveals. Perhaps equally telling is a recorded reading, for immediate playback, of a familiar English song text. Point out any intrusive phonetic inaccuracies in the spoken text. Then the same phrase should be sung slowly, first on a single pitch in comfortable range, returning to the original rhythm and melody. The reading aloud of foreign-language texts is extremely useful. It is a good idea to have the student write out the text in IPA symbols beforehand. (See appendices II and III.) An ancient Italian adage, "Chi pronuncia bene, canta bene," continues to be an important rule for the trained singer. (See *Si Canta Come Si Parla; Chi Pronuncia Bene, Canta Bene.*) Vowels and consonants, in either speaking or singing, need to be phonetically precise. The intrusion of nasality into nonnasals is one of the great bugaboos of good singing. (See Correcting Nasality.) Nasality is neither charming nor sexy; it is simply disturbing, and is disruptive of good voice timbre. Keep after it!

OBESITY AND THE APPOGGIO

QUESTION
I find it difficult to decide how to go about helping a very obese student of mine to establish good breath support. He is so corpulent that it is almost impossible to locate space between the bottom of his rib cage and his hipbone. Hands-on help is therefore limited. He has fine vocal potential.

RELATED QUESTION
I am a teacher who has to deal with two extremely overweight students, one male and the other female. It is difficult to discuss weight issues with either of them, because they take it as a form of personal disapproval. I feel certain that being overweight adversely affects their breathing. Should I ignore the issue?

COMMENT
These questions speak to a serious situation for a number of young singers and their teachers. The issue of obesity in singers has become more pressing because of current American dietary habits and the increasing importance of visual aspects in the performance world. You are correct that if the singer has a heavy, fleshy overlay, it is hard to locate where lateral/abdominal-wall expansion is occurring. In addition, most overweight singers have deficiencies of breath management that result in a wobble or marked admixtures of air in the tone. Stage movement and dramatic believability become more difficult for the overweight performer. Several major singing artists suffer from obesity, but in each case, they have had truly phenomenal instruments since youth, long before weight addition appeared. Even their technical and artistic abilities would show improvement were they to reach healthier weight levels. Noisy breathing, torso displacement, phrase-end collapsing, and irregular vibrato are among the tolls of obesity.

A teacher is morally compelled to undertake tactful counseling of the obese student, to explain the pejorative role corpulence plays in technique and in career advancement. The point must be made that it is just as important for a sufferer from obesity to seek professional help as for the person in need of voice therapy. Although it is known that genetic propensities may be a source of excessive weight, most persons who suffer from obesity do so as a result of food indulgences and a lack of sufficient physical exercise.

I have taught several seriously overweight singers who showed strong professional promise. I tried gradually, and I hope kindly, to raise awareness of the problem. I have had success with some, not with others. Sad to say, several persons of much vocal potential have not been able to correct the physical or emotional problems associated with extreme corpulence, and although their talents warranted, they have not gone on to performance success. Most gratifying is the case of one young man who because of his serious weight problem could not be cast as a romantic lead in on-campus roles, despite his exceptional vocal facility. I asked him this question: "Do you want to sing Parpignol or Rodolfo?" Having finally resolved the issue of obesity, following extreme measures and an adherence to great personal discipline, he has gone on to significant accomplishments in the professional opera world. I often cite him as an example to others, in hope of instilling similar courage. Best wishes to you in undertaking this task. (See Weight Reduction and the Singing Voice.)

WEIGHT REDUCTION AND THE SINGING VOICE

QUESTION
Does weight reduction decrease the timbre or volume of the voice?

RELATED QUESTION
Does losing weight cause disturbances in the vibrato rate? For example, I've read that Callas's wobble in the top came only after her big weight loss.

ANOTHER RELATED QUESTION
I am very overweight, and I have a real problem with noisy breathing and with sustaining long phrases. My teacher says I need to lose weight. However, I am built that way, as is every member of my family. (We are all big people who have always eaten heartily.) I think that my weight is natural to my body build and to my metabolism. I also read recently in an article written by [a noted voice researcher] that a certain amount of fattiness is good for the vocal folds. Won't it actually hurt my voice to lose weight? I am afraid it will cut back on my resonance.

COMMENT

Physical weight does not contribute to resonance. Wrapping a green, protective storage pad around a pianoforte does not increase its resonance. Neither does excess weight added to a singer's frame. Ideal weight for singing is the perfect weight for most athletic endeavors. Overweight singers are generally noisy breathers. When breathing is labored, it indicates that replenishment of air cannot occur cleanly and quickly; both agility and sostenuto tend to be labored. I am aware of the conjecture that fattiness may contribute favorably to the vocal folds, but I remain unconvinced.

With regard to the second question raised above, it is not true that Callas developed an oscillation in her upper range as a result of slimming down. Her tendency to wobble in high range was there very early. In fact, following weight loss, both her velocity ability and her dramatic, sustained singing were improved. In Rome and Milan, I was privileged to hear and see Callas on stage at different points in her career, performing within both of her body sizes. I can attest to the fact that the loss of weight was a positive factor both visually and vocally. Any "scientist" who recommends being overweight as favorable for the professional singer is applying his scientific information too loosely.

A tangential and regrettable aspect of this discussion must include comments on the overweight teacher. Many singers, and those of us who teach singing, appreciate the joys of fine eating. It is difficult to give advice that we ourselves cannot follow. The battle against corpulence must be engaged in by all who are involved in singing—students, teachers, and performers alike. But what courage, tenacity, and willpower it does demand!

WATER BABIES

QUESTION

My question has to do with the constant water-sipping that so many students now indulge in during lessons, between exercises, midway in arias and songs, and between selections in an audition. They even bring their water bottles on stage! I know that keeping hydrated is healthy, but can't you overactivate the swallowing muscles by all that guzzling? Is it really necessary? Cannot one overhydrate?

COMMENT

The benefits of good hydration are not at issue here. Dr. Van Lawrence, a leading laryngologist who specialized in problems of the professional voice user, liked to admonish his singers, "Pee pale and sing wet." The wisdom behind this folksy rubric is that if the body maintains its proper hydration level, urine should not be discolored. Although not an infallible test, keeping track of the color of one's urine proves a useful check. Lawrence said the shade of one's urine should resemble that of tap water. Never would the good doctor have intended that water-drinking be indulged in before and after every brief phonation. Proper hydration takes place well in advance of performance.

Many authorities advise drinking eight glasses of water each day. If you drink water only when thirsty, you may already be mildly dehydrated. Drink before the practice session and after it, before and after the lesson, before and after each opera scene or recital group, not during them. Taking a drink of water after each song or aria is public admission of performance anxiety, an emotional response that yields sensations of dryness in the buccal and pharyngeal membranes. It is ridiculous to be wedded to a bottle of water during a recital or an opera scene.

A major problem with water-bottle addiction is that an insufficient amount of liquid is actually being drunk per day. Sipping away at a pint container of water over the course of the day does not satisfy the body's need for hydration. No commercial portable bottle of water contains the equivalent of eight glasses. When a student takes a sip of water after each vocalise, or between songs and arias, one suspects that technical discomfort is manifesting itself.

A recent newspaper report stated that a young child, forced by its parents to drink large quantities of water, apparently as punishment, suffered brain damage. I have never met any singer who suffered brain damage from overdosing on water. But drinking excessive amounts of water at one time may cause various forms of social discomfort, including feeling bloated. (Recent reports advise that long-distance runners should not overindulge in water.) Make a habit of drinking a sufficient amount of water over the course of the day.

FLUSHING OF THE FACE AND NECK

QUESTION
What, especially with sopranos, causes the face and neck to show flushes of color on high, sustained passages? Even if the sound is good, this increase of color is embarrassing, because it comes across as fear or worry. Are there solutions?

COMMENT
Singing high-lying phrases of extended duration requires increases in breath energy and muscle action. Reddening or flushing of the face and neck during energized singing mostly happens to people of fair complexion. Such persons also show an increase of facial coloration during strenuous physical activity, as in dancing, running, or lifting heavy objects. Facial flushing can also be caused by height-

ened emotion. These changes in coloration are usually not of great significance. They are more apparent to the performer than to the observer, particularly from stage to audience.

An increase in dynamic level often accompanies sustained singing in high tessitura. It may be wise to decrease both decibels and energy, while constantly on guard against the perils of undersinging.

VOICE REST? WHEN? HOW LONG?

QUESTION

How long can a planned vacation from singing be taken without losing too much when coming back? Also, should one not sing when suffering allergies, nasal congestion, a head cold, a chest cough, a sore throat, or laryngitis?

COMMENT

It is my belief that health matters should be in the hands of doctors, not voice teachers. Nor should the ENT or voice therapist attempt to teach voice. The proliferation of voice-teacher advice on vocal health is a questionable recent development. However, as every singing teacher knows, there are certain physical circumstances on which a student needs immediate advice; it becomes clear that singing should be reduced or even avoided. I cautiously venture into some general comment regarding brief bouts of vocal incapacitation, and on recreation periods spent away from singing. I will steer clear of questions regarding chronic or pathological conditions.

Luigi Ricci told us that a singer never goes on vacation from the daily regimen: "Take a vacation from singing only when you are too ill to sing." If illness is not the question, even though repertoire is put aside for a week or two, the singer should vocalize briefly during every day of the vacation period. When learning of a two-week leave for this singer, Ricci advised, "If you can find no place to practice, go to the meadow and sing vocalises to the cows!" The voice should not lie fallow. Muscle tonus must be maintained. Following a week or two of not singing, the vocal instrument requires gradual reconditioning.

Because of the slight change in the surfaces of the vocal-tract tissues, some singers believe they sing exceptionally well at the very beginning of a head cold. It is all right to sing modest material at the very beginning of a cold, or with allergies and congestion, so long as there is no evidence of laryngitis, a condition that occurs when vocal folds are swollen. It is possible to continue to sing over light laryngitis but dangerous to do so. The singer who performs when suffering from laryngitis presses the unevenly puffy folds together to a achieve cleaner sound, causing further irritation and potential damage. Lingering laryngitis must be diagnosed and treated by an otolaryngologist. If the nose is tremendously congested, ears are plugged, or constant coughing persists, the singer should back away from practicing or performing. Cutting down on speaking is essential.

"A cold" is a catchall term that includes a variety of upper-respiratory infections. An old adage wisely advises that a cold lasts seven days without medication, a week with. In general, after the onset of a cold, at least ten days pass before a singer experiences normal, comfortable phonation. Any condition that lingers longer requires medical consultation. An established singer with forthcoming professional commitments that would be difficult to break should get medical advice at the onset of any cold.

Extended total voice rest is not appropriate, except as recommended by the ENT as a postoperative measure, or under other rare medical conditions. Yet, if a busy performer goes limping along from one engagement to another, a day or two of complete rest may work wonders. Longer periods of rest diminish the tonicity of the singing instrument and should be avoided.

MARKING

QUESTION
How much marking is acceptable for a performer with a heavy schedule?

COMMENT
Marking is a protective tool for the singer. The term comes from the German *markieren,* "to indicate." By marking, dynamic intensity and energy levels are reduced below those of *voce piena* (full voice), pitches being merely suggested. It is a useful procedure during rehearsals, particularly in heavy ensemble singing where frequent repetition may be required. A singer should learn how to mark, but the technique is not without pitfalls. Relying on marking for an entire rehearsal can be more strenuous on the larynx than singing out would be. By no means ought the singer to drop everything an octave lower than written, although an occasional lowering of a few high notes or an upper-voice phrase is not harmful. When a singer is out of voice, but still must sing the rehearsal, proper marking can be a lifesaver. For the benefit of colleagues, all ensemble entrances should be sung, and the rest of the phrase only marked. Try to skip the arias, or sing out only on isolated phrases.

It is dangerous to get into the habit of marking every rehearsal with the intention of saving oneself for the performance. A singer who constantly marks a strenuous opera role right up to performance time will not have learned to pace energy, or have built up the stamina necessary for the role. Many fine singers avoid marking almost entirely. I have long been of the opinion that the stronger the technique, the less frequent marking will be.

SENSATION OF PHLEGM AT THE MALE *SECONDO PASSAGGIO*

QUESTION
Why does phlegm seem to be worse at the male *secondo passaggio* than elsewhere? I am not aware of phlegm until I reach that point in the scale. Then it feels like there is something on the cords.

COMMENT
Some males think they are encountering phlegm at the upper *passaggio* point, feeling as though something were on the vocal folds, when in actuality they are suffering from weighty production. In response to exorbitant subglottic pressure at the *passaggio,* vocal-fold closure becomes pressed. The singer then indulges in throat-clearing when there is nothing there to clear, further irritating the folds. He may feel a need to break through this syndrome by applying yet more pressure.

As a lubricating process, mucous membranes normally secrete mucus, as much as several quarts per day. However, when globules of viscous mucus congeal, the normal process of vocal-fold elongation and thinning becomes markedly unresponsive. Although phlegm may reveal itself in a specific area of the vocal fold, on a normally healthy vocal fold it does not suddenly and repeatedly happen at a single pitch level. It is illogical to conclude that the sensation of obstruction occurs on a specific note or segment of the scale. More probably, the singer has not yet found that exact coordination between airflow and vocal-fold approximation needed for free negotiation in the region of the *secondo passaggio* or in pitches above it. A useful remedy is to reduce the degree of "covering" and to let up on excessive "support." If the condition does not abate, medical advice ought to be sought.

GARGLING

QUESTION
Does gargling strike the vocal cords?

COMMENT
Gargling does not reach the vocal folds. The epiglottis normally functions as a lid, protecting the larynx, trachea, and lungs from ingested material. If tonsil-

litis or pharyngitis is present, gargling may benefit the mouth and upper regions of the pharynx, and bring some temporary comfort to certain forms of sore throat. Most over-the-counter gargles are of dubious benefit, often containing astringents. Otolaryngologists generally prefer a mild saline solution, barely salty to the taste, as a useful gargling agent. Dr. Brodnitz recommended that any solution be mild, with saltiness barely perceptible. He likened this to the ratio of salinity the embryo experiences in the womb. Gargling may help in a limited way, but of course does not strike the vocal folds. If soreness continues, medical advice should be sought immediately.

NASAL IRRIGATION

QUESTION
I have heard that sniffing warm saltwater up the nose may help clear out congested nasal passages. Is that a good idea for a singer?

COMMENT
Some doctors suggest that with the head held up and back, a warm, mild saline solution can be administered to the nose by means of an eyedropper. Another old remedy is to administer the solution while lying down on the bed with the head hanging at a lower level than the body. Because there are varieties of causes for nasal congestion, it would be wise for you to consult your doctor before following either of these procedures. There is not agreement as to their efficacy.

INHALING STEAM

QUESTION
When a singer is hoarse, does steam inhalation help?

COMMENT
Dr. Van Lawrence, an eminent otolaryngologist, remarked that both steam and steroids reduce vocal-fold edema (the chief cause of laryngitis), but that steam is slower and safer. The use of steam is still much recommended in European medical quarters. European opera houses at one time had steam kettles for loan to ailing singers. (Perhaps they still do.) Americans are less willing to spend the time it takes to use steam.

Some steaming methods are far more efficient than others. Only concentrated steam will benefit the larynx. Not much is to be gained by hanging one's head over a bowl of hot water. In the view of many users, it is most effective to place a teakettle on the stove, and inhale the stream of steam with the face at least twenty-four inches away from the nozzle, to avoid scorching lips or tongue. No substance should be added to the water. Inhale normally through nose or mouth for about twenty minutes, three times per day. Because such steaming requires time, makes one wet and sweaty, and is not a particularly pleasant endeavor, it has lost its popularity in North America, where we tend to look for easy and immediate results through medication.

There is some evidence that the use of steam is not a good idea at the beginning of a head cold and should be reserved for use only at the cold's conclusion, when hoarseness lingers. Many singers discomforted by fatigue or hoarseness have found the steam kettle a faithful friend. Cold or hot steam? My preference is for the latter. Several portable commercial steamers are on the market. A number of professional voice users rely on them. Care must be taken that these instruments are kept entirely clean. Before beginning a regime of steaming, the singer should consult a physician.

TEA, HONEY, AND LEMON

QUESTION
I have several colleagues who always bring a tall thermos of hot tea and honey that they constantly sip throughout rehearsals. During performances, they keep it in the green room or the dressing room, and make a beeline for the thermos at all possible moments. Can this really be helpful for the voice?

COMMENT
Most probably not. Yet the tea-and-honey remedy has a surprising, folk medicine appeal to many performers. Tea is a desiccant (a drier-outer) that contains tannin, and it reduces hydration levels. Most herbal teas are not desiccants, but their medical properties seldom have undergone rigid laboratory testing. Honey may have some ability to nudge superficial mucus, and it may feel momentarily soothing, but there is no evidence that a combination of tea and honey is actually beneficial to the throat. Warmth from the liquid may provide some comfort. Inhaling the steam of a hot liquid may modestly benefit the nasal cavity, and the swallowing process assists in clearing away phlegm.

Another favorite folk remedy endorsed by some singers is a tea-and-lemon combination. In point of fact, desiccant and astringent properties are conjoined in this recipe. Lemon, like honey, may "cut" superficial phlegm. The chief value of these nostrums lies more in psychological consolation than in physiological effect. Diuretics do not contribute to performance ease or hydration.

I would bet that your colleagues who beeline it to the thermos, also beeline it to the WC during breaks and intermissions. During brief pauses and intermissions, it is far better to drink some other form of warm liquid than one with a tea component. Why not chew thoroughly, and swallow gently, a bit of apple? This was Jussi Bjoerling's answer to "clearing the throat" between acts.

VOCAL SKILL AND VOCAL LONGEVITY

QUESTION

Is a long singing career indicative of a fine vocal technique? Does an early finish to a career mean the singer probably was technically less solid? I have a personal interest in your answers.

COMMENT

There are a number of reasons for the early termination of a performance career. Some go beyond a singer's control; others are the result of choices. The voice of singing is not just the larynx but the total body. Like any other athlete, the singer must stay in the best possible physical condition. Physical state may become the chief factor in determining the duration of a singing career, but being in good physical shape is not the sole reason for vocal longevity. Laryngeal abuse and misuse may happen, regardless of physical condition. Singers schooled for the concert stage and the opera house usually have sufficient technical skill to manage the literatures assigned them, but in some technique aspects even they may resort to compensatory devices not conducive to vocal health.

Unfortunately, a talented performer sometimes takes on heavy-duty professional responsibilities before voice technique is secure. More than one emerging artist has been thrown to the critical wolves for undertaking roles that went beyond current capabilities. In other cases, the technique the singer has been taught leads to pressed phonation and heavy production, causing vocal fatigue or nodules. (See Pressed Phonation.) Despite a well-grounded technique, singing dramatic roles with high-lying tessitura within a short span of time can contribute to an early career termination. A major conductor convinced a foremost lyric tenor in his mid-thirties that the role of Radames was appropriate to him. The tenor never recovered the former ease and beauty of his voice. In another instance, the casting of a remarkable soprano as Carmen, and her attempts to carry chest voice upward to meet the conductor's conception of the role, produced a career crisis. Months of medically supervised partial voice rest, coupled with voice rehabilitation programs, permitted the artist to resume a successful career.

Singers express concern about developing vocal nodules, but nodes are not the only, or even the chief, reason for most early career demises. If the causes of misuse are identified and alleviated, nodules recede. Surgical removal is shunned by modern-day medicine, because most nodular growths can be eliminated through voice therapy. Of importance is the way health and tonicity are maintained through diet, rest, and an avoidance of smoke, either direct or secondhand, as well as of alcohol excess.

Gender and vocal category both factor into longevity considerations. There are physical conditions over which a singer has no control. Hormonal changes may cause early termination of a female's singing career. Any female singer who believes that to be the reason for a waning professional life should seek medical advice. Males also undergo hormonal alterations, but to a lesser degree. A highly recommended source of information on this and other health questions is Robert Sataloff's *Vocal Health and Pedagogy* (Singular Publishing, 1998).

Although there are notable exceptions, there is greater likelihood that the female singer will be less able to continue a public career into advancing decades than her male colleague. Just as the lightest vocal instrument is the first voice category to mature, often it is the first to show the ravages of time. Larynges of late developers, like *spinto* and dramatic sopranos and mezzo-sopranos, often fare better with advancing years than do those of soubrettes and coloraturas. If you are less able to sing strenuous repertoire that formerly seemed easy, choose something less demanding. A sensible rule to follow: don't stop singing, just sing something else.

Professional male careers often extend well into the sixties. A few top-flight male performers have enjoyed considerably reduced concert careers even past their seventieth year. However, the original sheen of the voice seldom remains inviolate. It is safe to affirm that many long-lasting careers have belonged to singers who over the years displayed high levels of technical proficiency. By contrast, one hears sadly of early career terminations for both males and females who briefly enjoyed star status, with successes confined to a few seasons or to a single decade. In some instances, health problems beyond personal control were responsible, but more often, foolish lifestyle, greed, and incomplete technique were chief culprits. The performance life requires stringent self-organization, cautious husbanding of physical and emotional resources, and a nurturing support system that includes family, spouse, friends, sponsors, conductors, and sympathetic agents. More than one performer has become swept up in a social whirl for which the psyche was ill prepared.

Several decades ago, a notorious agent in Milan signed promising young singers just out of Italian conservatories to comfortable monthly stipends for several years. He maintained the right to assign roles and arrange all appearances. A young tenor of great promise was constantly dashing from one end of the Italian Peninsula to the other, singing major roles in both major and minor houses in exchange for his monthly stipend. Meanwhile, Signor Agenzia was in Milan picking up some very good sums to line his pockets. The tenor's career grew increasingly difficult and terminated early because he was "sung out." Greed reaches far into the professional world, sometimes germinated or nourished in the agency office. Fortunately for young singers, there are artist representatives who are fully aware that killing the goose will terminate the supply of golden eggs—in this case, golden tones. They have a sense of responsibility regarding the welfare of their charges. Yet all run businesses for profit; they are not there for the sole purpose of mentoring and assisting artists. In order to protect themselves, wise singers learn to seek out understanding agents who will carefully negotiate with conductors and theater representatives.

What about the professional performer who operates on a less visible level? Relatively few singers, despite outstanding vocal talent and training, are faced with decisions about recording contracts, coast-to-coast travel, and international festivals. Today, many fine singers face the challenge of keeping their voices in good condition while working daily in local academic trenches. There is no doubt that using the voice for teaching day after day is an additional burden not faced by those who perform but do not teach. It is not surprising that the fully occupied voice teacher may be unable to match the career length of her full-time performing colleague. Yet careful attention to maintaining good condition of the singing voice will alleviate the effects of constant use of the instrument. It mostly is not a matter of using one's own voice during teaching that is detrimental, but the neglect of a daily technical regimen. No teacher of singing should ever begin a day's instruction without having done his or her own basic technical work. ENT Robert Sataloff, who frequently counsels on the professional singing voice, says the singer who does not warm up prior to a day of teaching is committing vocal suicide. Many career losses are brought about by a change in body tonus. As with any athlete, regular practice is a requirement for the singer. As persons grow older, and as performance opportunities lessen, it is tempting to neglect the daily maintenance of one's voice. Prevailing pejorative societal views on aging subtly undermine the confidence of maturing singers. By ignoring the modern-day emphasis on youthfulness and the traditional attitudes on aging, the process can be substantially delayed.

Finally, the entire performance experience does not have to be given up just because public performance is no longer in the picture. Forgo the stress of public performance, but don't give up the exultation of singing. If you have curtailed your own daily practice routine, return to it slowly and for short periods of time, but get back into the swim. Continue with daily vocalization and systematic technical work, and carry on with the joy of making music even if it must be restricted to your studio or music room. Longevity and continued attention to systematic technical work go hand in hand. Unless health problems surface, a well-trained singer can look forward to a long performance life through uninterrupted exercising of the vocal instrument.

PEDAGOGY ISSUES

ESTABLISHING OR ALTERING A TONAL CONCEPT

QUESTION

How does a singer develop a concept of beautiful tone, and how can a tonal concept be established or altered?

COMMENT

This thoughtful question has to do with the psychology of teaching and learning. Could a comprehensive answer be readily discovered, teaching singing would be a much easier profession. Most singers are drawn to the art of singing by hearing beautiful timbre and artistry from some model or models they admire. Although the means of artistic communication are discernible, no one can clarify with exactitude how the brain establishes an aesthetic goal or why a specific tonal concept becomes preferable to the exclusion of all others. Cultural milieu plays a determining role, but environment alone cannot explain why a singer may choose to accept, reject, or modify a specific aesthetic aim. With regard to form and structure, the elements of music are identifiable. How the mind processes the quality of ideal sound is not.

The chief task of the singing teacher is to devise and articulate ways that permit an individual performer to uncover dormant physical and acoustic potentials, and to harness them in the production of sound that is optimal for that particular instrument. Does the singer's current timbre issue from free vocalism, or does it depend on a superimposed concept of tone? If changes are to be made, how will they be defined, how conveyed?

Most accomplished singers possess amazing imitative powers. By conceiving a particular timbre, they are able, through the alteration of vocal-tract shapes and degrees of physical energy, to mimic other singers, even those of a different voice category. A person who is aware of a variety of timbre idiosyncrasies may parrot sounds which violate that singer's own native voice quality. He or she may base ideal voice timbre on a mature premier artist who by no means achieves voice quality in the way the modeler assumes. Parroting often induces placing the tongue in nonphonetic postures, hanging the jaw, clenching or distorting the jaw, manufacturing or disrupting the vibrato rate, introducing degrees of nasality, stiffening the velum, spreading the pharyngeal wall, or causing abnormal positions of the larynx itself. Applying imaginative approaches to the control of subglottic pressure can alter vocal-fold resistance to airflow and contribute to tonal discrepancies. Good technique is in part based on mimicry, but compensatory mirroring may be completely wrong for the imitator's structure.

Imitative ability may be put to positive use. Indeed, the principle of imitation can be part of the teacher's effective arsenal. Brief demonstrations can safely include modest degrees of desirable and undesirable timbre, accurate and inaccurate vowel definition, acceptable and inferior shadings of vowel modification in upper range, and degrees of nasality. Correct and incorrect breathing methods can be demonstrated as well. The subtle differences between what is less good, what is very good, and what is excellent can be modeled. Contrary to some published commentary, a voice teacher runs no risk in demonstrating differences among general tonal concepts. Of course, for reasons of personal health, the teacher should not constantly demonstrate undesirable tone, nor make truly harmful utterances.

What can serve as the lodestar in guiding the musicianly ear to conceive a liberated sound and to accept a new tonal ideal? (See Holistic Singing.) Unless voice pathologies or ingrained habits of misuse or abuse are present, the singer already uses the voice with a freedom during speech that is transferable to the singing voice. A healthy speaking voice is parent to the free singing voice. (See Dreadful Speaking Voices.) There should be no greater distortion in sung timbre than in spoken quality. (That is not the same as saying there are no differences between singing and speaking.) Just as some athletes come naturally to physical coordination appropriate to specialized sport tasks, so some singers come naturally to vocalism. But the schooling of the vocal athlete is no less involved or demanding than the training of any athlete. (See The Singing Athlete.)

When the three parts of the vocal instrument are in proper synchronization, good quality emerges. Timbre is not created to meet a preconceived notion; it emanates from uninhibited function. That is why it is crucial that the principles of voice instruction be in accordance with the physical and acoustic instrument. Feeling the pressure of time, it is sometimes tempting to rely on quick solutions, to indiscriminately try out various ideas that float about in the vast, uncharted pedagogic sea. In the process, one compensatory function replaces or augments another, becoming technical overlay, not technical solution.

It is the job of the singing teacher to recognize which of the sounds a student can produce are closest to unhampered vocalism, and to help the singer identify others that fall short of the goal. After a diagnosis locates the source of malfunction, precise corrective solutions can be prescribed. This is not accomplished by superimposing generic tonal ideals on every singer, but by uncovering the individuality of each instrument. Always there will be some note or notes in any problematic singing voice that are better than others. It is on these promising sounds that an individualized tonal concept is to be constructed. Old muscle habits have to be abandoned, new tracks routined. There is no magic muscle that upon discovery will immediately solve all technical difficulties. Persistence is essential.

It is not always easy to convince a singer to give up specious, induced controls. A student cannot perceive beautiful timbre simply by becoming aware of tensions and the need to eliminate them. Those very controls produced a sound which the singer has previously associated with good vocalism, and for which approbation probably was received. Change in tonal concept cannot be accomplished suddenly. Only if the singer is convinced that what is to come is better than what is to be given up, can significant improvement be made. (See The Reluctant Student.) None of us has the right to tell another person that one sound is preferable to another unless logical support for the new concept can be articulated clearly and the differences between the two tonal concepts heard, felt, and observed. Yet, when freedom is experienced through improved production, the new timbre as a preferable tonal ideal will gradually take over. That which is most freely produced will become easiest, and aesthetically most pleasing.

SYNTAX OF VOICE TECHNIQUE

QUESTION
You have stated that some approaches to singing technique are overly complex. You appear to advocate simplification of voice pedagogy by coordinating breath, larynx, the resonator system, and skillful registration. In general, how would you describe going about achieving all of this?

COMMENT
I like your question very much. Cultivated singing depends on patterned sequences. Voice technique must coordinate the breath process, vocal-fold vibration, and the filtering effect of the resonator tract. Registration plays a major role in the

latter. Voice pedagogy can be thought of as a form of syntax, the ability to devise and follow complex programs of action, using tools, signs, words, and physical coordination. Some dictionary definitions of syntax: to put together, to put in order, a connected system or order, an orderly arrangement; or a harmonious adjustment of parts or ambient factors. Although generally associated with grammatical construction, syntax occurs in all learning, including learning to sing.

Technique in any field depends on a connected, sequential system or structure. For that reason, a systematic approach to voice pedagogy is imperative, because without structured learning ("an orderly arrangement") there can seldom be a harmonious adjustment of the elements which produce refined singing. A good singer fine-tunes the motor, the vibrator, and the resonator into a harmonious whole. Any physical action that goes beyond the most primitive gesture requires complex programming, arrived at through repetition which begins in infancy. Singing is in many ways the ultimate form of physical, mental, spiritual, and communicative activity, requiring consummate coordination among all its parts. Constant reiteration of syntactical maneuvers leads to permanent behavior in performance.

Some systems of technique are more complex than is necessary. Simplification, not complication, should be the goal of all instruction. It is unnecessary to *invent* functions for the breath, the larynx, and the resonators. Why contrive abdominal muscles that do not exist, place the diaphragm in unknown regions? Why theorize that laryngeal function can be improved through local controls which are impossible to accomplish? Why contrive resonance spaces and domes that are not known to the rest of mankind? It is far easier, simpler, and faster to explain recognizable physical and acoustic facts regarding the singing voice, and it is far more honest. The syntax of artistic singing is most quickly and securely built on an assemblage of accurate information, not on a system of imagined structures and controls. The syntax of voice technique emerges by routing onset, breath management, agility, vowel definition and modification, voiced and unvoiced consonants, nasal and nonnasal consonants, sostenuto, *passaggio,* range extension, and *messa di voce* exercises. Remove the mysteries and let the voice freely function.

NATIONAL TONAL PREFERENCES

QUESTION
Are there really different national schools of singing, each with its own tonal preferences? Isn't the voice the voice, and isn't good vocalism good vocalism?

COMMENT
This question demands a personal anecdotal response. As a relatively young singer, I had the wonderful experience of singing for a number of seasons in a

major European opera house. I was fascinated by the variety of vocal techniques exhibited by well-established colleagues, many with spectacular voices, hailing from many national backgrounds. Why did one Marcello perturbate on his high F♯, while another did not, and a third Marcello sound fuzzy in low range? Why was it that one Abigaille (*Nabucco*) managed her coloratura passages beautifully but commanded little power in lower range, while another soprano cast in the same role seemed at times to fight her way through passages in high tessitura, while delivering tellingly throughout the rest of the range? What permitted one Violetta to be at ease in both the coloratura and sostenuto aspects of the role, while another managed one and not the other? Why were some Gildas vocally secure, some less so? Was it simply differences in native talent, or did answers lie in the technical orientation of the singers? And finally, did nationality and regional training play any role?

Clearly, singers cast in the same role used contrasting technical maneuvers. Among approaches were the following: inward pulling on the abdominal wall and hypogastric (pubic) regions; outward pushing on the same areas; preserving an *appoggiato* posture; dropping the jaw regardless of tessitura or amplitude; retaining a constant smile; keeping mouth postures quite similar to those of speech events; spreading the upper back; tilting the pelvis forward; lifting the sternum and shoulders at inhalation renewal; lowering the pectorals for breath renewal; lifting the head and larynx for high notes; holding the larynx down at all times; raising the larynx for mounting pitch; retaining a stable larynx; keeping an exact alignment of head, neck, and torso; avoidance of all chest timbre by some females.

Despite comparably exceptional natural endowments, some performers sang more efficiently and freely than others. It became apparent that technical maneuvers often followed national preferences. Individual singers from the same school of vocalism tended to adhere to identifiable breath systems and acoustic maneuvers, with mouths, lips, and jaws functioning in striking contrast to those of some others. Italian-schooled singers did not do things in the same way as many singers trained in Germany, France, or England. Differences in concepts of desirable tone, and the technical means for achieving them, were identifiable among Italian, French, German, British, and central and eastern European singers.

While on several academic research projects in later years, I observed voice teaching in most of the conservatories of Austria, Belgium, the former Czechoslovakia, England, Finland, France, Germany, Hungary, Italy, the Netherlands, Norway, Poland, Scotland, Sweden, and Switzerland. This study confirmed my earlier impressions regarding national and regional preferences in tonal ideals.

National or regional tonal ideals, as opposed to international maxims, keep some talented singers from acquiring vocal freedom and from enjoying international careers. For example, the cathedral-tone tradition of the English treble voice surfaces in the spectra of a number of British sopranos who are revered chiefly by the British. They not infrequently adhere to aesthetic goals that are different from those held by their colleagues trained in the French, the German, the Italian, or the prevailing American tradition. French baritones can seldom be confused with Italian baritones. German tenors have distinctive timbres not in line with those of their Italian counterparts. Russian and Bulgarian basses and mezzo-sopranos are identifiable by their vocal coloration and distinctive vibrato rates. They may well be singers with impressive instruments who are caught in a parochial tonal web. Most of them are not heard on the international stage because their regional vocal ideals do not permit qualities that are essential to international vocalism. If narrow pedagogic concepts produce imbalances in the spectra (imprecise relationships among lower and upper harmonics), there can be little hope that the singer, no matter how natively talented or artistic, can achieve an international performance career. There are great singers from every country who have international success because they have modified their regional or national vocal ideals. In our current global community, this is becoming increasingly the case.

An astute listener, aware of timbre preferences among singers, recognizes national variances. Fortunately for the art of singing, there are fine teachers in every nation who adhere to international vocal ideals. From these sources emerge the premier artists of the performance world, including a large number of North Americans.

AMERICAN SCHOOL/AMERICAN SOUND?

QUESTION
What are your thoughts on the actuality of an American school of classical singing? Is there general agreement in this country as to what comprises good singing technique?

RELATED QUESTION
Is there a recognizable American sound?

COMMENT
Surprisingly, many Europeans would answer these questions in the affirmative. They note a distinguishable tonal consistency among American singers. Some Europeans are convinced that international opera conductors cherish a distinct preference for "the American sound." Singing diverse operatic literatures, these singers traverse all national and cultural boundaries, largely because of technical reliability.

There is also the European complaint that the American singer gives more attention to the production of tone than to other equally important aspects of performance. Timbre congruity of the typical American singer disturbs some European ears. Tonal uniformity is thought to be lacking in interpretative subtlety, and neglectful of vocal coloration. A common comment is that there is no place for artistic risk-taking in the American approach to voice performance. The same type of criticism that some European critics bring against major American orchestras—too mechanically perfect—is leveled at the American singer.

Mainstream voice teaching in the United States nurtures many premier singing artists, because it remains closer to historic international pedagogic tenets than what is currently taught in some European conservatories and private studios, including those on the Italian peninsula. (See National Tonal Preferences.) This is not to say that fine teaching does not take place in Europe. Top-flight European teachers adhere to international technical goals.

While there appears to be a main route of pedagogic thinking in America, what takes place in private and institutional studios includes a plethora of assumptions that are in conflict with each other. Many pedagogic systems associated with narrowly national schools have taken root on North American soil. The mainstream, pragmatic American ideal of elite vocalism is based on free and healthy vocalism. At its best, this allows a singer to perform a wide variety of literatures, and liberates him or her for fuller realization of artistic and interpretative factors. At its worst, it can be unimaginative and boring.

LITERATURE STYLES AND VOICE TECHNIQUE

QUESTION

One of my numerous teachers once told me that a classical singer has to learn different techniques to sing contrasting styles such as German lieder, French art songs, and opera. Can that really be true? Shouldn't a good technique enable a singer to sing just about everything?

> A RELATED QUESTION
>
> To what extent must a trained singer alter technique in order to sing the French *mélodie* and the German lied, as opposed to singing standard Italian opera literature?

COMMENT

A well-trained and musically sensitive artist should be able to sing a broad variety of performance literatures without altering basic technique. It is true that some prominent personalities in today's opera arena are unable to present a compelling recital program because they cannot adapt their basic timbre to the subtle demands of song literature. They trot out the same mixture of *arie antiche* and opera arias, without stylistic differentiation, decade upon decade, for which they receive astronomical fees. Fortunately, they are in a minority. Major past and present artists are as successful in the recital hall as on the opera stage. For premier artists, it has never been a matter of changing fundamental technique to match performance venues or literatures, but of adapting stable technique to a variety of musical styles.

Not every performing artist is convinced of this principle. There are acclaimed performers, chiefly most successful in the recording studio, who, when singing lieder, the *mélodie,* or crossover literatures, assume that beauty of timbre is of secondary concern. A few members of the critical press accept that kind of vocal metamorphosis as an indication of profound musicianship and artistic sensitivity. Their published critical reports at times take on a nearly parodistic tone. For example, the lieder recital of a prominent baritone, identified in a 2002 review as "an artist of exceptional insight and subtlety," was pronounced to be so sophisticatedly creative that the delivery of some words could hardly be heard. Further (reported with approval):

> [He showed] no concern for beautiful singing. Rather he used his voice to express the intense feelings of the tragic character who plunged from springtime loss to winter bleakness. [X]'s voice sometimes sounded croaky. His dynamics ranged from a whisper to a shout. His tone alternated between dryness and warmth. Whatever quality of his sound, it was shaped and shaded to fit the meaning of the song. He never broke the spell he wove until a final moment after the final devastating song, which he sang seated.

Listeners who know the baritone's voice assure us that coloration and creaky tone were indeed intentional on his part. If so, he was forsaking the concept that, with rare exceptions, tonal beauty is the most expressive and communicative performance mode for the great literature of the lied, the *mélodie,* and the art song. Disenchanted audience members speculated that the artist was having a bad night or might be approaching an early career demise. How else explain forgoing all concern for beautiful singing? One listener's reaction: "Sad thing is, I've heard him sing stage roles quite beautifully." Certain performers mistakenly feel they must take on a second voice in approaching recital material. In trying to adjust the instrument to different literature demands, the basic quality of the voice becomes an expendable commodity. A somewhat bewildered listening public is asked to accept this vocal alteration as an affirmation of sensitivity and artistic finesse. Other artists artistically perform the same cycle without blatant tonal distortion. They are well versed in the musical and literary heritage of the literature they sing, but their aim is sensitiveness, not sentimentality.

Recognizing essential differences among styles of literature is an important part of professionalism. However, singing does not consist of an emotive reading of texts on roughly indicated pitches (except in some forms of *Sprechstimme*). A recital should capture poetic intent through beauty of colorful vocal sound, in collaboration with a fellow musician capable of creating miracles of sound on the pianoforte. In any literature, a momentary departure from the native character of the instrument may properly demand less than complete timbre, but such moments should be rare, not the norm. In trying to be sensitively expressive, Baritone X sacrificed musical and vocal integrity to the faulty premise that emotional indulgence is license for replacing beauty of timbre with character portrayal.

Another major artist suggested to singers participating in her master class that they should learn to use different voices in order to please as great a number of agents and conductors as possible! It should be no surprise that the basic quality of her own sound is experiencing deterioration. It is not necessary to destroy the voice in order to capture the meaning of the text. Stylistic demands of dynamic shading, word projection, phrase shaping, refinement of sentiment, and intimacy of communication often come more to the fore in lieder and in *mélodie* than in operatic literatures. There is, however, no need to whisper, to yell, to creak, to forsake centered intonation, or to produce ugly, dry sound. Singers should remember the dictum of Alfredo Kraus: "Never let the text or the drama rob you of the beauty of your voice."

How removed Kraus's philosophy is from that of a current British tenor, who in a 2002 newspaper interview remarked, "Sometimes it's more important to make a beautiful noise, but I think expressivity [*sic*] comes first"—as though beautiful vocal sound and expression of emotion were incompatible! In an interview, this artist professed admiration for "a Britten aesthetic of singing." He maintained that Benjamin Britten liked Peter Pears's singing because "he thought it overripe, decadent, like a rotten peach," rather than beautiful. Clearly, tonal ideals and general aesthetics vary widely, sometimes based on national preferences. (See National Tonal Preferences.) During the performance of any literature, an occasional vocal coloration is in order, but destruction of timbre is not. Don't sing lieder with the same style you sing opera: use the same instrument—*your* voice.

A well-trained singer ought to be able to meet the stylistic demands of several types of literature while remaining true to his or her own technical orientation. Art is dependent on beauty and truth, not on imitation and pretense.

THE RELUCTANT STUDENT

QUESTION
What do you do with a new student who, after a reasonable period of study, isn't willing to make changes in past tonal concepts?

COMMENT
With the passage of time, personal vocal sound becomes as familiar to its creator as the face that looks back from the mirror. Sounds we make are an expression of our persons, a significant outward expression of self-image. Critiquing the quality of the vocal timbre of a singer can be taken just as personally as com-

ments about the structure of the face or the build of the body. As soon as a teacher begins to judge the quality of sound, the student's personal fortress is invaded. An important part of teaching is to determine when and how far to invade.

Serious studio work can be successfully accomplished only after trust has been established, through honest but tactful evaluation and discussion. Whenever a student enters a new studio, he or she is bound to experience a certain degree of anxiety and expectation. This apprehension should not be interpreted as resistance. If the student did not feel the need for growth, there would have been no seeking out of a new teacher. Yet, there is always a fervent hope, on the part of all of us, that past accomplishments will be met with approval.

Hesitancy to change from what is known to what is unknown is an intelligent reaction. A singer cannot be expected to readily give up a sound that has already brought a degree of approval unless assured that what is to be substituted will be an improvement. Reluctance to change may be founded more on fear of what might be lost than on resistance to new ideas. Above all, the new student needs to understand why one concept of sound is preferable to another. It must be exactly articulated in what way current timbre is acceptable or deficient. Unless the singer can be given specific diagnoses as to what is lacking, and the technical causes for its absence, intellectual and emotional barriers to change will understandably be erected.

Every singer makes certain sounds that are better than other sounds. Rather than begin with an outright assault on what is missing, the best pedagogic approach is to isolate those sounds the singer makes—a phrase or a few pitches—that are closest to the teacher's own goals. It is easier for teacher and student to concentrate on determining which isolated examples are better than to immediately initiate a total technical overhaul. Major alterations in tonal concepts seldom can be accomplished quickly; they happen incrementally.

Finding something positive to say opens the door to reception of new ideas. A student may feel despair when, after having auditioned and been accepted by the new teacher, he or she hears "What you are doing is all wrong. We'll have to start over." Comments such as "your tone is too dark," "too bright," "too far back," "too far forward," "too dull," or "too shrill," or "your support is all wrong," have limited value in facilitating change. In-your-face teaching is not an acceptable form of pedagogy. Diagnosis must be precise and the suggested prescriptions explicit. The teacher may well know what "spin the tone," "float the voice," and "rounder sound" mean, but the terms themselves do not tell the student how to spin, float, or round the tone. If the pedagogy is not logically articulated, the student may be perfectly right to resist. Today's student wants not flowery imagery but practical assistance. A teacher may blame the student for not responding to instruction when, in point of fact, the language in which the instruction is couched is noncommunicative.

But what of great teachers of the past? Didn't they use pure imagery? It may come as a surprise to learn that most famous teachers of the past did not rely chiefly on imaging to build a reliable technique. Much material dealing with the technique of singing that is found in historic treatises offers precise information as to what happens with breath management, laryngeal action, and resonator tract adjustment. (See How Much Should a Singer Know?) Specificity of language is essential to communicative instruction. Every difference between one vocal timbre and another has either a physiologic or an acoustic source, or both. It is incumbent on the teacher to explain what contributes to these differences. Describing the sensations of one's own voice is of little value to a student who comes with entirely different talent, experiences, and problems. There is a great sense of relief on the part of any student when precise language is used to describe the ground rules of technique.

Skeptics of enlightened voice instruction suggest that one doesn't have to be an automotive mechanic in order to drive a car, with which premise there can be no argument. However, if the motor stops running, the brakes fail, or the muffler needs to be replaced, the driver had better find an expert who can determine the cause of the malfunctioning and knows how to repair it. If a voice teacher cannot diagnose what is lacking in timbre because he or she is uncertain as to the physical and acoustic parameters that determine balanced vocal sound—other than his or her own good ear and personal performance experience—that teacher may be helpless to repair faulty phonation. Gradually alerting a singer to the varieties of tone, explaining how each timbre is accomplished, and determining which of them is most in accord with the physical and acoustic nature of the individual's instrument is the route to changing tonal concepts. The more specific the language, the less resistance encountered.

The rare student of singing who stubbornly resists all logical instruction should be reminded that both time and money are being squandered. An invitation for a parting of the ways may serve as the necessary wake-up call.

WHAT IS THE BEST MUSICAL TRAINING FOR A SINGER?

QUESTION
Besides ear training and the mastery of solfeggio, what do you consider to be the best musical training for the potential professional singer or teacher of singing? Must it be the same for both? In what ways should preparation of a singer differ from that for the general musician?

COMMENT
Several important points are raised. For every musician, the ability to solfège and to read music at sight is a great assist to learning music rapidly. The

singer who can play another instrument carries musicianship over into the singing art. Without doubt, the development of basic keyboard skills is a decisive plus for the singing musician. A singer or teacher who can at least modestly play through the standard song literature has a distinct advantage when it comes to exploring and learning new material. Even more important, a pianoforte background provides a more complete way of listening to and understanding music. That ability increases comprehension of the undergirding harmonic organization and rhythmic pulse of a song; it raises awareness of how phrase movement and dynamic phrase-shaping relate to overall structure.

There is an unfortunate tendency on the part of many singers to listen mostly horizontally. A singer whose ear is singly directed to the melodic aspects of a Brahms lied or a Verdi aria lacks perception of the musical web from which the melodic line emerges; the composer's intent may remain unrealized. To sing Schubert, Schumann, Brahms, Wolf, or Strauss lieder without an understanding of underlying harmonic structures is to vocalize on them, not to conceive of them musically and emotionally. This is true of even harmonically simple music. Keyboard grounding is of inestimable value for the singer as well as for the voice teacher. A surprising number of fine singers began their musical lives as either keyboardists or string players. Of course, many others came late to the discovery of their vocal instruments, and had considerable catching up to do.

The voice teacher who lacks the rudimentary keyboard skill to provide harmonic underpinnings for vocalization sequences is seriously impeded. Even though a studio accompanist is available, the ability to convey from the keyboard the more subtle aspects of musical phrasing and its relationship to the text is a big plus in voice instruction and musical coaching. Within a few years, any musician can gain sufficient keyboard proficiency to meet the basic practical needs of the voice studio. It is never too late to learn them.

Although there are premier singers who are unable to find their way around the keyboard, intelligent singers should not be dependent on a coach or repetiteur to teach notes and rhythms. Inability to teach oneself the performance literature can be a financial drain. Save money, time, energy, dignity, and your voice by first teaching yourself the music; then take what you have prepared to a coach for linguistic, stylistic, and musical refining.

Of vital importance is the establishment of a tonal concept. (See Establishing or Altering a Tonal Concept.) This is best arrived at by developing a plan of listening to live and recorded performances of premier singers, present and past. Illogically, there are teachers of singing who seldom listen to great singing. They only teach. There are voice performance majors who want only to perform, not to listen. For either a voice student or a teacher of singing to remain uninformed on past and current professional vocal sound is to operate in an artistic vacuum. What the ear encounters is assimilated and transformed by an individual's musical intelligence into a personal tonal concept. An aesthetic ideal cannot be established if there are no comparative experiences on which to base it. Critical hearing (not passive listening) and solid musicianship are essential to both performance and pedagogy.

REPERTOIRE FOR BEGINNERS

QUESTION
I am a new teacher, in my first year of instructing undergraduates in the department of music in a small liberal arts college. Most of my students are not performance majors; many are beginners. I also privately teach both young men and women, some still in high school. My college students need to complete a couple of foreign-language songs each semester. It is difficult to find appropriate repertoire for both groups. Can you suggest some items? Perhaps collections as well?

COMMENT
Finding repertoire to fit the need of every beginning student need is not an easy task, especially with the immature male singer. Until a fairly sound technical basis has been established, it is wisest to choose mostly English-language songs and songs in Italian. Making sweeping repertoire recommendations is difficult because so much depends on gender, voice category, and an individual's level of accomplishment. However, a few suggestions are found in Appendix IV.

MUSICALLY UNMUSICAL

QUESTION
Why do some singers feel they have to torture every note in a phrase in order to be expressive?

COMMENT
It is possible for a singer who is a well-trained musician to deal in so much subtle detail that the overall design of the composition is destroyed. Fine musicians sometimes feel that unless they *do* something with nearly every note of a phrase, they are not being musical and expressive. In attempting dynamic subtlety, word painting, and vocal coloration, they destroy the shape of the phrase, diminishing any perception of wholeness. Overlooked is the fact that every phrase has its own trajectory, its own arc, its own points of arrival and decay. To torture words

and phrase segments by constant alteration of voice timbre and dynamic intensity is to obliterate the composer's creative response to poetic language.

Take a song such as the familiar "O wüsst' ich doch den Weg zurück" by Johannes Brahms. The opening phrase contours word inflection, pressing forward to the apex of the phrase, then decays. Settings of subsequent poetic verses inflect themselves in similar fashion: "den lieben Weg zum Kinderland! O warum sucht' ich nach dem Glück, und liess der Mutterhand, der Mutterhand?" It is painful to hear singers caress each word or syllable of this lied, indulging in crescendo and decrescendo nuances and rubato under the impression that they are being artistic and expressive, when in fact they are destroying its musical essence. Such trifling results in auditory revolving-doorism or a disconcerting concertina/accordion effect. The vocal line is forced to travel a disruptive "Weg" (pathway) of potholes. Bumping and crooning through a Brahms lied destroys its inherent beauty.

Legato singing is the most musical thing possible. Connected vocal sound permits both depth and brilliance of sound while retaining good vowel definition. Whether by a violin, a pianoforte, or a voice, beauty of timbre best communicates emotion. True artistry does not come from basking in one's personal emotions, but from honest, noble expression. Unfortunately for the artistic state of lied, *mélodie,* and art song, some performers believe they must put a personal stamp on everything they touch, missing the literary and musical universality of the material. Mired in an attempt to display unusual degrees of sensitivity, musicality becomes unmusical. (See Literature Styles and Voice Technique.)

Certain singers exaggerate the stylistic differences between operatic and lieder literatures, believing that beautiful vocalism belongs in opera, while word inflection and coloration are the paramount performance components of the lied. It is not the case that Schubert, Schumann, Wolf, and Brahms were uninterested in the inherent beauty of the singing voice. Much of the nineteenth-century lied literature was not written as salon art but was intended to be sung in public venues by prominent concert and opera artists. While intimacy of expression, including dynamics and coloration, is not identical across the broad scope of vocal literature, there is no need for either ventriloquism in the lied or shouting in the opera. Some artists, known to the public chiefly from the recording studio, have given young singers the impression that in singing lieder, the timbre of the voice must be reduced to a parodistic state. The settings of lied and *mélodie* texts were not intended to be read over keyboard accompaniments but to be sung.

Singing that attempts to prove itself musical turns into self-conscious artificiality. Mannerism is as detrimental to communication as is insensitive vocalism. Even in emotive speech, individual syllables and words are not treated as loosely strung separate units in constant dynamic ebb and flow, but as integers of continuous thought and emotion. (See The Second Half of the Note.) Mannered singing often comes from an honest fear of understating word inflection and musical phrasing.

For every singer with whom the chief instructional task is to induce deeper interpretative nuancing, there is another who needs to be warned against attempting supermusicality. I have found that a simple, forthright discussion of the matter is sufficient for reaching a more honest adjustment of vocalism and true communication. What should never be forgotten is that voice quality, always in the service of music, remains the chief emotive element of communicative vocalism.

THE SECOND HALF OF THE NOTE

QUESTION
What do you mean when you tell a singer, during coaching, to avoid diminishing the second half of each note and syllable?

COMMENT
In trying to be musical, sometimes a singer will treat each note as though it were a separate entity, altering dynamic levels to such an extent that individual notes displace phrases; separate words substitute for sentences. The soaring pattern of the musical phrase is destroyed. By inadvertently carrying over bad speech habits into singing, some performers habitually strike each syllable at an initially moderate dynamic level, then immediately retreat from it. After onset of a note, they allow amplitude to die away, causing a fall-off of intensity on each syllable. This habit prohibits all possibility of a well-shaped legato phrase. Phrase direction is victimized through misplaced lingering over single notes and syllables. Individual syllables then are formed like minimally connected links of sausage: dynamic surging—a coming and going detrimental to line. Don't get into the sausaging habit. Yet another useful description for this enemy of legato singing is "syllable caressing." Learn to caress the phrase, not the syllable. (See Musically Unmusical.)

One way to draw a singer's attention to this insidious habit is to suggest that the second half of each note must remain on the same dynamic level as the first half of the note. Dynamic shaping then becomes possible, permitting every degree of dynamic subtlety over the entire phrase without chopping it into small, unrelated segments.

EXCHANGE OF STUDIO INFORMATION

QUESTION
Where I teach, in a fairly large department, there is never any exchange of technical information among colleagues. In fact, talking about what we teach is purposely avoided. People in other disciplines talk freely with each

other about their theories and their work. Why is it so hard for teachers of singing to exchange information with colleagues in the same department or the same city? Any comment?

COMMENT

The question zeros in on an unfortunate aspect of the voice-teaching profession, and points to a fundamental flaw that plagues its instructional philosophy: teaching others to sing is sometimes conceived as a go-it-alone enterprise, much to the detriment of student and instructor alike. Uniting imagination and empirical experience in the art of singing is a uniquely creative exploit, explaining in part why the singer-turned-teacher may initially hold an erroneous assumption that the teaching of singing must be based on mystical, ill-defined personal discoveries.

There are teachers who believe that what is imparted in the privacy of the studio is unique, and they want to keep it that way. They are convinced that they, and perhaps their former teacher, have stumbled upon a remarkable system. There is no need to know about what anyone else does. Successful singers new to the teaching profession may assume that what was taught them regarding the technical aspects of singing is all there is to know. That same information is to be passed on to every student. Such questionable pedagogic philosophy is based on the principle of cloning: "This is how my teacher did it, and how I do it, so you must imitate it." Success rates in technical voice cloning are not high, because performance mimicry can belie the individuality of each vocal instrument. Although there is a large degree of function that is common to all who sing, it is naïve to assume that two individuals, in this case teacher and student, will have identical physical structures, voice types, psyches, proprioceptive sensations, and musical concepts. The teacher who comes to voice pedagogy as though it were based entirely on personal experience, operates in an intellectual and artistic vacuum.

Some teachers welcome brief sharing in off-campus or nonlocal symposia and conferences convened at a distance from home campuses, but consider off-limits any dialoguing about actual studio practices with their more immediate peers. The questioner rightly wonders why this should be so. The same hesitation to talk about the stuff of voice technique is evident in sessions at national and international professional meetings, most of which politely skim the surface of technical training under the guise of coaching, or style, evading substantive issues.

A classic example is the well-known voice pedagogue who candidly liked to pronounce in master classes that her technique was unique, a thing of her own invention. She enjoyed saying that she had never felt the need to read a book on singing, nor one on sex, both being areas in which she had personally experienced high degrees of success. This kind of ingenuous self-assessment, although amusingly expressed, presumes that pedagogy consists of personal imagery and the transfer of performance experience. Therein lies a grave error: no matter how charismatic the medium, all subjective, nonspecific information can be only minimally handed down from one person to another. To refuse to examine what others know is to practice intellectual insularity. Could it be possible that the noted teacher was hesitant to put technical observations on record because the information she delivered could not stand the light of objective scrutiny? If I already know what I'm doing, why should I confer with a colleague or anyone else on the art of singing? What more do I need than what I now have? An appropriate answer might be an old adage: "One never knows what remains to be learned if one never explores the world beyond oneself."

Some sequestered teachers are reluctant to share their pedagogic practices out of fear that studio secrets might be revealed. An example is in order. An accomplished young soprano from the Midwest, upon becoming a Metropolitan Opera Contest winner, moved to New York to further her career aspirations. Her Midwest conservatory teacher, with whom she had completed four years of highly productive work immediately prior to her competition win, recommended her to a well-known teacher. A few months later, learning that her former teacher and mentor was in the city, the young woman invited him to attend a lesson with the new teacher. When the soprano and her longtime teacher arrived at that teacher's studio door, they were informed that he would not be welcome to sit in on her lesson, or on any other lesson. No matter what the relationship between student and teacher might have been, no one was permitted to observe studio instruction, nor was lesson taping allowed. This closed-door policy can be found in the East, the Midwest, the South, and the West, as well as in European voice studios.

Yet another young singer, accustomed to recording lessons with several teachers, assumed taping to be normal procedure. Following her move to the city, she arranged for an initial lesson with another prominent teacher. Out of habit, she placed her miniature cassette recorder on a table near the studio piano. Midlesson, the teacher suddenly became aware of the recorder, leaped to her feet, removed the tape, and tossed it into the wastebasket, announcing with great agitation, "No one is permitted to record my teaching! What I do is privileged information!" The singer wisely never returned for another mystery lesson.

The best place to start exploratory exchange of information is with one's next-door colleague. Each of us may feel some hesitation. Having heard many of our colleague's students over the years, we think we already have a fair notion as to what principles are being taught. (Maybe we even took a few lessons with that teacher ourselves.) That should not dampen our curiosity as to how someone else plies the craft of teaching voice. Why not observe and inquire about a specific point that differs from mine? It might be useful to know why my colleague considers some particular technical maneuver to be advantageous when I do not. On what grounds does each of us hold our specific viewpoints, and how do those convictions fit into historic pedagogy? In discussing alternate teaching methods, both of us would be examining comparative voice pedagogy. An interchange of this sort might strengthen my current practices, or it could prompt me to consider alternatives. Justification for any technical information a teacher gives to a student ought to be based on the laws of acoustics and physiology. Why not openly discuss aspects of singing that depend on these two vital areas, weighing what each of us is doing with regard to those principles? With the student's permission (almost always willingly granted), why not sit in on each other's lessons for a period of time and afterward discuss what takes place? Or, as some of us have done with several past and present colleagues, why not team-teach several students? Hesitancy to talk about voice technique with near neighbors may stem from a benevolent desire to be nonthreatening to each other, yet by avoiding professional contact we show disrespect for each other's ideas.

Studio visits among departmental colleagues are rare, not because of busy schedules but out of fear or pride. Perhaps I might need to give up some cherished opinion, some technical point that I got years ago from one of my own teachers; maybe I would have to tell my students that I have changed my viewpoint on an aspect of technique. The topic raised by the questioner is of such burning concern that it should occupy a main-event session at every regional, national, and international conference devoted to the teaching of singing. Open discussion of the crucial areas of voice pedagogy might encourage an exchange of ideas at the local level, where it seems so difficult to initiate. Will it happen? The record thus far is not encouraging.

PEDAGOGIC JUSTIFICATION

QUESTION
What gives any voice teacher the right to say one vocal quality is preferable to another?

COMMENT
What a significant question! Every one of us who teaches voice should daily pose that question to ourselves. Can I claim that my good ear for vocal sound is superior to other good ears around me that prefer something else? Do I have the right to determine what is good because I claim to wear the mantle of a renowned teacher or great artist who has passed on certain esoteric information to me? Has my own singing career given me the right to make final judgment on tonal preferences when other successful professional singers have divergent viewpoints? Am I solely responsible for the fine success enjoyed by several outstanding former students? Do I have sufficient information regarding comparative vocal pedagogy to know why I accept some technical premises while rejecting others? Is it honest to assert that I have single-handedly invented my own unique methodology? Above

all, am I certain that everything I tell the student standing before me is objectively verifiable?

Every vocal technique can be classified by its approach to the three major components of the vocal instrument: breath management, laryngeal function, and resonator filtering. The teacher who claims to have uncovered vocal secrets, or to be in possession of unique knowledge, cannot be familiar with the vast literature of historic voice pedagogy. New techniques of singing are never new.

The search for the latest charismatic star in the voice-pedagogy firmament is a predictable annual event. Teacher-of-the-Year X bursts into orbit, to be superseded the next year by flamboyant Teacher-of-the-Year Y. Y is soon antiquated by the meteor-like ascendancy of Teacher-of-the-Year Z. One of the most amusing, yet disturbing, recurrent themes in major American metropolitan newspapers is exemplified by this prototypical ad (only the name has been camouflaged):

> Ignoto Ogniuomo, New York's most exciting new voice teacher, now accepting students! Learn how to breathe and sing! Call 212-000-0000 to learn bel canto and belting.

America is not alone. Here is a barely disguised paraphrase from a recent Australian music journal:

> If you want to learn classic or belting, write this number down and call Ian immediately. Begin a major performance career now!

Ian and Ignoto are permitted to hang up their studio shingles without undergoing any examination of professional credentials. If either has a technical gimmick and a propensity toward guruism, plus a few devoted students, financial success is assured. Of course, whatever an incoming student has previously been taught is totally in error. In addition, if the student experiences pain in the pharynx or larynx during lessons, or if the vocal range is decreased, that is just part of the developmental process of the new technique. Lessons are not recorded, teacher explains, because the originality of the method must be protected. (Might there not also be the possibility of consumer litigation?).

But it is not merely the suddenly surfacing Teacher-of-the-Year who may indulge in self-delusion regarding the delivery of a unique message to a blighted vocal world. For all of us, if there has been success with particular students, it is tempting to assume that our instruction alone has produced such remarkable results. What about the students who were dropped along the way—a common occurrence in some major studios—because they just could not learn what was being offered, that is, because the instruction was not productive? One has only to recall the prominent teacher who dismissed approximately one-third of all students who had been admitted into her studio on the basis of superior audition ratings, because they proved "inept" at catching on to the intricacies of her pedagogic message. "They didn't have what it takes. They just don't get it," she would say.

A visit to historic buildings in certain cities where multiple voice studios are domiciled, parallels journeying through several levels of Dante's *Inferno*. To achieve respiratory control, you push down and out in Room 001. Try in-and-up in Room 002. Fixate the diaphragm in Room 003. Spread the upper back in Room 004. Arrest the rib cage in Room 005. Assume the gorilla posture in Room 006. Tilt and tuck the pelvis to straighten the spine in Room 007. Squeeze the anal sphincter in Room 008. In Room 009, the larynx is elevated; in Room 010, it is depressed. In Room 011, the larynx is both raised or lowered at will, to produce interesting vocal colors. In 012, you bite on corks inserted at the molars, while across the hallway in 013, the jaw is narrowly positioned in the smile position by chomping down on pencils or chopsticks. Farther down the corridor, the pencil is placed on the upper lip to induce lip pouting and rounding. Next door, it's the idiot jaw that provides the answer. Is it up-and-over and out the forehead, or is it the funnel at the back of the neck? Shall I place the voice in the masque, at the little dome above the soft palate, or down the spine? All procedures are available for approximately the same fee, including a grand smorgasbord offering if you like. In the face of all this, surely cynicism is forgivable.

These pedagogical procedures, many in direct opposition to each other, are based on cherished opinions that have not been subjected to acoustic and physical analyses. The violations they induce may go unrecognized. The study of comparative voice pedagogy makes it clear that neither physiology nor vocal acoustics can be invented. No one has the right to suggest that one vocal timbre is superior to another, without determining what constitutes physical and acoustic freedom. The most beautifully produced sound is the most efficiently produced sound. We have the right to advocate that sound only if we are able to explain how it is produced and to spell out why it is to be preferred.

NURTURING THE SINGING INSTRUMENT

QUESTION
Sometimes I feel that as teachers of singing, we have too much to do. Is there any other field where a teacher needs to root out bad habits, implant new concepts, develop them, and still encourage the student? How do we accomplish all of that?

COMMENT
Another great question! Teaching singing has much in common with the art of gardening. In many ways, one cultivates the garden of vocalism just as one approaches the flower garden: prepare the soil, plant firmly, water, fertilize, weed, and mulch, then enjoy the bloom. These responsibilities are equally rewarding.

The questioner wisely speaks of implanting the seed of a good tonal concept. Careful soil preparation is an essential first step for both the singing teacher and the gardener. A good gardener looks over the terrain and determines conditions of light and shadow, observes what is already popping out of the soil, and sees what should be kept and what discarded. The wise teacher of singing listens to the new student, and determines the nature of the instrument and what technical weeds may be crowding out valuable growth.

In both cases, the weeding-out process must begin. The voice pedagogue faces a far greater task than does the sower of seed. Whereas the gardener may be able to immediately replace old, undesirable cultivars, the teacher of singing must proceed cautiously, substituting a new seed or planting in the place of each weed removed. The voice pedagogue cannot plow up the entire pedagogic plot and begin over. A teacher who declares, "We will have to start all over!" will not build a new garden but destroy the fertile plot itself. Vocal weed-killer does not work in the voice studio. (See The Reluctant Student.) An experienced gardener does not upset plant growth by vigorously pulling out every weed around a delicate plant, an action that disturbs the stability of its roots and causes the plant to wither. Tonal concepts cannot be yanked out; they can only gradually be altered. A form of tonal hybridization is required: improve the original tonal planting by altering it through the progressive ingraining of healthier influences around it. This can be done through a demonstration of good tone and by the application of an organized, systematic technique.

Seed cannot successfully be sown in cold, wintry soil. Harsh words do not produce vocal blossoms. Nor can young plant growth be transplanted without undergoing a hardening-off process accomplished by gradually accustoming the young plant to the changing conditions of light and temperature. So is it with the singing voice. One of the least productive approaches for either gardening or voice teaching is to try overnight to turn a recently severed cutting into a thriving bush. When the new sprout, the altered concept, has been properly planted, the nurturing process advances gradually. It cannot be forced.

Now comes the endless process of watering and mulching. Just as watering is essential to the life of a plant, so is encouragement to the singer. No matter how desirable it may be to rid the young transplant of unwanted growth around it, one must learn to wait until roots are more deeply embedded before ideal conditions become the norm. To change tonal concepts requires time. A garden is mulched to maintain uniform soil conditions and to discourage the return of weeds. Voice teaching involves a great deal of careful mulching. Good mulch does not act as a heavy blanket that suffocates growth. Voice mulching consists of guarding against the return of specious tonal concepts, and restrains physiologic and acoustic distortions from cropping up again. Good pedagogic mulch is weed-free because it contains only recognized nutrients required by the young plant. Experimental components are not found in proven mulch.

A strong vocal plant that has been properly nurtured can withstand adverse conditions—bouts with illness, unsuccessful competitions, unfair reviews, personal problems, financial crises—and in the long run will turn out to be more secure because of them. To both gardener and teacher comes the joy of watching plants mature, bud, and flower.

TEACHING AS LEARNING

QUESTION
My teacher tells me that when I begin teaching other people, my own singing will improve. What about that?

COMMENT
What your teacher suggests is almost universally true. Although there are some naturally coordinated singers who achieve a certain level of technical skill without needing to fully understand how, singing itself is a competence that has to be built through recognition and elimination of faulty technical maneuvers. The singer-turned-teacher must consider causes of a student's technical problem, and diagnose them accurately before recommending a prescription. In the process, that teacher is redefining and clarifying the principles by which he or she sings. St. Paul wisely poses the question "You who teach another, do you not teach yourselves?"

By learning to formulate technical principles that can be communicated, advanced students enrolled in pedagogy courses almost always experience improvement in their own singing abilities. The reason is obvious: if precise information is to be imparted to anyone else, its source must be grounded in one's own understanding of how the voice works as an instrument before specifics can be offered as to how best to use the voice in performance. In the process, one is instructing oneself as well as the person being taught.

TEACHING YOUNG VOICES

QUESTION
Do you apply the same principles regarding breathing to a younger student (twelve to eighteen, or younger) that you do to older students?

COMMENT
Although I have not had a great deal of experience in teaching very young voices, I can confidently affirm that breath-management techniques based on natu-

ral processes are applicable to singers of all age groups. Onset and agility exercises (the foundation stones for building the appoggio) can be used with children in either individual or group situations just as readily as with grownups. In fact, children love doing the laughter-like onsets, and vital, short agility patterns can be turned into delightful games. Of course, range extremes, registration factors, and extended periods of instruction are delayed. A child deserves the same genuineness of information as other people do. The style of presentation must be adapted to appeal to young minds, but the content must remain solid.

A personal anecdote may be in order. I was privileged to offer an extended pedagogy and performance course for a cadre of young professional soloists who sing Masses and other services at Notre Dame Cathedral in Paris. The director of the children's chorus asked if I would also work with his youngsters. A large group of boys, between ages eight and twelve, neatly and uniformly dressed, sat tall and cross-legged on the floor. We did our onsets, agility, and vowel-definition games together, to which they responded with much delight. Over the course of the week, during the break sessions in the cathedral yard, these little fellows would come running up, singing "Ha-ha-ha-Ha!" with wonderful coordination of airflow and vocal-fold approximation. A child, a youngster, and an adult all deserve to be given verifiable information, each at the appropriate level.

My own junior-high and high-school choral training was in the hands of Ms. Ruth M. Cogan, a woman who well understood how to help teenagers find joy and freedom in singing. I still use some of the technical drills she used with us. Her choral groups were known throughout the region as being of the highest quality. Significantly, a number of her students went on to professional careers in music.

IS ONE TECHNIQUE POSSIBLE FOR ALL?

QUESTION
Is one voice technique really better than all the others? Voice teachers all say different things, sometimes totally opposite to each other. I've even heard it said that a technique that works well for one singer can be bad for another. How could that be?

RELATED QUESTION
As a vocal coach, I have gotten the impression that each voice teacher I have ever known claims to have the only way. Singers use different approaches, so how can it be said that any one technique is better than others? It seems to me that voice technique is a very individual matter and that not everyone should be asked to sing in the same way. Your thoughts?

COMMENT

The questioners reiterate the urgent need for an in-depth examination of practical comparative voice pedagogy, to which subject this book is largely directed. One of its premises is that conflicting viewpoints in voice teaching are often based on erroneous acoustic and physiologic principles. Many have been discussed within these pages.

Not everyone, regardless of native endowment, sings equally well. Nor does every successful singer perform without still having some problems. It is eminently clear that singers use different techniques. Yet commonalities of function pertain to all physical activity, despite structural differences. Not everyone displays an identical carriage when walking or running, nor do all tennis pros serve the ball in exactly the same way. Yet there is a rudimentary coordination that involves optimum muscle movement for both actions. Although a walker who curls the toes under will manage to move forward, his normal gait will be impeded. A player can hold the tennis racket rigidly and still manage to hit the ball, but only inefficiently. Aberrations cannot be recommended as models for any endeavor.

When the three segments of the inspiration/phonation/expiration cycle conform to uncontrived principles, the breath mechanism functions most freely. During customary inspiration, the abdominal wall is not forcibly pulled inward, nor are the large, flat muscles of the abdominal wall pushed downward. The vocal tract is not held in a set yawn or a fixed smile position. What a singer does with the lips, the jaw, the tongue, the velum, the zygomatic region of the face, and laryngeal positioning determines timbre. If a uniformly fixated position of one or more parts of the resonator tract is perpetuated, the filtering process of the resonator system cannot respond flexibly; vowel distortion and articulatory deformity will be the outcome. There are performers who handle one technical aspect well, but another poorly. When singing freely, they are in accordance with unforced physical function; when resorting to incompetent procedures, they sing less well. Regardless of what method they may have been taught, great singers avoid violating their physical structures. A singer may be convinced that he or she is adhering to a particular identifiable technique, when in actual performance circumstances quite another thing happens. That is why some major artists who give master classes unwittingly advocate approaches to breath management and vocal-tract adjustments that are entirely different from those which they themselves exhibit in performance or even during the master class itself.

Although each voice is unique, principles of free function are essential to all beautiful singing. It is shortsighted to say that differences in technical approach are all of equal merit. Some maneuvers simply work better than others. The teacher of singing should know what they are, and evaluate each as to its physical and acoustic efficiency. Each individual has a distinct identity. We learn in various ways. Some persons are visually oriented, others best respond aurally or kinesthetically. Despite individualism, we share basic physical commonalities. From the standpoint of physical action, when bodies function well during singing, they follow explicit physiologic and acoustical laws, channeled through the propensities of each individual.

Information can be delivered in a number of diverse packages, but appealing wrappings cannot make false information acceptable. Exercises should be devised and adjusted to the performance level and technical needs of the student. Teaching styles ought to be modified to mesh with the personality of the individual student. A good instructor will not deliver information to all students within the same span of time or by the same procedure. One of the great joys of teaching comes in accommodating one's personal style to the diverse psyches being taught. Delivery of technical information must be paced in accordance with the student's rate of comprehension and assimilation; but basic content must remain. Not all voice techniques are created equal. (See Pedagogic Justification; Dissimilar Voice Techniques in Performance; National Tonal Preferences; and Exchange of Studio Information.)

DISSIMILAR VOICE TECHNIQUES IN PERFORMANCE

QUESTION
You have a strong interest in comparative voice pedagogy, passing judgment on differing techniques, apparently based on technical competency. Is it not true, however, that in actual performance, a variety of techniques are often apparent? Would that not attest to the fact that there are many ways to sing successfully?

COMMENT
Certainly, considerable variations in technical approach exist in the real performance world. It happens with great frequency that during an evening at the opera, a listener can observe a variety of approaches to vocalism emanating from the stage. I recently attended a performance of *Meistersinger* in a major European house, and became intrigued by the diversity of technical approaches evident among members of the cast.

One of the male artists, who had very successfully performed a major role that evening, sought me out following the lengthy performance. Said he, "You must have been fascinated by the variety of voice techniques we performers were throwing at each other and out at the house." When asked to describe more precisely the differences he himself had seen and heard, he spoke kindly of his colleagues, several of whom he was personally quite fond and whose artistry he admired. About others, he was less enthusiastic. His technical analyses were delivered in the spirit of determining what actually works best on the operatic stage. His comments are slightly paraphrased here; they pertain directly to the question under consideration.

> Beautifully balanced singing came from the soprano, who was a joy to watch and to hear; she had what you term the chiaroscuro timbre. Then there was the muddy bass-baritone looking like he was perpetually on the verge of vomiting, whose sound seemed to come from inside his stomach, not from his mouth. His vibrato was slow and wide. The Walter, on the other hand, constantly spread his nostrils and never dropped an exaggerated smile position; his nasal, edgy tone swooped out over all of us like a laser beam. The young lyric tenor singing David sounded superbly free. So did the Hans Sachs. In the large ensembles, I felt I was in a vocal warfare with little possibility of matching the voice qualities or dynamic levels around me. I loved the sets, costumes, and lighting. Staging was first-rate. Let's not discuss the conducting!

I had to agree that the performance had been a laboratory demonstration of comparative voice pedagogy. Members of the audience, including numerous en-rollees at an international voice seminar, were fully aware of the differences in technical approaches exhibited by members of the international cast. A nonscientific postperformance survey of voice teachers in the audience indicated that we had witnessed a highly uneven vocal evening. Every singer on stage was talented, but some were now and again at sea with regard to the technical handling of a fine instrument.

It cannot be concluded that only personal tonal preferences were decisive in generating critical judgment here. A better conclusion might be that what is most efficiently produced is most aesthetically pleasing to the largest number of knowl-edgeable listeners. Different techniques do indeed exist. Some lead to greater tonal freedom and beauty than do others, and they obey the physical and acoustical laws. (See Is One Technique Possible for All?)

COMPLETING THE TECHNICAL WORK

QUESTION
I have a flourishing studio in the city, with many fine performers among my students. I find that the hardest singer to deal with is the advanced performer who has enough technique and artistry to handle much of the song repertoire and a number of opera roles, gets cast in good regional opera productions, and has been chosen for two major apprentice programs, but in my opinion (I know his voice very well) still has a fair amount of technical work to do. As soon as I concentrate on what remains to be done, I meet resistance and discouragement. A kind of "Why is what I am doing not good enough?" attitude. I suspect other teachers have had similar experiences.

COMMENT

The fault most likely lies not with you but with the performer. So-called master-class teachers often have an opportunity to work with advanced singers selected to sing in public sessions because the singers are at a sufficiently high level to benefit from the experience. The problem you identify periodically surfaces on those occasions. The "Is there something wrong?" syndrome in response to critiquing reveals either naïveté or a lack of objectivity on the singer's part. He or she lacks awareness of the fine-tuning essential to professional vocalism that still lies ahead. In a brief master-class encounter, first citing the singer's good qualities generally permits the visiting teacher to get to work on what might be made better. In the privacy of the voice studio, the performer who begins to feel he or she has "arrived" can be assured that progress has been excellent, but he or she needs to be reminded that there is no perfect singer and that constant growth is part of true professionalism. Sometimes having several advanced students within the studio observe each other's lessons makes clear how technical teaching and literature coaching apply at all levels. Realization may dawn that everyone has room for improvement. Sometimes in teaching an established artist a further problem arises when that person begins to believe his agent's publicity releases.

A singer's confidence in native endowment and performance ability is a healthy thing. Every performer needs to develop a good self-image. But when egotism becomes so strong that further improvement is curtailed, the issue must be squarely faced by an open discussion. A conscientious teacher must continue to teach. If the advanced performer does not trust the critical ear of the teacher, or has lost faith in the instruction offered, a parting of the ways is in order. In all probability, the same difficulty will resurface wherever that individual turns for instruction. Not every mind or spirit can be won over.

UNITING TECHNIQUE AND LITERATURE

QUESTION

How can a studio teacher find a good balance between working on technique and covering the performance literature? Can't too much time on technique actually mean a loss of attention to musical and artistic matters?

COMMENT

Conjoining technique and artistry should begin early, and continue to the conclusion of the performance career. Voice technique and artistic communication mutually exist on a developmental continuum. It is a mistake to presume that the earliest periods of study ought to be devoted to technique, with later instruction given over to literature coaching and to performance considerations. No voice lesson or practice session can be rationally separated from musicmaking. That a dichotomy exists between technique and communication is an illusion, a point not recognized at an international conference session titled "Which Comes First, Technique or Artistry?" In early training, it is sometimes necessary to give the preponderance of lesson time to fundamental techniques of onset, agility, vowel definition, resonance balancing, and register unification. But unless incorporated into actual performance, technique remains an extraneous pedagogic appendage. Explicit technical work should combine with the communication of poetry and musical thought. Moments from the literature ought to be excerpted as exercises for vocalization. Much of the vocal music of Haydn, Mozart, Donizetti, Bellini, and Rossini is built on pyrotechnical skill coupled to emotive communication. Routining of selected passages demands fervent involvement of creativity and function.

In tailoring technique to interpretation, every exercise becomes a vehicle for phrase shaping, dynamic nuance, and meaningful text inflection. No vocalise ought to be executed without a specific goal. It must be sung as though in public performance. Never feel alone in the practice room. Fill the room with an imaginary audience, and sing even your vocalises to them. At the approach of public recital or stage appearances, technical considerations must recede, concentration now centered on musical and dramatic coaching. Only when performance is undergirded by technical freedom can interpretive aspects become second nature; continued technique fussing with a student the week of the recital or opera performance is too late. It is time to lay off.

An effective voice technique does not grind out singing machines but produces artists. Singing is a kinesthetic event in which the musicianly ear, technical skill, and the communicative impulse unite in the individual psyche. It is undesirable at any stage of development to separate technique from musical and interpretative factors. Even when singing a series of vowels on a single note, there must be a sense of phrase, a desire to communicate emotion through sound. Beautiful sound is not a substance to be produced; it is the servant of artistic expression. (See Holistic Singing.)

FEMALE AND MALE VOICE MODELING

QUESTION
As you have demonstrated, male teachers can use falsetto to model for female students without harming themselves. Is it healthy for a female teacher to model tenor and high baritone ranges in female chest voice? I am thinking specifically of the male *zona di passaggio*. I am a mezzo. I can sing those notes an octave lower in chest.

COMMENT

The advantage of vocal modeling lies in exhibiting a well-balanced spectrum, not in producing sounds for imitation. Even were a female with a well-developed chest voice to sing the $E\flat_4$ ("Melba point" for the soprano; E or F_4 for the mezzo-soprano) to demonstrate the baritone *secondo passaggio* event at the identical pitch in the scale, she would not be modeling an exactly alike process. Although some females, particular mezzo-sopranos, can mimic baritone sound even above the lower *passaggio* point, doing so in a distended way could be detrimental to vocal health. (See Belting.)

Falsetto production is not a physical replica of female sound. As you point out, it can be useful for some male teachers in demonstrating certain pedagogic principles for female students. The male teacher can model female transitions from head to chest by progressing from falsetto to *voce piena* timbres, especially on descending patterns. Falsetto is of greatest value in demonstrating postures of the mouth, lips, and the zygomatic arch in upper range. Male falsetto is not a timbre the female can be expected to emulate, but vibrancy rate, vowel definition, and mouth positions, for example, are all demonstrable in falsetto. By using his imitative falsetto of female sound, the male teacher reduces energy levels that he would otherwise need in order to illustrate high pitch levels in his own *voce piena.* Buccal and mandibular positions for demonstrating pitches in upper-middle or upper ranges are roughly the same, regardless of which timbre he uses.

If she has a good grasp of the principles of vowel modification and breath application, no female teacher should feel intimidated by working on the male *passaggi,* or any other aspect of male vocalism. She should demonstrate her own well-balanced sound. It is neither necessary nor healthy for her to imitate male sounds, or to carry chest voice much beyond her own lower *passaggio* pivotal point.

SYNTACTIC DOUBLING IN ITALIAN

QUESTION

What do you and others who mention it mean by "syntactic doubling" in the singing of Italian? You seem to lay considerable stress on this principle when you coach Italian literature. Why is it so important?

COMMENT

Your question prompts some anecdotal expounding on the subject. As a student, I studied Italian at a major American university, then went to Italy on a performance Fulbright Award. As I worked with the noted singing teacher and coach Maestro Luigi Ricci I was shocked to learn that I had been ignoring a major facet of diction and articulation in the singing of Italian: *le regole del raddoppiamento sintattico* (the rules of syntactic doubling). Another noted authority on the structure of the Italian language, Professor Pitola, at L'università per gli stranieri, Perugia, insisted on the same doubling rules. I began to note that Italian singers tended to follow this principle instinctively. Most of the rest of us need to be made aware of the linguistic authenticity that syntactic doubling achieves. For much of the following discussion, I have relied heavily on *La voce dell'attore e la voce del cantante,* by Ansaldo and Bassetti (Sabatelli Editore, 1977).

The doubling of a consonant in Italian (spoken or sung) occurs not only because of a word's spelling (secco, pollo, gemma, etc.), but can happen also by reason of syntax, that is, a word's position in a sentence.

Any word of two or more syllables ending in a stressed vowel causes doubling of the first letter of the following word, if that letter is a consonant.

perché (p)piangi?	*così (p)presto*
verrò (c)certamente	*recitò (c)con forza*

Most monosyllabic words that end in a vowel call for the same doubling.

che (b)bello!	*alle sette e (m)mezzo*
ho (f)fame	*so (t)tutto*
a (m)me	*mi (p)piace*
più (t)tardi	*da (l)lei*
o (f)fratello	*chi (r)ride?*
fra (p)poco	*quello che (v)viene* [*che* as a relative]
sì, (c)caro	

The exceptions are *di, se* (if), definite articles (*lo, la, le,* etc.), *che* as a conjunction (*Sono sicuro che viene*), the impersonal *si,* and combinations of unstressed pronouns (*ce ne, ti ci, me ne,* etc.). Very complete Italian dictionaries place a star after the entry for a word that causes doubling of the immediately following consonant.

While syntactic doubling is the norm in everyday speech in Italy, it may be less often heard in some parts of the country (notably the northernmost area), but there is no question that it is everywhere required for singers and actors.

SOPRANO AND MEZZO-SOPRANO INSTRUCTION

QUESTION
I am a male teacher. What differences do you make in teaching a soprano and a mezzo? What things are common and what are different about teaching each category? Do you try for darker timbres in the mezzo and for brighter colors in the soprano? Are the approaches completely different?

COMMENT

Each category exhibits distinctive timbres requiring different literatures, but individual voices within the two general categories of female voice ought not to be forced to follow predetermined patterns. There are as many differences in timbre within the subcategories of light and dramatic sopranos as between many mezzos and some dramatic sopranos. Since registration events for sopranos and mezzo-sopranos occur at different points in the scale, specific adjustments are required for the individual voice. Size and weight of the voice determine how vowel modification is treated, but there is no need to seek out unique vocal colors to distinguish the categories. Vowels are vowels, balanced harmonic spectra pertain across *Fach,* and good breath management is prerequisite to all skillful performing. Above all, there should be no insistence on heavy chest voice coloration for the mezzo-soprano, or on an exaggerated head voice for a soprano. Well-balanced female voices assigned to an overall category sound characteristically appropriate to it through the efficient coordination of all aspects of the instruments. Details vary in the teaching of sopranos and mezzo-sopranos, but principles of technique remain the same. Finding freedom in production—the avoidance of superimposition of manufactured hues—reveals true *Fach* orientation.

SEARCHING FOR A NEW VOICE TEACHER

QUESTION

I am finishing my bachelor's degree, so I have to leave the fine voice teacher with whom I have worked very well for over four years. Neither she nor I know where I should turn. We have heard so many horror stories about singers getting really messed up in private studios and graduate schools. How do I go about making the right decision? I've thought about trying to get a trial mini-lesson with a number of teachers.

COMMENT

This is a common practical concern. It requires forthright answers. Rule 1: do not telephone the prospective teacher and ask, "Exactly how do you teach?" No one can sensibly give a nutshell answer. Equally to be avoided under Rule 1 is "I have a number of questions for you to find out if you teach as my present teacher teaches." Rule 2: do not ask for a free trial lesson. Requesting to audition the teacher—which is what the request amounts to—is inappropriate. Don't expect a teacher in whom you are interested to give you a mini-lesson. To honor such frequent requests, the teacher would need to add an extra day or two per week to an already overloaded schedule. If you wish to take a lesson with a noted teacher, offer to pay for it. But do not be surprised if a private lesson is difficult to arrange, and quite expensive. (If a prospective teacher has time to give a free audition lesson to anyone who requests it, you probably are not looking at the right level of instruction.) Besides, a brief trial lesson reveals little regarding the teacher's actual pedagogic orientation. Many departments of music at major schools discourage this form of personal faculty recruitment, considering it to overstep the boundaries of professional ethics. This is because the practice quickly develops into an unhealthy competition among department members, degenerating into a kind of personality competition. Indeed, such a brief encounter can produce quite false impressions. There is a better route.

Invest your time and money in arranging visits to studios that already have reputations for solid instruction. Watch and hear what the teacher does in a *continuing* situation, not during an initial encounter. Any reputable teacher should welcome potential students and teachers as studio visitors. That does not mean that every lesson should be open to visitors, but a general open-door policy ought to be in place; the wishes of the person being taught must be taken into account. (There are times during any studio relationship when a student and teacher need to be alone.) Talk to a student after the observed lesson.

Here is what you should be looking for in evaluating voice instruction. Does the technique accord with free function and the laws of voice acoustics? Are the purposes of the vocalization patterns made clear? Does the teacher use specific, understandable, and accurate language, avoiding both the pseudoscientific and the mythological? Listen to see if technique and interpretation are kept in balance, and determine if the lesson produced some recognizable results. Is there a sense of honesty, a lack of pomposity, an absence of cloying solicitousness, an avoidance of Mt. Olympian behavior on the teacher's part? Are the needs of the student being met? Above all, is the lesson about the student or mostly about the teacher?

Don't be overly concerned about having to leave your present good teacher. Be grateful to her and let her know how much her instruction has meant to you. The level of voice instruction in North America is at an all-time high, because most serious teachers currently avail themselves of information that leads to solid instruction. There are many good teachers out there. Do the right research and you will find one. Good luck!

IS THERE A RACIAL SOUND IN CLASSICALLY TRAINED AFRICAN AMERICAN SINGERS?

QUESTION
Do you think there is a distinguishable ethnic black sound among classically trained African American singers?

COMMENT

This is a perennial topic wherever serious vocalism is discussed. The affirmative viewpoint is commonly held among some white and African American performers, but is disputed by others of both ethnic groups. Seen in historic perspective, the question is of recent interest, because only in the second half of the twentieth century did classical performance opportunities become open to a number of African American elite singers. Even so, acceptance developed slowly, not because of a lack of competent black performers but because of continuing racial attitudes with roots in previous centuries and societies. For example, Todd Duncan (whose name inexplicably does not appear in a recent edition of *New Grove's Dictionary*), Roland Hayes, and Paul Robeson were African American male singers of remarkable ability who were given only limited performance opportunities in America. The role of Porgy was the sole vehicle for low, male black voices, and only an African American can legally sing the role.

As late as the early decades of the twentieth century, racial stereotyping was the rule even among most anthropologists. This gave rise to concepts of racial purity, hybrid races, and the superiority or inferiority of peoples. Indeed, the most devastating war of the past century was at least in part spawned by the doctrine that the Nordic branch of the Aryan race was superior to all others. By contrast, decades ago, the eminent anthropologist George A. Dorsey's "Race and Civilization," republished in Charles A. Beard's *Whither Mankind* (Longmans, Green, 1928, pp. 229–263) stated:

> There is no warrant for the assumption that there are any "pure" races or that any existing classification of mankind according to biologic or heritable features and psychologic or cultural traits has any permanent scientific merit. Race is the garment we are born in and is set in our biologic or blood inheritance: Civilization—or culture, to use a more comprehensive term—is the garment we learn to wear and depends on physical and social environment: time, place, parents, teachers, society.

Although the scientific community had already discarded racist viewpoints early in the twentieth century, some ethnic groups in major parts of the civilized world clung to a feeling of superiority over other peoples, usually based on skin pigmentation but frequently on the enhancement of financial exploitation. Except for hate groups and zealots who continue to preach racial or religious superiority, these stereotypes have mostly been abandoned in modern democratic societies. Nonetheless, racial prejudice is still very much alive on every inhabited continent, continuing to provoke genocide and warfare into the twenty-first century.

This is not to assume that the person who thinks it possible to identify voice timbres as black or white is indulging in racial prejudice, but such judgments cannot be based on identifiable, verifiable fact. Prime consideration should be given the nature of the physical instrument itself. Although some similarities of physical type, including neck, head, facial, and torso structures, may be common within persons of a particular racial or ethnic heritage, laryngeal examination cannot determine the group to which a singer belongs. Fiberoptic/stroboscopic observations reveal no racially classifiable features of uniform laryngeal construction with regard to vocal tract proportions, dimensions of the pharyngeal wall, shapes of the pyriform sinuses, or epiglottic activity. Although these factors may contribute to the determination of voice *Fach,* they are not narrowly restricted to any particular racial origin. Corresponding physical types are to be found universally. In addition, as the results of the most recent U.S. census confirm, ethnic intermingling has made it nearly impossible to classify people racially. Given the extent of racial mixing in contemporary society, finding a black or white voice cannot be based on ethnic purity.

It is not just the "black voice" that some commentators think they can identify but also the Russian voice, the Slavic voice, the Scandinavian voice, the German voice, the Italian voice, the French voice, the English voice, the Jewish voice, the Asian voice, and, especially among European critics, the American voice. (See American School/American Sound?) This discussion is not meant to deny the existence of regional and national tonal preferences but to suggest they are of cultural rather than racial origin. Oddly enough, the "blackest" of singing timbres belongs to the *Schwarzerbass,* while the expression "white voice" is pejoratively used in all four major pedagogic languages (*voce bianca, voix blanche, weisse Stimme*). Many "black basses" have been Finns, Swedes, Russians, Germans, or Frenchmen, generally of fair complexion. Why should there be so many lyric baritones in France and such a large percentage of operatic tenors of Italian and Spanish origin among men of similar body type? (See National Tonal Preferences.) Why is there an exceptional percentage of Russian, Bulgarian, and Chinese basses? Why are middle and southern European sources so rich in the production of dramatic sopranos and mezzo-sopranos? Why, unless the performer is visible, is it often impossible in current pop vocal styles to tell whether the singer is African American or white?

A recent research project sponsored by the Vocal Arts Center at Oberlin Conservatory dealt with a comparative study of popular and classical vocal styles that included nationally noted Nashville pop stars. The purpose of the study was to subject performances recorded on audiocassette to spectral analysis. Sound and spectra were then played informally before a group of voice teachers, some of whom were African American. All listeners wrongly identified all of the singers as being black, but actually none were. Clearly, whites can learn to make a "black" sound, as the contemporary entertainment scene attests. "Black" sound is culturally, not racially, generated. Discussion continues as to whether American speakers are identifiable by race. The question is somewhat moot when applied to the singing voice because, as is well known, many premier singers of both African and

European heritages have regional accents when they speak that are not present in their cultivated singing voices.

An early discussion of possible black vocal sound occurred a couple of decades ago in the highly respected music critic Harold Schonberg's "Bravo for Opera's Black Voices" (*New York Times Magazine,* January 17, 1982). Both white and black singers were interviewed. Schonberg recalled the watershed break-through for African American singers achieved by Marian Anderson's Metropoli-tan debut as Ulrica in Verdi's *Un ballo in maschera.* Prior to her debut, among major American opera houses, the New York City Center Opera alone had engaged African American singers, including Camilla Williams, Lawrence Winters, Todd Duncan, and Adele Addison. Schonberg quoted Leona Mitchell, a current interna-tional African American and Metropolitan Opera artist: "Thank God for Marian Anderson."

Other noted African American artists consulted by Schonberg were Grace Bumbry, Shirley Verrett, Barbara Hendricks, Jessye Norman, Simon Estes, George Shirley, Isabelle Davis, Ella Lee, Gloria Davy, Mattiwilda Dobbs, Carol Brice, Reri Grist, and Leontyne Price. Most did not believe that they themselves repre-sented some black-voice aesthetic. According to Schonberg, African Americans often cite Martina Arroyo as one of the quintessential black voices. Yet Vinson Cole, an African American singer, says that the first time he heard Miss Arroyo he did not realize she was African American. (Nor did this writer at a stellar *Don Carlo* performance witnessed at Covent Garden in 1972.) Many of her admirers, including this one, believed Arroyo to be of Brazilian or Portuguese origin.

Jan De Gaetani, a noted Caucasian performer and teacher, attributed the black voice to cultural rather than technical sources. Shirley Verrett reported to Schonberg, "I am a black singer, but I don't think I have a black sound.... I moved to California and that is where my speech patterns were conditioned. Singing in so many respects is a function of speech patterns." Her famous rival, Betty Allen, supported the same viewpoint: "Julian Patrick, a white bass, comes from the Deep South. I'd like to put him up against a black bass from the same area and see if anybody can tell the difference." Having enjoyed Patrick's performances in decades past, I would agree that his was a marvelously dark timbre. (Julian Patrick is now professor of voice at a major West Coast school of music, where presumably he teaches voice without reference to ethnic sounds.)

A number of African American undergraduate voice-performance majors in conservatories of music have had strong, supportive black church vocal experi-ences in which a measurably slower vibrato rate and the extensive use of chest tim-bres are considered emotive and desirable. Even though these sounds can be altered through pedagogic means, such timbre characteristics are sometimes mistakenly assumed to be inherently racial. An equally large segment of highly talented under-graduate and graduate African American performance majors have no such typi-cal tendencies because they did not grow up in that particular cultural stream. (Recall Verrett's comment.) It is not race that determines vocal timbre; rather, culture and the individual tonal concept are the dominant factors. Can there be any doubt that the Eastern Orthodox liturgical tradition, and the English and Scandinavian choral traditions, have left their marks on the vocal aesthetics of many singers originating within those groups?

There will always be arguments as to which noted African American classical singers do or do not "sound black." Much of the discussion is not objectively grounded but remains captive to external physical appearance. When all factors are properly weighed, the only logical conclusion can be that it is not race but social environment, speech patterns, parents, society, teachers, and self-image that influence individual tonal concepts and timbre characteristics of all singers. Pigmentation and physical structure play no role in determining white and black sounds. Individual cultural history and tonal ideas do.

HOW MUCH SHOULD A SINGER KNOW?

QUESTION
I have studied over a number of years with an experienced teacher who says that past great singers and teachers of singing never bothered about how the voice works, and that it's really foolish to spend time on that sort of thing. She says that each voice eventually finds its own way, and that no singer needs to know how the voice actually operates. She says all you need to do is support from your diaphragm, place the tone properly, then open the mouth to let the sound spin out. I suspect you do not agree with some or all of that.

COMMENT
You are right in your suspicion that I, as well as most others who work in the voice performance world, believe it important to know something about how the singing voice works. For example, understanding where the diaphragm is located and what the diaphragm can and cannot actually do, and learning what factors contribute to the good tone that your teacher of many years hopes to achieve with you. The reason for investigating how the voice operates is to avoid muddled notions that make learning to sing more complex than it ought to be. Your teacher, in telling you not to bother with fact, may have been unaware of the detailed history of voice pedagogy. Important teachers of the eighteenth, nineteenth, and twentieth centuries made use of then available information regarding the physiologic and acoustic nature of the vocal instrument. It was Manuel Garcia, probably the most famous and revered voice teacher of the nineteenth century—not some physician—who invented the laryngoscope, by which vocal-fold activity can be examined. Historic

treatises mirror Garcia's intense interest in discovering how the body most efficiently functions to produce desirable tone.

Another notable historic document is Mathilde Marchesi's *Bel Canto: A Theoretical & Practical Vocal Method.* Marchesi, a pupil of Manuel Garcia, taught major artists in a period that came to be known as the Second Golden Age of Singing, among them, Emma Calvé, Nellie Melba, Sibyl Sanderson, Emma Eames, and Blanche Marchesi, her daughter. From the preface of her method, developed over many years and first published around 1903, comes the following statement: "It is essential that the mechanism of the voice should be trained to execute all possible rhythmical and musical forms before passing to the aesthetic part of the art of singing." Marchesi employs language that is as precise as that of contemporary voice researchers whose findings appear in current professional journals. Note these substantial statements, which deserve extensive quotation:

> The lungs, formed of a spongy, elastic tissue, perforated in every part by thousands of little tubes destined to receive the air, are concave and largest at their base, and separated from the abdominal cavity by a convex muscular partition, called the Diaphragm, upon which they rest.

Later:

> Three things are needed for the production of a sound: a *Motor* that acts either by sending a column of air against a vibrating body or by immediate friction with this body; a *Vibrator* that executes a certain number of isochronous [regular] or irregular vibrations in a given time when set in motion by the *Motor;* and finally, a *Resonator* (because of its function, it would be more correct to call it the co-operating element) that receives the sounding column of air that escapes from the vibrating body to imbue it with the character of its own sound, by reverberation.
>
> A singer who has learned how to breathe well, has equalized the voice, neatly blended the registers and developed the activity of the larynx and the elasticity of the glottis and resonant tube in a rational manner, so that all possible shades of tone, power and expression can be produced by the vocal organs, would most assuredly be able to sing well, and without fatigue and effort the long and declaimed modern phrases.

Marchesi concludes: "Every art consists of a technical-mechanical part and an aesthetic part. A singer who cannot overcome the difficulties of the first part can never attain perfection in the second, not even a genius."

The great artist Dame Nellie Melba, a pupil of Mathilde Marchesi, was specific regarding the urgent need to understand female registration events and voice function in general. Even a truncated list of historically famous teachers includes the names of those who based their pedagogic hypotheses on an understanding of acoustic and physical information. Among them are Louis Bachner, Mario Basiola, Enrico delle Sedie, Jean de Rezski, Manuel Garcia, Harry Plunket Green, Leo Kofler, Francesco Lamperti, Giovanni Battista Lamperti, Franziska Martienssen-Lohmann, M. Nadoleczny, Luigi Ricci, Vera Rosza, Giovanni Sbriglia, William Shakespeare, Emma Seiler, E. B. Warman, and Herbert Witherspoon. Distinctive, individualistic interpretations as to how the singing voice functions were not always consistent with fact, nor were they in agreement with each other, but all attempted to understand how the instrument worked. Others include Georg Armin, Walter Bartoschek, Emil Behnke, Lennox Browne, Van Christy, D. A. Clippinger, E. Herbert-Caesari, Frederick Husler, Anna Kaskas, Lilli Lehmann, Paul Lohmann, Morell Mackenzie, Lucie Manén, D. M. McClosky, Frank Miller, Elizabeth Rado, Arnold Rose, Sonia Sharnova, Douglas Stanley, Julius Stockhausen, Kenneth Westerman, and E. G. White. Most twenty-first-century teachers of singing understand the necessity of being informed about the physiology and acoustics of the singing voice, especially those teachers of the newer generation. They adhere to the philosophy that voice technique must not be in conflict with what is factually knowable, and that such information is transmittable. Medical and scientific research, by providing factual information and helping to evaluate pedagogic assumptions, has had considerable impact on the modern voice-teaching community.

Every teacher of singing is indebted to one or more pedagogic lineages. Whatever your teacher is teaching you now has been taught before. By becoming familiar with the literature of her chosen profession, she might discover the sources of her own pedagogy, improve on them, or detect new avenues that could heighten her teaching success. Perhaps you and she could investigate some of these sources together. As an opening gambit, you might want to ask why she believes her particular approach to some given area, such as breathing, resonance balance, or laryngeal action, is superior to those of other systems. You have a right to know why you are being taught what you are being taught. You also have the right to check what you are being told to do against what actually can take place.

PERFORMANCE CONCERNS

LEARNING TO PORTRAY EMOTION

QUESTION

What advice would you give a student who, for fear of looking silly, is uncomfortable about showing emotion in performance—besides offering the obvious suggestion to take acting and movement courses? This twenty-one-year-old male senior performance major is not given to displaying emotion in daily life. Several others in the studio have the opposite problem! They oversell themselves. How do I bring him out?

COMMENT

No matter how hard it may seem to awaken artistic instincts in some individuals, it must never be overlooked that performance communication can be taught and learned, just as can vocal technique. Standing alone in the niche of the piano, in front of an audience, is not a form of everyday behavior that leads to normal channels of communication. It requires the mastery of certain conventions that go with performance, which are both teachable and learnable. They are not simply the result of an innate ability to communicate; they are acquirable through learning by doing. There are far fewer born-expressive performers in the professional world than is sometimes presumed.

Human personality is delightfully diverse. We may be introverted, extroverted, or somewhere in the middle. In normal daily contact, some persons express themselves only reluctantly, while others seek out every possible opportunity to communicate. Yet outgoing tendencies displayed in everyday social encounters are not necessarily transferable to public performance. Contrariwise, the reserved personality, to which type one of your students seems to belong, may eventually discover a deeper communicative channel (through fully believing in the musical setting of the text or the drama, and learning techniques for their portrayal) than does the openly demonstrative person.

If technical facility is mostly adequate to the task, the teacher needs to reassure the student that he or she has the right to communicate to an audience. Suppose, as appears to be the case with this young male, the singer has a good voice and considerable technical facility, but is afraid to be openly expressive. That may be a more favorable condition than it at first appears to be. He may see through the falsity of frequently exaggerated interpretative and superficial performance routines indulged in by many singers (perhaps by some in his studio), and be quite right in assessing them as more mannered than authentic—indeed, "silly."

The keys to freedom of expression are physical, acoustic, and psychological. Body awareness is essential for anyone who wishes to outwardly express an emotion or to present a dramatic characterization. Regardless of basic physical structure, when appearing before the public, a singer needs to feel comfortable regarding the outward body. A performer must know what message the external body is sending, so that it is not out of sync with what intelligence and emotion hope to convey. Although workshops and courses in acting techniques and body movement are useful, and should be part of all preprofessional training, that instruction can also originate in the voice studio. A singer has to know what the face is conveying as well as what the body is saying. Facial expression is of prime importance for communication. The deadpan singer may wrongly presume that his or her face needs to mirror a vast gamut of emotions. In hoping to avoid appearing foolish in trying to convey each of them, emotional portrayal is dampened. It should be made clear that a wide compass of emotions can be covered by a pleasant, alert expression, without resort to mugging.

A valuable medium for alerting a singer to both physical stance and facial expression is the video camera. A singer should be filmed—not watching the camera—and later study the performance playback. A frank discussion between singer and teacher of best and least good results should follow. Although the modern-day voice studio ought to be equipped with a video camera, in its absence a full-length mirror in which a performer can view the body in profile by means of a hand mirror can also produce favorable results. Performers who do not want to see themselves on tape, or who refuse to watch themselves in mirrors, need to be reminded that everyone else sees what that performer looks like. They must give up considering singing a thing to be privately enjoyed. In the current performance world, the visual is as important as the aural.

By confusing reality and art, an overachieving interpreter may try to metamorphose into someone she or he is not, coming off as shallow and unbelievable. This may lead to superficial "acting acting." It should also be kept in mind that the drama must never rob a singer of the voice. (See Musically Unmusical.) Many performers falsely assume that unless they actually experience the upheavals of unrequited love, fear, or rage expressed in a text, they are being less than truthful. Others, believing themselves incapable of delivering such intense levels of emotion, and being unwilling to fake it, simply withdraw. Being reluctant to display emotion in an art song or an opera aria may come from misunderstanding the extent to which a performer must personally feel the drama's events. Perceiving that they are not of the same psychological or physical makeup as the character they are called on to represent, they do not want to indulge in falsehood. The outcome may be avoidance of taking that creative step from the real world to the world of imagination, essential to all acting, be it in opera, in concert, or in a stage role. When divorced from communication, technical and musical competence is of limited value.

People who want to be singers seldom are low-key personalities. If the dramatic situation is understood, the language properly coached, musical and technical expertise suitably honed, singers are able to communicate successfully. In hard cases, such as the young man mentioned, as much attention has to be given to the technique of communication as to any area of professional preparation. Essential performance attributes can be learned through routining. Such simple devices as shifting the body weight at changes of mood; mental repetition or the addition of a text during musical interludes; envisioning the events of the unfolding drama, staging the art song, then assuming the same dramatic thoughts while remaining physically quiet; singing to the three sides of every hall—as opposed to fixated forward staring; relaxation of the hands and arms; and accustoming the face to experiencing an alert, expectant feeling, may all prove fruitful. (See Breaking Stance and Shifting the Body Weight; Internal and External Listening.)

INTERNAL AND EXTERNAL LISTENING

QUESTION
What do "internal hearing" and "external hearing" mean?

COMMENT
The noted Hungarian researcher Georg von Békésy confirmed that a person hears his or her own voice in two distinct ways: externally by means of the meatus (the complex instrument known as the ear), and internally through sympathetic vibration conducted by bony structures of the head. Practical studio evidence suggests that some singers depend almost excessively on internal listening, relying heavily on vibratory sensations registered in the skull. In so doing, they tend to

shut out the encompassing world. They appear to be singing for themselves, closing off communication with their audience. Symptoms of internal listening are (1) low pitch center, (2) lack of vibrancy, (3) unawareness of body language, (4) closed or fixated eyes, and (5) deadpan expression. Sound seems encased within the performer's body. A simple directive to listen on the outside may be sufficient corrective for both timbre and communication.

A more explicit pedagogic device is to have the singer lightly place an index finger against the lips to feel the sympathetic vibration that occurs on them during singing and, for the same reason, to position a hand just below the jaw. Directing attention to these more outward physical sensations may have greater psychological than acoustic value. Insist on outwardly directed vision (eyes open and alight), without a fixated point of vision, and a pleasant, outgoing facial expression. Communication, not self-absorption, is the aim.

THE PROBLEM OF FAULTY INTONATION

QUESTION
Are sharping and flatting caused by a poor ear (bad pitch sense), wrong breath support, faulty vowels, or a combination of all of the above?

A RELATED QUESTION
When a singer is alternately flat and sharp within the same phrase or in neighboring phrases, is the cause always the ear, or could it be due to improper breath support, inaccurate pronunciation, or perhaps even muscle tension?

COMMENT
The questioners wisely cite some probable causes for pitch vagaries among singers. Oddly enough, the person with a fine ear may be oblivious to self-produced flat or sharp singing, while aware of it when others sing. Inner vibratory sensation, registered internally through bone conduction, sometimes misleads on pitch-targeting judgments. Emotionally internalized singing is frequently flat. (See Internal and External Listening.) Even though the fundamental remains at the proper number of cycles per second, the pitch may sound flat because of a loss of acoustic energy in upper regions of the spectrum. Modern voice research refers to this concentration of acoustic energy as "the singer's formant," which ideally consists of strong third, fourth, and fifth formants. In the prescientific world, the phenomenon was known as the *chiaro* (clear) aspect of the complete chiaroscuro tone. Subjective language describes it as the "ring," the "ping," the "focus" of the tone. (See Chiaroscuro; Formant Information. Why?)

Specifically, configurations of the lips, the tongue, the jaw, the velum, the larynx, and the zygomatic arch produce the inner perception of pitch accuracy.

Spectrographic analysis confirms that regardless of the precision of the fundamental, the exact distribution of acoustic energy depends on vocal-tract shaping. If
the shape of the buccopharyngeal cavity—the chamber of the mouth and pharynx—
does not match the targeted vowel, pitch vagaries will abound. Specific pitch problems in singing often originate from pedagogic concepts of what a singer should
do with the buccopharyngeal resonator when progressing from front to back vowels. (See Keeping Uniformity of Timbre throughout the Changing Vowel Spectrum.) In the production of front (lateral) vowels, the mouth is in a more horizontal position, the front portion of the tongue relatively high, although, of course, the
apex of the tongue remains in contact with the inner surface of the lower front
teeth. With rounded (back) vowels, although remaining in contact with the inner
surface of the front teeth, the front segment of the tongue is now lower; the back
portion of the tongue, more elevated in the velar (soft palate) area. Because of their
phonetic nature, the lateral vowels have a higher number of upper partials than do
the rounded vowels. For that reason, /ɔ/, /o/, /ʊ/, and /u/ are disposed to flatting,
a tendency exacerbated by their occurring late in a long phrase, or when terminat-
ing the phrase. (See Maintaining the Male 3000 Hz Factor.)

In unskilled singing, the pitch center falters, being either below or above the
targeted note. Lack of energy produces insufficient glottal closure. That is why
singers are admonished to concentrate on "supporting" to the phrase termination.
Even at a phrase onset, high rates of fluctuating airflow not turned into tone may
lead to off-key singing. Although perception of the fundamental is not a direct result of vowel defining, pitch accuracy will alter if transition sounds interfere with
precise resonator shaping. These phenomena are visible through spectral analysis.
Accumulating air pressure in conjunction with excessive vocal-fold resistance
produces pressed phonation (pushing). For that reason, sharping often happens at
register pivotal points or at pitches above the *secondo passaggio,* when breath energy ought to increase. (See Flow Phonation.) Flatting or sharping often occurs at
specific scale points. Faulty intonation is almost always a matter of phonetic dis-
crepancy, or of unbalanced airflow rates not commensurate with the phonatory
tasks.

FLATTING ON FINAL DESCENDING NOTES

QUESTION
How can dulling or flatting of the tone on the last note or two of a
descending phrase be prevented?

COMMENT
Preference given to the mouth as chief resonator at the expense of the pharynx uniformly lowers all formants. If the buccopharyngeal resonator remains in

the same position for low as for high pitches, acoustic strength of the upper partials diminishes, and bottom notes become dull and flat. Gradually closing the mouth on returning to low register brings compliance with spoken vowel postures. However, in extremely low parts of the range, the jaw will again need to lower to reinforce low harmonic partials.

No matter how efficient breath management may be, air supply becomes depleted at the end of a very long phrase. At such moments the sternum and chest want to fall; the rib cage, to collapse; and the abdomen, to move rapidly inward. To counteract these tendencies, the singer must make doubly sure that an axial position is retained. (See Always Noble and Axial?) If you feel your chest is lowering, raise it. You won't get more breath, but you will inhibit the collapse syndrome. (See The Problem of Faulty Intonation.)

AMPLIFICATION OF OPERA PERFORMANCE

QUESTION
What is your opinion of the new tendency in some opera houses to amplify singers' voices during performance?

COMMENT
As of today, the practice is relatively rare. If widely adopted, it could change the very nature of the lyric theater, and that of historic elite vocalism. Soubrettes could conceivably be cast as Butterfly, *leggiero* tenors as Tristan, coloratura mezzos as Azucena, and lyric baritones as Boris, their vocalism audible but the quality of their respective voices far from the composer's original intent regarding orchestra/voice relationships and the character of the drama. The classically trained opera professional learns how to balance formants so that the voice can carry over heavy orchestration, even in large halls. This characteristic quality results from the production of vibrant, resonant sound. By contrast, the microphoned singer has no need to rely on classic tonal balance. However, any well-trained singer who has appeared in convention halls seating 10,000 spectators, or in a mammoth metropolitan stadium, will attest that without some electronic boosting, it is next to impossible to perform, because of a lack of acoustic feedback. (See Ear-Cupping as an Acoustic Device.) When a performance venue is truly unfavorable, amplification ought to remain imperceptible to the audience. The body microphone cannot substitute for efficient *voce completa* production. Onstage amplification could destroy the *Fach* system that has served both singers and the listening public so well. Producers who adhere to high standards in opera and recital halls will resist this innovation.

REHEARSAL ROOM VERSUS HALL DYNAMICS

QUESTION

Over a period of years I have sung with some top-flight opera companies in both Europe and North America. Repeatedly in the piano ensemble rehearsals, coaches and assistant conductors insist that we singers need to cut back on dynamic levels. Then we move to the hall for the orchestral dress, and the conductor grumbles that none of us is singing out. "More sound!" is what we hear from the pit. Much of what we were trying to achieve in the rehearsal room has little relationship to what is required for performance in the theater itself. Why do so many coaches and repetiteurs fail to understand the acoustic differences between rehearsal rooms and halls?

COMMENT

You have largely answered your own question. There are coaches with fine musicianship and keyboard skills who know less than they should about the singing voice or how it responds to room acoustics. If dynamic levels during rehearsals are unrealistic, the differences in energy levels between holding back and singing out, as the questioner points out, are in conflict when the move to the hall is made. Some degree of marking is often desirable during musical rehearsals and staging sessions, especially when difficult ensemble sequences are repeated a number of times. (See Marking.) That is not the question here. Singing at dynamic levels and with timbres that are not transferable to the performance hall can mean having to learn to sing the role all over again when the move to the hall is made.

The same issue pertains in some voice studios. Teacher or coach sees a *p* or *pp* marking on the page, and asks the singer to produce a studio-ambient sound that could never be serviceable in the recital hall. Adherence to dynamic levels is an important aspect of the art of singing, but constant scaling back of a viable professional voice is not. Many professional singers have undergone this unpleasant experience. The answer lies in convincing coaches that hall dynamics are not studio dynamics, and that not all voices are identical. To blur those differences is detrimental to vocal health and the final product.

THE RELATIVITY OF VOICE DYNAMICS

QUESTION

All my life I have been told that I have a big voice. I am one of those who stuck out in choir, and I was constantly yelled at for being too loud. Now, as a graduate student and as a person a lot of respected people think has a promising voice, the same thing still happens with the coach who is teaching the vocal literature courses. I'm asked to sing so softly that all the quality goes out of my voice. What should I do about it? It doesn't sound like me, and it sure doesn't feel right.

COMMENT

Dynamic levels are relative to the size of the performing instrument. Voices come in all sizes. There is no such thing as an explicit decibel standard for *pp, p, mf, f,* or *ff.* The human voice is not capable of making as wide a range of dynamics as the pianoforte, nor should it be expected to do so. Reducing dynamic intensity below mezzoforte requires more skill than does singing mezzoforte and above. It may be that you are not yet sufficiently adroit in reducing decibels while maintaining energy to ensure resonant timbre. That is a developmental matter, requiring high skill and a commitment of time. Your literature coach may misunderstand the nature of your instrument, or be making unreasonable dynamic requests of you. In either case there is not much to be done, except to smile and say you will keep trying (the grin-and-bear-it maneuver). Try to bring more subtlety into your singing by applying *messa di voce* exercises to segments of the literature. But do not destroy your basic timbre in order to comply with an unrealistic goal. It may take time and further vocal maturity for you to produce all the dynamic variations you and the coach wish. (See *Messa di Voce.*) Perhaps this is an occasion when I should quote from the *Dear Abby* column: "Show him this column!"

MESSA DI VOCE

QUESTION
In *messa di voce,* why does my vibrato waver or the tone go straight when I return to piano dynamic?

RELATED QUESTION
How does one keep from becoming airy on the decrescendo of a long phrase?

COMMENT

Both questions focus on a common dilemma: how to maintain consistency of timbre and vibrancy during a change of intensity. The *messa di voce*—beginning the phrase at *p* or *pp* dynamic, crescendoing to *f* or *ff*, returning to *p* or *pp*—is a test of how well breath emission and vocal-fold approximation are coordinated. A 1795 London publication, "Mr. Tenducci to His Scholars," defined it this way: "To sing messa di voce—swelling of the tone—begin pianissimo and gradually increase to forte in the first part of the tone; then gradually diminish to the conclusion of each note." If early depletion of the breath supply happens before completion of sustained phonation, or if vocal-fold closure becomes slack before the exact moment of release, the tone is breathy and loses vibrancy. *Messa di voce* is the ultimate exercise for ensuring skill in combining breath management and optimal phonation control. The celebrated Italian teacher and coach Luigi Ricci remarked: "A singer who can execute a truly perfect *messa di voce* on every note of the performable scale is a fully accomplished singer." Then he would pause, smile, and add: "Don't expect to be able to do it without years of work." *Messa di voce* study should be introduced only after security in breath management has been established. It is inappropriate to the early phases of technical study. A singer must first be able to execute clean, vibrant onsets on short phonations to achieve proper vowel definition and sostenuto control. The crescendo and decrescendo portions of a long phrase depend on preserving the abdominal-wall inhalatory position as long as possible. Because of gender laryngeal structural diversities, most women win a *messa di voce* victory earlier than do most men. *Leggiero* tenors have a greater affinity for the *messa di voce* than do sturdier tenor voices; lyric baritones have an easier time than dramatic male low voices.

In practicing the *messa di voce,* divide the process into (1) a crescendo from *p* to *f,* followed immediately by (2) an intervening silent breath renewal, and (3) a subsequent decrescendo from *f* to *p*. (Use a single pitch in lower-middle voice, later on higher pitches. Each of the cardinal vowels may be used alternately.) Then the breath-renewal interruption is eliminated and the complete *messa di voce* is routined. It is applicable to phrases of various lengths and pitches, and to cumulative passages where phrase shaping and sculpting is essential for musical and textual communication. Even though not always directly indicated by the composer, dynamic shading within each phrase should outline an intensity trajectory pattern.

Crescendoing and decrescendoing must be reserved for the overall phrase, not applied to individual syllables. (See The Second Half of the Note; Musically Unmusical.) Constancy of airflow within shifting dynamic levels can be accomplished only when airflow and subglottic pressure precisely coordinate pitch, vowel, and dynamic intensity. *Messa di voce* is a device for achieving such precision. It is for singers who already have attained a good level of technical proficiency.

PREPHONATORY TUNING

QUESTION
Please define prephonatory tuning.

COMMENT
In the skillfully executed onset, the musicianly ear and the larynx undertake a split-second tuning process in advance of actual phonation. Accurate pitch

targeting is immediately coordinated with precise consonantal and vowel defini-tion. When the flow of air is commensurate with demands of the intended funda-mental, probing for the right level of breath energy to ensure pitch centering is avoided. There is no pitch slurring or hesitancy in landing squarely on pitch cen-ter. Exactitude of prephonatory tuning depends on the simultaneous conjoining of airflow and vocal-fold approximation. Pitch accuracy and full resonance are im-mediate results of prephonatory tuning. Before a pitch is sung, the ear accurately conceives it. Instantaneous conception of the pitch not only brings about exactitude of intonation; it also incites well-balanced timbre, to which vibrancy is essential. Prephonatory conception permits an efficient onset.

ORATORIO VERSUS OPERA

QUESTION
I am a relatively mature voice-performance major hoping to become an opera singer, but I really love the great oratorios. What is the difference in vocal technique between opera and oratorio? Is it unsettling to try to learn both?

COMMENT
There is not one voice technique for oratorio and another for opera. In fact, when religious considerations forbade opera performances, oratorios were some-times presented as an alternative to opera; vocalism remained the same. Although there are numerous stylistic differences between the two categories, depending on the period from which they stem, the demands of both opera and oratorio require an equal technical proficiency. One cannot think of the great sacred choral/orchestral masterpieces without including such diverse works as those by Bach, Haydn, Han-del, Mozart, Schubert, Beethoven, Mendelssohn, Brahms, Verdi, Dvořák, Kodály, Honegger, Britten, Poulenc, Walton, and a number of contemporary composers. The vocal demands for the oratorio solo singer parallel and in some cases exceed those found in operatic writing. It is clear that both style and voice timbre are vari-able, and that one does not sing Bach like Verdi, Haydn like Brahms, or Mozart like Puccini; but it is naïve to believe that a skilled singer must bring a different technique to each period or style. Learning specialized voice techniques for each style is not the logical answer. Instead, a deep understanding of the differences in musical style must be mastered. These vary as greatly within the operatic litera-ture as in the oratorio. Styles vary, but technique remains constant. (See Literature Styles and Voice Technique.)

PERFORMANCE ATTIRE

QUESTION
Some of my overweight female students want to improve their physical appearance during performance by wearing tight garments that make them look slimmer and high heels that make them appear several inches taller. Have you any comment on the effects of this recital costuming on voice production?

COMMENT
Inasmuch as the singer's art is visual as well as auditory, concern for appearance is well founded. But a sturdily built singer cannot alter his or her body structure through external camouflaging. Restrictive clothing seldom produces a better visual result. Getting professional advice on accentuating the positive aspects of appearance is a wiser move. Practical experience has shown that sleeker lines may be insinuated by wearing clothing that offers perpendicular as opposed to horizontal designs. Nevertheless, sartorial disguising does not deal with the fundamental problem. Any clothing that restricts full expansion of the chest or of the abdominal wall interferes with breath management. At the close of the nineteenth century, in a corset style termed straight-lacing, the abdominal area was tightly firmed inward, projecting an hour-glass appearance. Restrictive fashion styles led to high-chest (clavicular) breathing and to voice pathologies that were deplored by several medical sources of the era.

It is reported that when asked about chief requirements for the singing of long Wagnerian roles, Birgit Nilsson replied that a pair of comfortable shoes was essential. The question of high heels is pertinent not only to the female performer. In order to woo his Gilda, more than one Duca di Mantova has had to wear two-or-three inch lifts in boots that already had raised heels. There are potential problems of body balance in wearing higher heels than is customary. With singers who have a tendency to incline the body backward on the heels (especially for high notes), raised heels that pitch the body somewhat forward may actually be advantageous. Some singers achieve better head, neck, and torso alignment when the weight of the body is shifted onto the balls of the feet. Oddly enough, there are some techniques of singing that shift the weight to the heels on purpose, inclining the body on a backward arc, causing an undesirable alteration of axial posture.

Singers of either gender should not wait until the performance itself, whether concert or opera, to perform in an untried costume or recital attire. Dress rehearsals for staged productions are invaluable in providing a chance to adjust to hat, veil, tiara, draping, or train, or in managing tights, sword, cape, beard, mustache, and boots. A tightly fitting collar, a costume with a neck design never intended for a compact build, a wig that covers the ears, a hat that alters the acoustic response, shoes that don't fit well, can be enough to upset a performer. The singer is not just being temperamental when complaining about an ill-fitting or problematic costume. An experienced singer will want to thoroughly know his or her costume in advance, as well as to become acquainted with all the props.

In the dress rehearsal for recital or concert, performance shoes should be worn. A singer should sing at least once in the recital costume prior to the performance. In the current casual academic world, student recitalists often feel no need to "dress" until the actual performance. Many a young woman has lurched onto the stage for her senior recital wearing shoes in which she has never walked, with hair that sits on top of her head as never before, wearing sleeves, scarves, or drapes (or bare shoulders and arms) that do not feel normal. The young male who has had no experience wearing dress tails, jacket, cummerbund, and accessory linens may suddenly face several unanticipated body strictures. There is always the danger of disorientation when attire feels foreign. It is just as important to know how the body feels in a costume as to assess the acoustic response of the hall. Public performance is a special event and it requires appropriate attire.

PERFORMANCE-DAY DIET

QUESTION
What type of food do you suggest before a performance, and how soon before should we eat? In general, what is the best diet for a singer?

COMMENT
Singers do not need to be tied to a particular diet. The most healthful food for normal living is the most healthful diet for singing. Nutritious dietary choices are available from numerous health sources. However, desiccants should be avoided. They include most commercially prepared fast foods; all deep-fried, salty, or spicy foods; olives; tea; coffee; and alcohol. All are what Dr. Van Lawrence, a noted otolaryngologist, designated as "dryer outers." Hydration is essential to the singing voice; diet on performance days should not include desiccating choices. Refrigerated drinks, particularly colas, should be shunned. Nuts, powdered sugar, and astringents are not recommended. For many singers, avoidance of ice cream, sherbet, and milk is advisable on a performance day.

Maestro Luigi Ricci, a noted twentieth-century voice coach and teacher, advocated eating a nourishing but light meal several hours before strenuous performances. Body strength must be maintained, but the digestive process needs a chance to do its work prior to extended vocalization. Water and juices should be drunk throughout every day, especially on performance days—not just before the performance, but also in pauses, intermissions, or between scenes. (See Water Babies.)

SOLO SINGER IN A CHORAL SETTING

QUESTION

At major schools of music in North America, highly talented solo voices are required to participate in choral groups. How does a director deal with a large number of fine solo voices in an ensemble without violating unique individual timbres?

> RELATED QUESTION
>
> I am director of choral studies at [a major school of music]. Performance majors are required to elect choir each semester they are in residence. That means I deal with real singers, not amateurs. My problem is not with them but with some professional colleagues in regional and national organizations who criticize any choral sound that does not fit their concept of neutered, detimbred, straight choral tone. Why do professional singing teachers' organizations not campaign to get across to the academic choral world that this constant conflict has to be resolved in favor of healthy vocalism?

COMMENT

Bravo! A choral director who works with talented solo voices must resist tonal premises advocated by those who deal almost entirely with amateur choristers. As indicated in the above perspicacious questions, within today's choral community the questionable concept of nonvibrant and sterile choral sound still has numerous fervent adherents. This philosophy is handed down through workshops and symposia from one choral conductor to another, permeating North American secondary and collegiate choral scenes. It has taken on the nature of cultism. This search for compliance with a preconceived notion is largely responsible for the turning off of serious singers who should be happily participating in what can be the exciting world of ensemble singing.

Not all ensemble groups are of uniform technical level. A choir or chorus with trained solo voices should not be handled in the same way as one composed of amateur singers. Further, the wide diversity of talents within any single chorus must be taken into account. Instead of aiming for one bland concept of timbre, a responsible choral conductor ought to look carefully at the singers and discover ways to balance their diverse tonal potentials, raising the less skillful to a higher level. Unfortunately, in order to find peer approval, many choral conductors prominent in academic choral associations feel compelled to conform to a super-imposed, uniform concept. This then becomes the model for high-school choral conductors.

Every voice instructor at the collegiate level groans under this burden. There are solutions for dealing with this burning problem. Administrators should enlist the help of teachers of singing in actively searching for a choral conductor who knows how the voice works as an instrument, and who has an ear for the poten-tials of the human voice. As responsible teachers of singing we must not abdicate our responsibility to insist that enlightened choral conductors be sought, hired, and retained. We must not continue to function as a wagging tail to the choral dog.

TENOR CHORAL FALSETTO

QUESTION
How can I help my young tenors survive daily singing in two choral ensembles, as they have to do at my university? Is it okay to tell them to use falsetto in upper range?

RELATED QUESTION
The tessitura in much of the choral literature is fatiguing for fresh-man and sophomore tenors. Should I advise my young tenors to mostly use falsetto in rehearsal and even in performance?

COMMENT
The two questioners express a concern shared in academe by many teachers of singing. The sustained tessitura of much choral writing for tenor voice lies con-sistently higher than that of many tenor arias. Because of the number of ensemble requirements in music degree programs, how to solve the challenge of the solo voice in the choral ensemble continues to be a major problem for academic voice teachers and their students. (See Solo Singer in a Choral Setting.) Part of the dilemma is em-bedded in the histories of several choral heritages that exist side by side on the North American continent. Among them are the Anglican chapel/cathedral tradition, the Scandinavian-Lutheran choral tradition, the middle-European *Knabenchor* (boys' choir) and *Männerchor* (men's chorus) traditions, the symphonic-choir tradition, and, more recently, the "twentieth-century Baroque" vocal ensemble movement.

Contrasting tonal ideals mark the prepubertal English treble choir and the middle-European treble *Knabenchor*. Male choral groups (*Männerchor*) no longer flourish in America, but robust *Männerchor* tonal influences continue in some re-gions of the country. In the nearly defunct *Männerchor* heritage, vitality and exu-berance were an aim. The tonal aesthetic of the English choral tradition is based on ideals of tonal "purity" in which vibrato is eliminated from the tone. Because of heavy reliance on excessive breath mixture, the resultant timbre, in point of fact, is acoustically quite impure. (See British Treble Choral Tradition.) High airflow and lack of vibrancy combine to produce sharping and straight tone in treble and female voices, because improper ratios between breath-flow rate and vocal-fold closure yield pitch vagaries. (See Free-Swinging Vibrancy; and Identifying and Steadying Vibrato Rate.)

Vibrancy is an essential ingredient of the professional chiaroscuro timbre. When the vibrato is suppressed, an imbalance among first and third formants occurs, with voice quality reduced to one uniform color. The search for authenticity in Early Music is a driving force among certain academic choral groups. It and other tonal traditions act as conflicting influences on American liturgical and academic choral circles. Some choral conductors consider such timbre to produce ethereal, spiritual, or "Baroque sound." The objective listener is left longing for centered intonation and for honest timbre, in which the fundamental and its overtones are in balance at all dynamic levels, a goal transcending centuries and literature styles.

The same "pure-tone" aesthetic is present in the widely disseminated Scandinavian-Lutheran choral tradition prominent in the northern half of the United States and dominant in some quarters of North American professional choral organizations. Although less committed to high levels of breath emission than the British tradition, a branch of the Scandinavian-Lutheran choral aesthetic seeks to diminish the upper portion of spectra (reduction of harmonic partials [overtones]). Jaws are hung and back vowels are favored as a means of masking the individual quality of solo voices. In the case of the young male singer, particularly the tenor, rather than emasculate his normal production through resonance distortion, it may be best to resort to falsetto timbre in upper range. (See Tenor Choral Falsetto.) These problems are not as intense in middle-European *Knabenchor* and Germanic *Männerchor* traditions. The vibrant sound of boys who sing in the *Knabenchor* tradition contrasts with the "toot-tone" (*Tutentönen*) or "tube-tone" (*Röhrentönen*) of the nonprofessional German parish choir (and of the traditional metropolitan British boy choir). Happily for the future of healthy vocalism in Britain, today there exists a recognizable antagonism between the hooty treble choral concept and the vibrant tonal completeness of the middle-European treble choral tradition. A number of chapel and cathedral choirs in England, while performing traditional liturgical literature, are abandoning the vibratoless Church of England sound in favor of vibrant, healthy young voice timbre.

In falsetto, the closure phase of the vocal folds is demonstrably less efficient than it is in *voce completa* (complete voice), the normal male classical singing sound in an ascending scale. During phonation, air passing over the vocal folds that is not turned into tone is a mark of inefficient function. Free-flow phonation is desirable; breathy phonation is not. Fiberoptically, light male falsetto somewhat resembles a stage whisper. (When one whispers, the vocal folds do not fully approximate; extended whispering is not a healthy form of phonation.) A reinforced falsetto at high decibels incites better vocal-fold closure but is as dynamically inappropriate in ensemble singing as *voce piena in testa* (full head voice) would be. It may even produce a higher level of vocal-fold resistance to airflow than is commensurate with the best vocalism. (See Countertenoring.)

What is the answer for the poor student tenor (and his teacher) called on to maintain a tessitura in choral literature that he would not encounter in "Celeste Aida"? He has the choice, in upper range, of either straining his as-yet-marginal voice technique or of reverting momentarily to falsetto. Although it would not be advisable to rely on falsetto production in solo appearances, it may be advantageous for him to resort to falsetto timbre in choral situations. He must at all costs avoid the physical trauma of trying to produce legitimate tone at subtle dynamic levels in a tessitura in which he does not yet function freely.

Imaginative choral conductors ought to be able to solve the problem of the solo singer in the choral ensemble by understanding how to obtain a balanced choral sound that results from healthy vocalism. It should not be necessary for the young tenor to use destructive vocal means in order to comply with a conductor's tonal concept. The female who possesses a voice of viable professional dimensions faces a similar dilemma, particularly when she is required to mimic straight-tone, boy-treble quality in high-lying passages.

BRITISH TREBLE CHORAL TRADITION

QUESTION
Would you discuss the British boy-choir tradition and how that unique sound is achieved? How does it relate to vocal health?

COMMENT
As mentioned in the choral-singing discussions, acoustic and physiologic factors that produce the straight-treble cathedral tone rely on a high admixture of breath in the sung tone, an action that tends to reduce or eliminate vibrancy. A false assumption is made that vibrato is foreign to the prepubertal vocal instrument, and that straight-tone timbre yields an "angelic," "pure" tone appropriate to liturgical literature. Because it sounds disembodied, the end product resonates in the popular mind as representing an ethereal, spiritual world. Unless forbidden to do so, children will sing vibrantly. With a child's voice, as with a voice of any age, the tasks of singing exceed the demands of ordinary speech. Vibrato is a relaxant principle essential to vocal freedom. Vibrato is held out of sung phonation only through constrictive controls. With regard to tonal purity, straight-tone quality is actually impure because of a high degree of breath emission. A heavy rate of breath

passing over vibrating vocal folds does not bring about efficient vocalization. Breathy tone registers spectrally as noise. (See Free-Swinging Vibrancy; Vibrato in the Young Singer.) It should also be remarked that in most commercially recorded performances involving traditional cathedral-tone boy treble timbres and liturgical male falsettists, pitch hovers above the targeted intonation center. Why that should be aesthetically pleasing among musicians to whom pitch accuracy is traditionally a sine qua non remains a mystery. It is clearly an acquired aesthetic taste, associated with an esoteric, specialized style of musicmaking. Treble cathedral-tone imitation continues to flourish in North American Anglican liturgical circles and in some campus choral groups.

A number of British and North American observers report that treble choristers from this tradition seldom develop into adult professional singers of note. Their post-pubertal voices seem unable to make the transition to healthy young-male vocalism. (I am aware of only a few exceptions.) In contrast, many males permitted to sing vibrantly as children enjoy adult professional careers. The effects of years of vibratoless treble singing on the future adult male voice have never been properly subjected to extensive research. (Doctoral dissertation subject?)

GESTICULATION IN SINGING, AND THE KINESTHETIC SENSE

QUESTION
Do the gestures students want to use as they vocalize really serve a purpose? The problem I have is that they want to carry them over into performance. Some singers seem to think they have to keep hands and arms in motion most of the time. They add things during performance that I have never seen them do in the studio, and they look foolish doing it.

RELATED QUESTION
Some teachers encourage students to make sweeping hand gestures while executing vocalises, particularly in search of legato. Does that really make a difference in the sound? And isn't it wrong to rely on a practice that cannot be transferred to performance venues?

COMMENT
Occasional physical movement that tends to break the cycle of rigidity can be put to good use in the studio as a means of inducing freedom in voice production. It can be introduced to counteract excessive motion of arms and hands. (See Breaking the Stance and Shifting the Weight; Physical Movement during Singing.) Requesting a graceful hand and arm gesture in the studio may also induce a better

sense of line for a particular phrase. Then the singer repeats the phrase without gesticulating, retaining the sense of line and physical freedom. This kinesthetic shaping of a phrase may focus concentration in a favorable way. The problem arises when the singer comes to rely on physical gestures to accomplish mental concepts, and is unable to produce the concept without the gesture. Pedagogic reliance on gesticulation should not substitute for specific communicative language.

Memorable is a master class, taught by a premier artist, in which a baritone who lacked legato was told to pretend he held a violin in his left hand, a bow in his right. He was to move his bow over imaginary strings while singing "Per m'è giunto." Did it help? Perhaps there was some temporary improvement. But as soon as he stopped fiddling, he was again unable to achieve a legato. Perhaps a more efficient approach would have been to explain why he was failing to maintain sufficient energy and dynamic continuity to connect one tone to the next. A somewhat more fantastic illustration of movement as an inducement to physical freedom occurred in another master class in which a singer was to pretend she was an elephant sweeping up peanuts with her trunk. The master teacher heard improvement, but it occurred to a number of observers to wonder how frequently a soprano may be cast as a hungry female elephant. Even if discernible, the benefits of elephanting were purely ephemeral. Without trunk and peanuts, the problems remained. Can gesturing induce a sense of line? Will the linear concept remain when the gestures are laid aside? Success depends on the underlying mental concept. Mostly, upon returning to physical quietude, a performer may miss the security of the physical gesture. Rather than deal indirectly through gesticulation, the wisest route is to explain the causes of the deficiency and to correct them through specific techniques.

The negative aspects of gesticulation are many. Much of what constitutes good stage behavior lies in learning to divorce performance from rhythmic pulsation and body movement. In order for dramatic enactment to take place, independence from the musical constraints of the drama is essential. A speaker fails to increase believability by rhythmically bobbing the head up and down with every verb and noun. Susanna is not believable if she is constantly moving her head and torso in 6/8 rhythmic impulses for "Deh, vieni non tardar." She must learn to separate kinetic energy of the rhythmic beat and of body swaying from her dramatic interpretation if she is to be credible. She must not exhibit the seams of her musical garment, but become clothed with reality. Further, physical movement can become a substitute for actual musical motion. Pop musicians confuse motion with emotion. Amateur choristers and even some professional ensemble singers nod and weave to show sentiments of the text. Intelligent performance does not require choreography. The performer may be experiencing physical and emotional pleasure, but sophisticated members of the audience aren't. The viewer, in danger of becoming seasick, sees only personal indulgence, not communication. True artists learn to free the body from extraneous motion; the voice should move, the body should not.

For singing, as for all athleticism, the kinesthetic sense must be tied to cognitive information and is acquired through skillful repetition. Reliance on physical motion during performance is not freedom-inducing but enslaving. ("The damned are in ceaseless motion."). Much is to be gained by studies in eurhythmics for a sense of freedom, but even here an impression must not be left that physical movement equates with phrase movement.

REASONABLE WARM-UP TIME

QUESTION
You have mentioned the importance of warming up the voice and have suggested a number of exercises that are to be done in sequence. What is an appropriate warm-up time for beginners? For advanced students? Does the length of time a singer spends in warming up depend on the size of the voice? On the work to be sung? How long should a singer warm up just before a recital or an opera role? Why do some singers seem not to need any warm-up, while others require as much as thirty minutes?

COMMENT
Physical activity should take place before strenuous motion is placed on any muscle group. Even a public speaker will benefit from a few minutes spent in preparatory exercises involving bodily movement. It is the entire body, not only the larynx, that needs to be ready. Warming up for singing should begin with simple physical exercises that bring into play the musculature of the torso, the abdominal wall, and the neck. The body must be alert, invoking tonicity among muscles that make up the structural framework for breathing and phonating. Some freedom-inducing physical exercises should precede a regimen of voice warm-ups. Then choose a few patterns from each area of systematic technique, to include onset, agility, vowel differentiation, resonance balancing, sostenuto, registration, and range extension. Preperformance warming up should not be lengthy or fatiguing, yet the voice should be exercised throughout its range.

Warming up should be a daily event for every healthy singer of any age. A beginner may find no more than ten to twenty minutes a comfortable amount of warm-up time before feeling fatigue. A more advanced singer may take thirty minutes to touch all areas of technical work. When established singers have perfected a warm-up routine, they can, if necessary, warm up in a few minutes. Lighter voices, female or male, seldom need a long warm-up. Aging performers may need to increase the duration of warm-up periods, pacing themselves less strenuously, although some maturing singers require less time than formerly. A good warm-up procedure puts the voice in healthy condition for the remainder of the day, but it does not replace periods of further technical exploration.

Singers who believe they need no warm-up delude themselves. They subject their listeners to what should have taken place in private. Using the opening material of a recital or an opera role for onstage warm-up is perilous to vocal quality and to vocal health. A noted Marschallin, famous for using her initial appearance in Act 1 for warming up publicly, annoys audiences and critics alike. Until her voice loses thickness and oscillation, one wonders why she was cast. She later produces impressive sound. It would be suicidal for Turiddu or Radames to attempt onstage warm-ups with either of their opening arias.

Male singers often require a longer warm-up period than do females. When the male leaves his chest voice, he increases energy for the negotiating of pitches above middle range far more than his female colleagues do. He should not ask his vocal mechanism suddenly to jump into those tasks without preparation. As technique becomes increasingly secure, warming up becomes briefer. Excessive warm-up before a performance will remove the bloom from the voice.

FLYING ON AUTOMATIC PILOT

QUESTION
I'm a soprano who has spent over two decades singing leading roles in European and U.S. opera houses. After many years of technical training with two wonderful teachers, I almost always have the feeling during performances that with regard to vocal technique I am flying on automatic pilot. I can seldom recall what technical things I have done during the performance itself. Is this a common experience? Could you please comment?

COMMENT
You are apparently a testimonial to what thorough technical grounding should accomplish. Your question involves consideration of some quite profound aspects of the learning process as it relates to artistic performance. The kinesthetic motor memory that underlies the physical aspects of singing does not parallel that which calls up stored information for adding, subtracting, dividing, multiplying, or conjugating verbs. It is clear that high-level singing skills fall into a category of behavior which goes beyond the generalized aptitude that serves the body in normal human activity. This capability exceeds both natural and social intelligence because it unites technical skill with a reservoir of musical and emotional responses that function without conscious involvement. The exact relationships among specific parts of the brain, including those which control language, music, counting, and the ordinary kinesthetic mechanical tasks associated with daily living, remain con-

jectural. What the body as an instrument and the musicianly ear have assembled through disciplined routine allows a fine singer the technical freedom you experience. A good singer takes in technical information, assimilates and processes it over years, and then relies on it during public performance, mostly without direct thought.

I do not believe that the premier singer standing on stage directs attention to "placing" the tone, to manipulating the articulatory resonators, to controlling the breath-management muscles, or to conscious positioning of the larynx. Those things are all in the past. There are occasions, of course, within any opera or oratorio role, a *mélodie* opus or a lieder cycle, when a singer needs to consciously call on ingrained technical devices, but the skilled performer has earlier solved problems of technique through learned and assimilated information. That singing artist is then free to direct the imagination to artistic expression that leads to direct communication with an audience.

Such behavior may be viewed as the accumulation and integration of knowledge and experiences assembled from parallel but unrelated modes. It is this integration of the separate modules of information that provides the elite singer with a secure technique that can be called upon without conscious attention being directed to it: "flying on automatic pilot."

THE BROADWAY SOUND

QUESTION
There is a strong commercial market for young and physically attractive singers who can produce "the Broadway Sound." Many musical comedy scores require legitimate, classically oriented singing, while others demand a constant mix, or even the use of the dreadful B [belt] quality. Those of us who have been trained in traditional voice technique try to develop a technical system that is equally applicable to musical theater and to legitimate singing. For example, we attempt to incorporate the French nasals into an English-language middle-voice mixture, what some sources call "twang." We strive to maintain the same breath management as used in classical singing, and we aim for a free sound that permits vocal health.

There are healthy models like Maureen McGovern, Barbara Cook, Terence Mann, and Judy Kuehn (the latter of *Les Mis,* numerous musicals, and *Pocahontas* fame). These artists can sing in several stylistic ways. Could you go on record with any comforting comments regarding pop-culture pedagogy, or do you feel it is all *bunk?* Those of us who deal with this type of singer on a daily basis need advice, and maybe reassurance. Thanks.

COMMENT

The question touches on a major dilemma facing today's private voice instructor. Voice teachers at universities and conservatories of music mostly have the luxury of concentrating on standard classical voice literature. Their nonacademic colleagues wield spades and shovels in the trenches of the real world of pop vocalism. Hats off to those who can do the latter while recognizing the need to safeguard the vocal health of their charges. A number of classically trained students (several from my own studio, including one of the group mentioned above) have gone on to successful careers in musical comedy and to what may be termed "the Broadway Sound." Good breath management and the ability to sustain and to move the voice, to play with resonance balances, and to produce understandable diction are essential elements of every vocal idiom.

A chief task for the teacher of pop idioms is to determine the extent to which so-called chest voice can be carried into the high ranges without violating a basic principle of voice production: as the fundamental pitch is raised, the vocal folds elongate and their mass diminishes. In some pop techniques, even those advocated by purported specialists in pop training, this principle is abandoned, producing clear register violations. For this reason, the laryngologist finds a large part of his or her performance clientele represented by both male and female pop artists. Avoidance of extreme register violation can be accomplished by "mixture" exercises in midrange. As suggested by the questioner, degrees of nasality may reduce the temptation to achieve projection through vocal-fold tensing, and apparently is not unwelcome in many popular idioms.

Microphone technique is essential to most pop styles, particularly when the singer competes with a loud band and is surrounded by noise. Knowledgeable pop artists insist on sound levels that remain competitively low. The pop singer often performs under adverse circumstances, including noisy and smoke-filled halls. They are also at the mercy of choreographers and designers who have little concern for the long-range health of the artist, and who make demands that the human voice cannot meet without undergoing fatigue. When the goal for individuality in a pop artist's sound is based on pathologic dysfunction, there is little any teacher can do except to urge its abandonment and to recommend recuperative voice therapy. A teacher can point out alternative choices, but lucrative rewards may weigh against their being adopted.

Unfortunately, there are some teachers of pop idioms who, like some of their classical colleagues, have little information on diagnosing vocal problems or prescribing solutions. Their instruction ends up advocating styles that other pop artists have developed for their particular vocal instruments. While disclaiming any authority in teaching pop styles, I suggest that healthy vocalism is appropriate to every singing style, and that whatever might militate against it should be discarded, after which there ought to be a reexamination of functional vocalism in the light of the instrumental potentials of the human voice. That cannot be done if a teacher or coach lacks specific information on the acoustic and physiologic workings of the voice as an instrument. (See Belting.) Uninformed instruction is harmful for any style of singing.

HOLISTIC SINGING

QUESTION
When you deal with such separate areas of voice technique as breathing, resonance balancing, registration, and vowels, how can you be treating singing as a holistic experience?

A RELATED QUESTION
Can one ever really systematically isolate concepts such as onset, agility, vowel definition, consonants, resonance, vibrancy, and dynamic levels, when in music they all happen at the same time?

COMMENT
Singing is a coordinated act. Premier singers standing before an audience do not concentrate on which parts of the torso to squeeze, push, or pull; how to place tone into parts of the head or down the spine; or how to modify vowels in the *passaggio* regions. (See Flying on Automatic Pilot.) They do not enter into separate onset, agility, sostenuto, vibrancy, or resonance-balancing modes. They sing to communicate text, drama, musical concepts, and their own personal understanding of the music. The voice is not a mechanical instrument separated from the innermost nature of an individual communicator, yet it is dependent on the mastery of specific skills. The following must not be forgotten:

1. Voice is not an ethereal substance to pour forth from the imagination.
2. Voice is produced as a result of certain biologic functions that preceded speech itself.
3. Voice is the product of neuromuscular events resulting from reflexes associated with normal human behavior.
4. Voice is the result of aerodynamic/myoelastic coordination between airflow and vocal-fold vibration.
5. Quality in the singing voice is determined by the filtering effect of the resonator tract in response to laryngeally generated sound.
6. Singing is only one aspect of coordinated components, and is not unrelated to other phonatory functions.
7. Individual components of the voice mechanism must be combined into a totality in order to produce the high-level performance demanded of the professional singing voice.

These functions are stimulated by a concept of tone brought into being through acquired mental processes. How a tonal concept is developed lodges in the mysterious complexity of individual personality. It is not possible for a teacher to teach any single technical function apart from the others, but it is feasible to examine how some particular inefficient behavior on the part of one of them may stand in the way of the coordinated whole, and to deal with it directly. This does not mean that the ultimate goal is separate control of component areas. However, it is necessary to temporarily draw a singer's attention to any localized activity that prohibits freedom in a specific area of function.

Diagnosis is made and prescription is offered. Every significant writer on the art of singing, past or present, has sought ways to help singers deal with details of the whole instrument. Let us conclude this book devoted to the diagnostics and prescriptions of the singer's concerns by remaining specifically analytical, while applying practical solutions to performance problems. If a singer is incapable of elongating the normal breath process so as to permit the execution of long phrases, a diagnosis must be made as to why. If there are tensions of the jaw, the tongue, the neck, or the larynx, they must be identified and corrected. If the singer still suffers from articulatory problems originating in regional speech habits, countering devices must be brought into play. Advising the singer to activate the imagination will not keep the tongue from going where it should not go. If nasality invades the sounds of singing, recommending that the singer get in touch with his or her inner psyche will not bring about velopharyngeal closure. If the scale is in segments, awareness of psychoacoustics will not effect its unity. Impediments need to be identified and curative techniques developed. It is not enough to apply generalized holistic imaging.

No violinist, no pianist, no trumpeter, no tennis player, no dancer, no swimmer, no skater, no poet, no writer, no painter, no sculptor has ever brought forth a high-level product without acquiring the skills required by that specific craft. Technical skills are eventually integrated into an artistic and kinesthetic whole dictated by the holistic imagination. Anyone who practices an art form must first learn to deal with all of its components. That is why the singer needs to learn systematic coordination of the motor, the vibrator, and the resonator. Only then can the art of performance become a holistic event. The discipline of singing is a demanding but highly rewarding venture. Shall we head for the practice room?

GLOSSARY OF TERMS

abdomen frontal body lying between the pelvis and the thorax; cavity of the torso.

abduction parting (as in glottal opening).

acoustics the science of sound, including its production, transmission, and effects; the sum of the qualities of an enclosure that determines the nature of the sound generated within it.

adduction coming together (as in glottal closure).

aggiustamento a system of vowel modification for achieving an equalized scale throughout registers of the singing voice.

alveolar articulated or produced with the tongue apex touching the upper front alveolar ridge.

alveoli air cells of the lungs.

anterolateral in front and to the side.

appoggiare to lean against, to be in contact with, to support.

appoggio an international breath management technique in singing; coordination among the large, flat abdominal muscles of the anterior/lateral wall and the thoracic cage throughout the breath cycle.

approximate to approach or produce vocal-fold contact or closure at the median position. (See Adduction.)

articulators tongue, lips, teeth, hard and soft palates, which modify the acoustic properties of the vocal tract.

arytenoid cartilages paired laryngeal cartilages to which the vocal folds are attached.

atmospheric pressure pressure exerted by the atmosphere in every direction, approximately 15 pounds per square inch at sea level.

attacco **(attack)** vocal onset.

Bauchaussenstütz "belly breathing"; distention of the lower abdominal wall; a breath-management technique associated with a part of the Germanic/Nordic school.

bel canto a style of vocalism uniting tonal beauty and technical skill; frequently restricted to describing solo-voice literature and cultivated singing styles prior to the mid-nineteenth century, as in the music of Rossini, Bellini, Donizetti, and their contemporaries.

bilabial formed with the aid of both lips, as in /p/, /b/, and /m/.

breath management control of the inspiratory/expiratory components of the breath cycle, efficiently uniting myoelastic and aerodynamic aspects of phonation.

buccal cavity cavity of the mouth; oral cavity.

buccopharyngeal resonator resonance space formed by the mouth and the pharynx.

cabaletta the second major section of the opera scena form, written in florid or dramatic contrast to the lyrical cantilena section that precedes it.

cantilena a graceful, flowing melody in "singing" style.

cartilage nonvascular connecting tissue, more flexible than bone (as in the cartilages of the larynx).

cartilaginous characterized or formed by cartilage (as the cartilaginous portion of the vocal fold, which is not engaged in vibration).

cavatina the first section of the opera scena form, in lyric, legato, sustained cantilena style.

central tendon large tendon of the diaphragm.

chest voice subjective term for sensations of sympathetic vibration experienced in lower range where the "heavy mechanism" is predominant.

chiaroscuro tone the "dark-light" tone of professional vocalism, denoting proper balance among the fundamental and its multiple harmonic integers, which ensures appropriate formant relationships.

complemental air (inspiratory reserve) air that can be inhaled in addition to the quantity taken in during quiet breathing.

continuant a speech sound that may be prolonged during a single breath (as in a nasal continuant).

copertura gradual vowel modification in a mounting scale; a component of *aggiustamento* in achieving *voce chiusa* as opposed to *voce aperta* timbre.

costal pertaining to a costa or rib.

couverture (See *copertura*.)

covering an inexact term used to describe various circumstances of acoustic alteration during singing; darkened or somber voice timbre; laryngeal events that result from excessive vowel modification or laryngeal depression.

cricoarytenoids muscles that rotate the arytenoid cartilages on the cricoid cartilage.

cricothyroids muscles attached to the front of the cricoid cartilage that can change the relationships of the thyroid and cricoid cartilages.

damping diminution in the amplitude of oscillations, as in vocal-fold damping.

Deckung a technique of laryngeal and acoustic alteration of timbre, associated with one part of the Nordic/German School.

diaphragm organ composed of muscles and sinews, separating the respiratory and digestive systems; partition between the chest and abdominal cavities.

dorsal refers to the back.

electroglottography (EGG) a device for measuring changes in electrical impedance (resistance) at the glottis. (Two electrodes are placed on opposite sides of the thyroid cartilage of the larynx, and register a waveform for visual display.)

epiglottis one of the three single cartilages of the larynx, located between the root of the tongue and the entrance to the larynx.

exhalation (expiration) breath emission during the breath cycle.

expiratory reserve volume the amount of air that can be exhaled from the lungs beyond that exhaled in quiet respiration.

external oblique muscle a muscle whose fibers run mostly downward, forming layers of the lateral walls of the abdomen, fusing with the internal oblique to form the linea alba.

extrinsic external (as in extrinsic laryngeal muscles).

Fach term used in distinguishing one category of singing voice from another.

falsetto in historic voice pedagogy, a male timbre imitative of the female voice; in some speech therapy quarters, any voiced sound that lies above modal register.

fascia (fasciae) a sheet or layer of connective tissue that covers, sheathes, supports, or binds together internal parts or structures of the body.

fauces (isthmus of the fauces) the narrow passage located between the velum and the base of the tongue, leading from the mouth to the pharynx; space surrounded by the soft palate, the palatine arches, and the base of the tongue; the pillars of the fauces consist of two folds on either side of the faucial isthmus.

fioriture ornaments, florid embellishments, and cadenzas.

flageolet a female voice register that extends beyond the normal pitches of "head" voice; an extension of upper range, accomplished through extreme damping.

formant the concentration of acoustic energy peaks, originated by the action of the breath on the resonance chambers, producing spectral regions of prominent energy distribution; spectral determinant of vowel differentiation, resonance balance, and timbre.

frequency the number of vibrations or cycles per second. The greater the number at the fundamental, the higher the pitch.

fricative a voiced or unvoiced speech sound produced by air friction passing through a narrowed aperture, as in /f/, /v/, /s/, /z/.

fry (See Vocal Fry.)

gemischte Stimme "mixed voice."

genioglossus pair of fan-shaped muscles whose fibers radiate from the chin, inserting on the hyoid bone and attaching to the sides of the pharynx, with insertions into the tongue.

geniohyoid pair of slender muscles that arise from the mandible and insert on the hyoid bone.

glottis the alterable space between the vocal folds

harmonic an overtone or upper partial; vibration frequency that is a multiple of the vibration rate produced at the fundamental frequency.

"head voice" upper range of the singing voice.

heavy mechanism a term sometimes used to describe the predominant role of the vocalis muscle; "chest" voice

hyoid bone U-shaped bone situated at the base of the tongue and above the larynx.

hyothyroid muscle and ligament connecting the thyroid cartilage of the larynx and the hyoid bone.

hyperfunction excessive activity in any part of the physical mechanism.

hypofunction insufficient activity in any part of the physical mechanism.

hypogastric (pubic) lower abdominal region.

Hz unit of measurement applied to the number of cycles per second (as in 440 Hz); named for physicist Gustav Hertz.

imposto (impostazione della voce) "placement of the voice."

inhalation (inspiration) the part of the breath cycle during which breath enters the lungs.

insertion the part of a muscle attached to the bone it moves.

inspiratory reserve volume (See Complemental Air).

intercostals short external and internal muscles between ribs.

internal oblique abdominal muscle whose fibers mostly run upward, producing layers of the lateral walls of the abdomen, and fusing with the external oblique to form the linea alba.

intrapulmonary within the lung.

intrinsic on the inside; within (as intrinsic muscles of the larynx).

jugular pertaining to the throat, neck, or jugular vein.

labial pertaining to the lips.

labiodental a speech sound formed with the lower lip and the upper teeth (as in /f/ and /v/).

laryngoscope an instrument for laryngeal examination.

latissimus dorsi broad, flat, superficial muscle of the back.

levator muscle that raises or elevates (as in levator scapula, levator veli palatini).

light mechanism term sometimes used to describe dominant vocal-ligament activity; may refer to "head voice."

linea alba a median, tendinous line that separates right and left sides of the abdominal musculature.

lingual of the tongue.

lotta vocale (**French,** *lutte vocale*) the vocal contest or struggle; a description of abdominal muscle antagonism experienced during the appoggio.

mandible the jaw.

manubrium upper portion of the sternum; its positioning is crucial to the maintenance of an axial posture and to proper breath management for singing.

marking (*markieren*) sparing the voice during rehearsal through reducing dynamic levels; indicating certain pitches rather than singing them fully.

mask (masque) popular term for the zygomatic facial region.

maxilla (maxillae) area between the lips and the cheeks.

melisma rapidly moving notes on a single syllable.

membrane thin layer of tissue that covers, separates, binds, or lines the cavities of members of the body.

membranous characterized or formed by membrane (as in the membranous portion of the vocal fold that is engaged in vibration).

mylohyoid paired muscles attached to the inside edge of the mandible (jaw) and to the hyoid bone, forming the floor of the mouth.

myoelastic property of elasticity in muscles, as in the vocal folds.

myoelastic/aerodynamic theory of voice production vocal-fold vibration as the result of muscle tautness and breath pressure.

naris (pl. nares) nostril.

node a knotty swelling (also called a nodule).

nuchal back of the neck; nape of the neck.

occlusion closure (as in glottal occlusion).

onset (*l'attacco del suono*) commencement of phonation.

opera scena an operatic form for solo voice, generally made up of a cavatina, a bridging recitative, and a *cabaletta;* a frequent component of bel canto style.

orbicularis oris a muscle encircling the mouth.

oscillation backward and forward motion; pitch fluctuation; may refer to pitch variant that is too wide and too slow, producing a "wobble."

overtone an acoustic phenomenon; a multiple of a fundamental frequency.

palate roof of the mouth.

pars obliqua four muscles attached to the anterior of the cricoid cartilage; located at the sides of the cartilage, with diagonal fibers that pull directly on the thyroid cartilage.

pars recta four muscles attached to the anterior of the cricoid cartilage; located in front, having vertical fibers that pull directly on the thyroid cartilage.

partial a harmonic (overtone) component of a complex voiced tone.

passaggio register pivotal point (as in *primo passaggio, secondo passaggio*).

pectoral pertaining to the chest.

pelvis cavity of the pelvis; bony structure of the lower trunk.

pericardium conical sac of serous membrane enclosing the heart and the roots of the great blood vessels.

phonation voicing; sound produced by the vibrating vocal folds.

piriform sinus (See pyriform sinus.)

placement subjective term denoting sensations of sympathetic vibration.

platysma broad, thin muscle lying on either side of the neck under the fascia, a superficial facial muscle, sometimes termed "the grimacing muscle."

plosive a speech sound formed by a complete stop closure, or by audible air released by an articulator or the glottis.

proprioception awareness of stimuli produced by one's own tension, relaxation, movement, or function, resulting in muscle, vibratory, or auditory sensation.

pyriform sinus space between the laryngeal collar and the alae of the thyroid cartilage.

rectus abdominis a long, flat muscle located on either side of the linea alba, extending the length of the front of the abdomen; arises from the pubic crest and inserts into the cartilage of the fifth, sixth, and seventh ribs; its upper three-fourths is enclosed in the rectus sheath formed by the aponeuroses of the external and internal oblique muscles ventrally, and the internal oblique and transversus abdominis dorsally.

register consecutive series of tones of similar quality.

residual breath breath that remains in the lungs after forced expiration.

respiration the breath cycle; exchange of internal and external gases.

respiratory passage the nostrils, the nasal cavities, the pharyngeal cavities, the oral cavity, the larynx, the trachea, and the bronchial tubes.

risorius a narrow band of muscle fibers arising from the fascia over the masseter (chewing) muscle, inserted into tissue at the corners of the mouth; a muscle of the cheek; sometimes termed "the smiling muscle."

scalenus (scaleni) deep muscle (anterior, medius, posterior) on each side of the neck, extending from the transverse process of two or more cervical vertebrae to the first or second rib; accessory muscle of respiration.

Schnarrbass (*Strohbass*) a low register in the male voice, below the normal pitches of speech inflection, produced by laryngeal depression.

serratus muscle that arises from the ribs or vertebrae; popularly termed "the boxer's muscle."

sibilant speech phoneme characterized by a hissing sound, as in /s/ or /z/.

sinus a cavity, recess, or depression, as in the paranasal sinuses or the ventricular sinuses.

sostenuto sustained.

spectrography a means to measure and display the fundamental and overtone amplitudes generated during phonation: the first formant displays acoustic energy in the lower regions of the spectrum; vowel definition is indicated largely by shifting harmonic energy of the second formant at specific points in the spectrum; the singer's formant, composed of the third, fourth, and fifth formants, displays strong acoustic energy in the upper regions of the spectrum; balanced relationships among the fundamental and the first through fifth formants produce the chiaroscuro tone of the cultivated singing voice.

sphincter a ringlike muscle around an orifice, capable of inducing closure (as with the laryngeal and anal sphincters).

sternocleidomastoid a thick, superficial muscle on each side of the neck, arising from the sternum and the clavicle and inserting into the mastoid bone; strong component of the external-frame support of the larynx.

straight tone devoid of vibrato; reduced spectral energy.

Strohbass (see *Schnarrbass*).

subglottic below the glottis.

submandibular below the jaw.

supplemental air air that can be expelled forcibly beyond what is exhaled during quiet breathing (also known as reserve air.)

supraglottic above the glottis.

synergy the working together of two or more muscles (or muscle groups) or organs.

thorax the part of the torso housing the organs of breathing; situated between the neck and the abdomen, supported by the ribs, the costal cartilages, and the sternum.

thyroarytenoid muscle muscle arising below the thyroidal notch and inserted into each arytenoid.

thyroid cartilage the largest single cartilage of the larynx.

tidal air (tidal volume) air exchanged during quiet, normal breathing.

trachea the windpipe; main tubular system by which air passes to and from the lungs.

transverse abdominis deep abdominal muscle that works synergistically with other abdominal muscles in successful breath management.

trapezius large, flat, triangular superficial muscle on either side of the upper back.

tremolo a vibrato rate that is excessively rapid, with narrow pitch excursion.

trill a rapid pitch variant of a semitone or more, produced by an intended oscillation of the larynx.

trillo a baroque ornamentation device, consisting of a rapid pulsation on a single pitch.

uvula fleshy pendant lobe located in the middle of the posterior part of the soft palate.

velum a membranous partition; the muscle portion of the soft palate.

ventricle a cavity or pouch (as in the laryngeal ventricles).

vibrato pitch variation, the result of neurological impulses that occur during proper coordination between airflow and vocal-fold approximation; a laryngeal relaxant principle characteristic of cultivated singing.

vital capacity maximum amount of air that can be expelled after maximum inspiration.

vocal folds vocal bands, true vocal cords; the lower part of the thyroarytenoid muscles.

vocal fry prolonged vocal-fold rattle; a "frying" sound produced through nonperiodic vocal-fold vibration; a glottal scrape, rattle, or "click," considered by some researchers a separate low voice register.

voce aperta "open," unskillful tone.

voce chiara clear or bright timbre.

voce chiusa well-balanced resonance; avoidance of *voce aperta*.

voce coperta equalized timbre in upper ranges through proper *aggiustamento* of the vowel, avoiding shrillness or blatancy.

voce di petto "chest voice."

voce di testa "head voice."

voce finta "feigned voice"; a specialized vocal timbre that avoids *voce piena* timbre.

voce intermedia (See *zona di passaggio*.)

voce mista "mixed voice"; a descriptive term for timbre in the *zona di passaggio;* often assumed to be a mixture of "chest" and "head" functions.

voce piena "full voice."

voix mixte "mixed voice."

wobble (See oscillation.)

xiphoid process lowest division of the sternum.

zona di passaggio **(passage zone)** middle voice; area of the voice between the *primo passaggio* and the *secondo passaggio*.

zygomatic arch bone that extends along the front and side of the skull, formed by the union of the zygomatic process of the temporal bone with the zygomatic bone, at the cheek area.

zygomatic bone a bone of the face, below the eyes.

zygomatic muscles slender bands of muscle on either side of the face, arising from the zygomatic bone and inserting into the orbicularis oris and the skin at corners of the mouth; involved in pleasant facial expression.

APPENDIX I

PITCH DESIGNATIONS

In modern international acoustic and voice pedagogy usage, pitch designations are indicated by an Acoustical Society of America system that is endorsed by the U.S.A. Standards Association. Each keyboard octave, beginning at the note C, is assigned a number. For example, middle C (C_4) initiates the fourth octave.

When performance literature for the male voice is notated in the treble clef, the indicated pitch is sung an octave lower than the same note designated for the female voice. (For example, from Puccini's *La bohème* act 1 duet, Mimi's High C occurs at C_6 and Rodolfo's at C_5).

Older treatises retain the Helmholtz method, often using upper and lowercase designations extending from C_1 to c_4. The Helmholtz method has universally been replaced by the more current U.S.A. Standards. A comparison of the two systems follows.

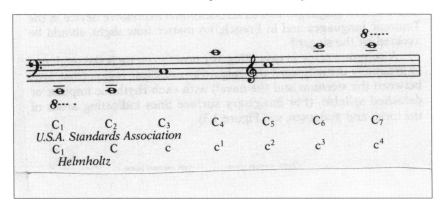

Pitch Designations

APPENDIX II

IPA SYMBOLS FOR VOWELS, SEMIVOWELS,

AND FRENCH NASAL VOWEL SOUNDS

IPA Symbols	English	German	Italian	French
Vowels				
/i/	k*ee*n	L*ie*be	pr*i*ma	l*i*s
/ɪ/	th*i*n	*i*ch		
/e/	ch*ao*s	L*e*ben	p*e*na	*été*, cr*ie*r
/ɛ/	b*e*t	B*e*tt, G*ä*ste	t*e*mpo	*ê*tes, p*è*re, n*ei*ge
/æ/	b*a*t			
/a/	t*a*sk (American)			p*a*rle
/ɑ/	f*a*ther	St*a*dt	c*a*mera	r*a*s, *â*ge
/ɒ/	h*o*t (British)			
/ɔ/	s*o*ft, *a*ll	S*o*nne	m*o*rto	s*o*mme, j*o*li, v*o*tre
/o/	n*o*te	S*o*hn	n*o*n	be*au*x, p*au*vre, gr*o*s
/ʊ/	n*oo*k	M*u*tter		
/u/	gn*u*, f*oo*l	M*u*t	*u*so	*ou*
/ʌ/	*u*p			
/ə/	(schwa) *a*head	g*e*tan		d*e*main
/y/		(approximates /i/ plus /u/) m*ü*de		*u*ne
/ɤ/		(approximates /ɪ/ plus /ʊ/) Gl*ü*ck		

continued

IPA Symbols	English	German	Italian	French
/ø/		(approximates /e/ plus /o/) schön		peu
/œ/		(approximates /ɛ/ plus /ɔ/) Köpfe		heure

Semivowels and glides

IPA Symbols	English	German	Italian	French
/j/	yes	ja	più, pieno	lion, pied
/w/	wish		uomo, guida	moins
/aɪ/	nice	/ae/ Mai, Ei	/ai/ mai	
/aʊ/	house	/ao/ Haus	/au/ aura	
/eɪ/	way		/ei/ dovei	
/ɔɪ/	boy	/ɔø/ Häuser, Kreuz	/ɔi/ vuoi	
/oʊ/	so			

Vowel sounds peculiar to the French language

IPA Symbols	English	German	Italian	French
/ã/				temps
/ɛ̃/				faim, vin
/õ/				nom, long
/œ̃/				parfum, jeun

APPENDIX III

IPA SYMBOLS FOR CONSONANT SOUNDS

	Voiceless		Classification by Formation	Voiced	
Pairs[a]					
/p/-/b/	/p/	pope	bilabial	/b/	bob
/t/-/d/	/t/	tote	lingua-alveolar	/d/	dead
/k/-/g/	/k/	coke	velar	/g/	glug
/f/-/v/	/f/	fife	labiodental	/v/	valve
/ɵ/-/ð/	/ɵ/	think	linguadental	/ð/	the
/s/-/z/	/s/	cease	dental	/z/	zones
/ʃ/-/ʒ/	/ʃ/	Sh!	lingua-alveolar	/ʒ/	vision
/ç/-[b]	/ç/	ich (German)	palatal		
/x/-/ʁ/	/x/	ach (German)	velar	/ʁ/	Paris (French)
/h/-/ʔ/	/h/	ha-ha! (aspirate)	glottal	/ʔ/	uh-oh! (stroked glottal)
/tʃ/-/dʒ/	/tʃ/	chase	lingua-alveolar	/dʒ/	judgment
/ts/-/dz/	/ts/	tsetse	linguadental	/dz/	adds
Nasal consonants					
/m/			bilabial nasal	*m*a	
/n/			alveolar nasal	*n*o	
/ŋ/			velar nasal	so*ng*	
/ɲ/			palatal nasal	og*n*i (Italian), o*n*ion (English), a*gn*eau (French)	
/ɱ/			nasal labiodental	co*n*forto (Italian)	

continued

Voiceless	Classification by Formation	Voiced
Other voiced consonants		
/ʎ/		fo*gli*a (Italian)
/l/		*lul*l
/ɹ/		*ra*re (retroflex r, sometimes referred to as midwestern r)
/r/		ve*ry* (single tap r, as in British speech)
/ř/[c]		ca*rr*o (Italian); G*r*und (German) (alveolar trill)

[a]Pairs of consonants, one unvoiced and the other voiced, are executed with similar tongue and lip positions.

[b]/ç/ is generally believed to be without a voiced counterpart.

[c]The symbol /ř/ is used in this work, and in many phonetic sources, to represent the alveolar rolled r, because the IPA symbol for the trilled r /r/ is used indiscriminately in many American sources.

APPENDIX IV

REPERTOIRE FOR YOUNGER OR BEGINNING SINGERS

English (including some translations)
SAMUEL BARBER
   The daisies
   With rue my heart is laden
BENJAMIN BRITTEN
   Folksongs of the British Isles
      Six volumes of folk song arrangements that contain generally
      simple vocal lines, often with complex accompaniment
   Sally Gardens
   The Ash Grove
   O Waly, Waly
HENRY BISHOP
   Home, Sweet Home
JOHN ALDEN CARPENTER
   Green River
   May the Maiden
   To One Unknown
THEODORE CHANLER
   Eight Epitaphs
      Vocally modest, musically complex
   The Lamb

AARON COPLAND (FROM *OLD AMERICAN SONGS*)
    Shall We Gather at the River?
    'Tis the Gift to Be Simple

JOHN DOWLAND LUTE SONG COLLECTIONS
    Many of extreme beauty and of psychological depth, with limited
    vocal range

JOHN DUKE
    I Can't Be Talkin' of Love
    Loveliest of Trees

STEPHEN FOSTER
    Beautiful Dreamer
    Jeanie with the Light Brown Hair
    The Camptown Races
    My Old Kentucky Home
    Oh! Susannah

RUDOLF GANZ
    A memory

BENJAMIN GODDARD
    Florian's Song

EDUARD GRIEG
    Solvejg's song (requires some technical skill)
    A Swan
    I Love Thee

CHARLES T. GRIFFES
    Five songs from the Chinese
        Vocally modest, musically sophisticated
    The First Snowfall
    The Half-Ring Moon
    An Old Song Re-sung
    We'll to the Woods and Gather May

HANDEL
    A wide selection of English and Italian arias, some of moderate
    range and difficulty, others demanding more dramatic voices
    Ask if Yon Damask Rose
    As When the Dove
    Come and Trip It
    Let Me Wander
    Or Let the Merry Bells
    Thanks Be to Thee, Lord God of Hosts
    Vouchsafe, O Lord

HAYDN
> *Songs and Canzonettas*
>> Most have moderate technical demands, with accompaniments requiring skillful pianism
> Pleasing Pains
> She Never Told Her Love
> My Mother Bids Me Bind My Hair
> Mermaid's Song
> Sailor's Song (a study in melismatic skill)
> Fidelity

ANNIE HARRISON
> In the Gloaming

CHARLES IVES
> At the River
> Evening
> Two Little Flowers

JOHN LAWES
> *Book of Airs*
>> Both simple and complex

MENDELSSOHN
> But the Lord Is Mindful of His Own
> O Rest in the Lord
> Numerous items from the lied collections

PURCELL
> High and Low volumes contain songs at several levels of difficulty
>> I Attempt from Love's Sickness to Fly
>> I'll Sail upon the Dogstar
>> Man Is for the Woman Made
>> Music for Awhile
>> Sweeter than Roses
> (Benjamin Britten's Purcell realizations should be programmed as Purcell/Britten.)

ROGER QUILTER
> Go, Lovely Rose
> Love's Philosophy
> Now Sleeps the Crimson Petal

NED ROREM
> from *Flight from Heaven*
>> Cherry Ripe
>> Upon Julia's Clothes
>> To Daisies
>> To the Willow Tree

Little Elegy
from *To an Unknown Past*
 The Lover in Winter
 Hey, Nonny No!
On a Singing Girl
Psalm 134
Psalm 142

LADY JOHN SCOTT
 Annie Laurie

JAMES E. SPILMAN
 Flow Gently, Sweet Afton

TCHAIKOWSKY
 A Legend

RANDALL THOMPSON
 May Day Carol
 Velvet Shoes

KURT WEILL
 Cabaret Songs (in English, French, and German)

Folk Songs and Spirituals

Believe Me, if All Those Endearing Young Charms
Bluebells of Scotland
Comin' thro' the Rye
Couldn't Hear Nobody Pray
Deep River
Drink to Me Only with Thine Eyes
Go 'Way from My Window
I Know Where I'm Goin'
The Last Rose of Summer
Loch Lomond
Nobody Knows the Trouble I've Seen
Roll, Jordan, Roll
Steal Away
Swing Low, Sweet Chariot
There Is a Balm in Gilead
Were You There When They Crucified My Lord?
Zoltan Kodaly, folk song arrangements (English translations)
Bohuslav Martinů, folk song arrangements (English translations)

Italian

BEETHOVEN
 In questa tomba oscura (for the young bass or bass-baritone)

BELLINI

    Farfalletta

    Il desiderio

    Vaga luna

LUIGI DALLAPICCOLA

    Arie antiche (realizations avoiding nineteenth-century harmonic excesses)

HANDEL

    Non lo dirò col labbro

    Ombra mai fu

    Verdi prati

MOZART

    Un moto di gioia (of moderate difficulty for the young soprano)

    Ridente la calma (of moderate difficulty for the young soprano)

ALESSANDRO SCARLATTI

    Già il sole

    Le violette

    Per la gloria

    Sento nel core

    Selve amiche

German

BEETHOVEN

    Es war einmal ein König (from Goethe's *Faust*)

    Gebet

    Ich liebe dich

BRAHMS

    Dein blaues Auge

    Der Gang zum Liebchen

    In stiller Nacht

    Mein Mädel hat einen Rosenmund

    Vergebliches Ständchen

    Wiegenlied

        The Brahms *Volkslieder* (High and Low voices) are an excellent source for German-language songs of limited technical demands that require strong musicianship.

ROBERT FRANZ

    Many songs in medium range, suitable for early studio work.

GRIEG

    Many songs in German, some with English translations from the Norwegian; they are often of moderate difficulty. Still others have an almost bel canto melodic construction.

LISZT

Du bist wie eine Blume

Es muss ein Wunderbares sein

> Most others require extensive vocal range and maturity, demanding accomplished keyboard skills.

MENDELSSOHN

Many lieder are limited in range and technical demand; others are technically more difficult.

> Auf Flügeln des Gesanges
> Schilflied

MOZART

Items included in numerous lieder collections require good breath management and language flexibility. Some are essentially miniature arias, yet they form an important part of the repertoire of the developing soprano or mezzo-soprano voice. They are available in high voice and low voice. Although not appropriate for the complete novice, several wonderful items are included here.

> Abendempfindung
> Als Luise die Briefe (a miniature drama, appropriate for promising young female voice)
> An Chloë
> Die Männer sind mechant
> Das Veilchen

SCHUMANN

Dein Angesicht

Du bist wie eine Blume

Marienwürmchen

Der Nussbaum

Meine Rose

Röselein! Röselein!

Der Sandmann

Scheeglöckchen

Widmung

Zigeunerliedchen (I and II)

Zwei venezianische Lieder (I and II)

SCHUBERT

Songs of medium range, but of wide variance in difficulty

> An die Musik
> Heidenröslein
> Horch, horch die Lerch (also in English as "Hark, Hark the Lark")

Nur wer die Sehnsucht kennt (Mignon)
Romanze aus Rosamunde
Seligkeit
Der Tod und das Mädchen (interpretatively subtle)
Das Wandern
Was ist Sylvia (also in English as "Who Is Sylvia?")
Wiegenlied
Wohin?

HUGO WOLF
Fussreise
Gebet
Gesang Weylas
Der Musikant
Ständchen
Das verlassene Mädglein
   Most other lieder are musically complex and interpretively
   demanding.

French

FAURÉ
Adieu
Chanson d'amour
Ici-bas
Lydia
Nell
Sylvia
   Fauré mélodies often lie exceedingly high for the young male
   voice.

REYNALDO HAHN
Offrande
Si mes vers

LULLY
Bois épais

GIOVANNI BATTISTA MARTINI
Plaisir d'amour (also in Italian as Piacer d'amor)

MOZART
Dans un bois

Collections of Songs and Literature Sources

JOAN BOYTIM
   Fine collections of standard literature for young voices: soprano;
   mezzo-soprano; tenor; baritone, and bass; highly recommended for
   practical studio use in teaching late teenagers.

VAN CHRISTY

Foundations in Singing: A Basic Textbook in the Fundamentals of Technique

Contains a number of standard early teaching pieces, in translation and transposition.

ALBERT FUCHS

Italian Songs

A collection of seldom performed, beautiful *arie antiche,* at several levels of difficulty. A good alternative to the "famous twenty-four."

MAYBELLE GLENN

Pathways of Song

SERGIUS KAGEN

Singers' Repertoire (reissued by NATS)

Listing of songs with various degrees of difficulty.

CAROL KIMBALL

Song: A Guide to Style and Literature

A list of important repertoire items

ALESSANDRO PARISOTTI

Fifty-six *arie antiche* in two volumes, from which the "famous twenty-four" are selected, plus a volume of duets, in medium-high and medium-low keys. A major source for the studio.

La Flora

Collection of *arie antiche* with romanticized keyboard realizations.

J.G. PAYTON

Arie antiche collections, often treating the same material found in the Parisotti collection, but with an intent to avoid Romantic realizations.

JAN SCHMIDT

Basics of Singing

Contains fifteen musical theater items, fifteen folk songs, and fifteen art songs.

Miscellaneous Collections

COLE PORTER

Collections contain many vocally grateful songs, accessible to the young student.

FRANZ LEHAR

Collections contain operetta selections of varying difficulty.

SIGMUND ROMBERG

Collections contain vocally advantageous songs and arias of varying difficulty.

Songs from the Modern Art Repertory

A fine selection of moderately difficult art songs in English, French, German, Italian, and Spanish (not a collection of contemporary items).

ARTHUR SULLIVAN

G & S repertory is often simple and accessible, but occasionally difficult.

SELECT BIBLIOGRAPHY

Aikin, W. A. *The Voice: An Introduction to Practical Phonology.* (1910). Reprint London: Longmans Green, 1951.

Ansaldo, Lea, and Eldes Basetti. *La voce dell'attore e la voce del cantante.* Milan: Sabatelli editore, 1977.

Appelman, D. Ralph. *The Science of Vocal Pedagogy.* (1967). Reprint Bloomington: Indiana University Press, 1974.

Armin, Georg. *Die Technique der Breitspannung: ein Beitrag über die horizontal-vertikalen Spannkrafte beim Aufbau der Stimme nach dem "Stauprinzip."* Berlin: Verlag der Gesellschaft für Stimmkultur, 1933.

Bachner, Louis. *Dynamic Singing.* London: Dobson, 1940.

Balk, Wesley. *The Complete Singer-Actor.* Minneapolis: University of Minnesota Press, 1973.

Bartholomew, Wilmer T. *The Acoustics of Music.* New York: Prentice-Hall, 1942.

Bérard, Jean-Baptiste. *L'Art du chant.* (1775). Translated and edited by Sidney Murray. Milwaukee, WI: Pro Musica Press, 1968.

Bertoni, Giulio, and Francesco Ugolini. *Prontuario di pronunzia e di ortografia.* Turin: Istituto del libro italiano, 1944.

Bolognini, Tommaso. *Trattato di tecnica del canto dalla pratica antica alla moderna.* Fasano: Schena Editore, 1982.

Brewer, David J., ed. *Research Potentials in Voice Physiology.* Syracuse: State University of New York Press, 1964.

Brodnitz, Friedrich. *Vocal Rehabilitation: A Manual Prepared for the Use of Graduates in*

Medicine, American Academy of Ophthalmology and Otolaryngology. Rochester, MN: Mayo Clinic, 1971.

Brown, Oren L. *Discover Your Voice: How to Develop Healthy Voice Habits.* San Diego: Singular/Thomson/Delmar, 1996.

Bunch, Meribeth. *Dynamics of the Singing Voice.* New York: Springer-Verlag, 1982.

Burgin, John Carroll. *Teaching Singing.* Metuchen, NJ: Scarecrow Press, 1973.

Campbell, E.J. Moran. *The Respiratory Muscles and the Mechanics of Breathing.* Chicago: Year Book (Medical) Publishers, 1958.

Campbell, E.J. Moran, Emilio Agostoni, and John Newsom Davis. *The Respiratory Muscles: Mechanics and Neural Control.* London: Lloyd-Luke, 1970.

Christy, Van A. *Foundations in Singing.* Dubuque, IA: William C. Brown, 1974.

Cleveland, Thomas F. "Constructing Exercises That Enhance the Management of the Interdependence of the Vocal Folds and Breath Management in Singing." *Journal of Singing* 58: 1 (2001): 61–62.

Clippinger, D.A. *The Head Voice and Other Problems.* Philadelphia: Oliver Ditson, 1917.

Coffin, Bertrand. *Overtones of Bel Canto.* Metuchen, NJ: Scarecrow Press, 1980.

———. *Historical Vocal Pedagogy Classics.* Metuchen, NJ: Scarecrow Press, 1989.

Corri, Domenico. *The Singer's Preceptor.* (1810). Edited by E. Foreman. Urbana, IL: Pro Music Press, 1968.

Crutchfield, Will. "Some Thoughts on Reconstructing Singing Styles of the Past." *Journal of the Conductors' Guild* 10 (1989): 111–120.

Curtis, H.H. *Voice Building and Tone Placing.* New York: D. Appleton, 1901.

Davis, Richard. *A Beginning Singer's Guide.* Lanham, MD: Scarecrow Press, 1998.

de Boor, Helmut, Hugo Moser, and Christian Winkler. *Siebs deutsche Aussprache.* Berlin: Walter de Gruyter, 1969.

Delle Sedie, Enrico. *L'estetica del canto e dell'arte melodrammatica.* Leghorn: The author, 1885.

Denes, Peter B., and Elliot N. Pinson. *The Speech Chain: The Physics and Biology of Spoken Language* (Bell Telephone Laboratories, 1963). Garden City, NJ: Anchor Press, 1923.

Donington, Robert. *A Performer's Guide to Baroque Music.* New York: Charles Scribner's Sons, 1973.

Fields, Victor Alexander. *Training the Singing Voice.* New York: King's Crown Press, 1974.

Fillebrown, Thomas. *Resonance in Singing and Speaking.* Bryn Mawr, PA: Raven Press, 1911.

Forman, Edward, ed. *The Porpora Tradition.* Milwaukee, WI: Pro Musica Press, 1968.

Freed, Donald Allen. "Imagery in Early Twentieth-Century American Vocal Pedagogy." *Journal of Singing* 56: 4 (2000): 5–12.

Froeschels, Emil. "Chewing Method as Therapy: A Discussion with Some Philosophical Conclusions." *Archives of Otolaryngology* 56 (1952): 427–434.

———. "Nose and Nasality." *Archives of Otolaryngology* 66 (1957): 629–633.

———. *Selected Papers of Emil Froeschels, 1940–1964.* Edited by Helen Beebe and Felix Trojan. Amsterdam: North-Holland, 1964.

Fuchs, Viktor. *The Art of Singing and Voice Technique.* London: Calder and Boyars, 1963.

Gabrielli, Aldo. *Il museo degli errori: L'italiano come si parla oggi.* Milan: Oscar Mondadori, 1979.

Garcia, Manuel. *Garcia's Complete School of Singing* (a compilation of editions of 1847 and 1872). London: Cramer, Beale, and Chappell, n.d.

——. "Observations on the Human Voice." *Proceedings of the Royal Society of London* (1854–1855): 399–410.

Green, Harry Plunket. (1912). *Interpretation in Song.* Reprinted London: Macmillan. 1956.

Hammer, Russell A. *Singing—An Extension of Speech.* Metuchen, NJ: Scarecrow Press, 1978.

Helmholtz, Hermann L.F. *On the Sensations of Tone.* Translated by Alexander J. Ellis. London: Longmans, Green, 1875. Reprint 1939.

Henderson, W.J. *Early History of Song.* London: Longmans Green, 1921.

——. *The Art of Singing.* London: Dial Press, 1938.

Herbert-Caesari, E. *The Alchemy of Voice.* London: Robert Hale, 1965.

——. *The Science and Sensations of Tone.* 2nd ed., rev. Boston: Crescendo Publishers, 1936. Reprint 1968.

——. *The Voice of the Mind.* London: Robert Hale, 1969.

Heriot, Angus. *The Castrati in Opera.* London: Secker & Warburg, 1956. Reprint New York: Da Capo Press, 1969.

Hines, Jerome. *Great Singers on Great Singing.* New York: Doubleday, 1982.

Husler, Frederick. *Das vollkommene Instrument.* Stuttgart: Belsar-Verlag, 1970.

Husler, Frederick, and Yvonne Rodd-Marling. *Singing: The Physical Nature of the Vocal Organ.* London: Faber and Faber, 1960.

Husson, Raoul. *La voix chantée.* Paris: Gauthier-Villars, 1960.

Ivey, Donald. *Song: Anatomy, Imagery, and Styles.* New York: The Free Press, 1970.

Kantner, Claude, and Robert West. *Phonetics.* New York: Harper & Brothers, 1960.

Kennedy-Dygas, Margaret. "Historical Perspectives on the 'Science' of Teaching Singing: Manuel Garcia II (1805–1906) and the Science of Singing in the Nineteenth Century." *Journal of Singing* 56: 4 (2000): 23–30.

Klein, Herman. *An Essay on Bel Canto.* London: Oxford University Press, 1923.

Kockritz, Hubert. *Language Orientation—An Introduction to the Pronunciation of Foreign Languages Based upon the International Phonetic Alphabet.* Cincinnati: Privately published, 1965.

Kofler, Leo. *The Art of Breathing as the Basis of Tone-Production.* 6th ed. New York: Edward S. Werner, 1889.

Lablache, Louis. *Lablache's Complete Method of Singing: Or a Rational Analysis of the Principles According to Which the Studies Should be Directed for Developing the Voice and Rendering It Flexible, and for Forming the Voice.* Boston: Oliver Ditson, n.d.

Ladefoged, Peter. *Elements of Acoustic Phonetics.* Chicago: University of Chicago Press, 1962.

Lamperti, Francesco. *The Art of Singing.* Translated by J.C. Griffith. New York: G. Schirmer, 1890.

Lamperti, Giovanni Battista. *The Techniques of Bel Canto.* New York: G. Schirmer, 1905.

————. (1931). *Vocal Wisdom: Maxims of Giovanni Battista Lamperti.* Edited by William E. Brown. Reprint Boston: Crescendo Press, 1973.

Large, John W., ed. *Vocal Registers in Singing.* The Hague: Mouton, 1973.

Lehmann, Lilli. *How to Sing.* New York: Macmillan, 1903.

Lessac, Arthur. *The Use and Training of the Human Voice.* 2nd ed. New York: Drama Book Specialists, 1967.

Lieberman, Philip, and Sheila Blumstein. *Speech Physiology, Speech Perception, and Acoustic Phonetics.* New York: Cambridge University Press, 1998.

Lohman, Paul. *Stimmfehler-Stimmberatung.* Mainz: B. Schott's Söhne, 1933.

Luchsinger, Richard, and Godfrey E. Arnold. *Voice-Speech-Language.* Translated by Godfrey Arnold and Evelyn Robe Finkbeiner. Belmont, CA: Wadsworth, 1965.

Mackinley, M. Sterling. *The Singing Voice and Its Training.* London: George Rutledge & Sons, 1910.

Mancini, Giovanni Battista. (1774). *Practical Reflections on the Art of Singing.* Translated by Pietro Buzzi. Boston: Oliver Ditson, 1907.

Manén, Lucie. *The Art of Singing.* London: Faber Music, 1974.

Marafioti, P. Mario. *Caruso's Method of Voice Production: The Scientific Culture of the Voice.* New York: Appleton, 1923.

Marchesi, Mathilde. (1903). *Bel Canto: A Theoretical & Practical Vocal Method.* (1903). Reprint New York: Dover, 1970.

Marchesi, Salvatore. *A Vademecum.* New York: G. Schirmer, 1902.

Mari, Nanda. *Canto e voce.* Milan: G. Ricordi, 1970.

Marshall, Madeleine. *The Singer's Manual of English Diction.* New York: G. Schirmer, 1953.

Martienssen-Lohmann, Franziska. *Das bewusste Singen.* Leipzig: C. F. Kahnt, 1923.

————. *Der Opernsänger.* Mainz: B. Schött's Sohne, 1943.

————. *Der wissende Sänger.* Zurich: Atlantis-Verlag, 1963.

McKinney, James. *The Diagnosis and Correction of Vocal Faults.* Nashville, TN: Boardman Press. Reprint San Diego: Singular Press, 1982.

McIver, William, and Richard Miller. "A Brief Study of Nasality in Singing." *Journal of Singing* 4 (1996): 21–26.

Meano, Carlo. *La voce umana nella parola e nel canto.* Milan: Casa Editrice Ambrosiana, 1964.

Melba, Dame Nellie. *Melba Method.* London: Chappell, 1926.

Miller, Dayton Clarence. *The Science of Musical Sounds.* New York: Macmillan, 1916.

Miller, Donald G., and James Doing. "Male Passaggio and the Upper Extension in the Light of Visual Feedback." *Journal of Singing* 4 (1998): 3–13.

Miller, Donald G., and Harm K. Schutte "Toward a Definition of Male `Head' Register, Passaggio, and 'Cover' in Western Operatic Singing." *Folia Phoniatrica Logopaedica* 46 (1994): 157–170.

Miller, Frank E. *The Voice: Its Production, Care and Preservation.* New York: G. Schirmer, 1913.

————. *Vocal Art-Science and Its Application.* New York: G. Schirmer, 1917.

Miller, Richard, and Harm K. Schutte. "The Effect of Tongue Position on Spectra in Singing." *The NATS Bulletin* 37, 3 (1981): 26–27.

Miller, Richard. "Spectral Analysis of Several Categories of Timbre in a Professional Male (Tenor) Voice." *Journal of Research in Singing* 7, 1 (1983): 6–10.

———. *The Structure of Singing.* New York: Schirmer Books/Macmillan, 1986.

———. *Training Tenor Voices.* New York: Schirmer Books/Macmillan, 1993.

———. "The Solo Singer in the Choral Ensemble." *Choral Journal* 35: 3 (1995): 31–36.

———. *National Schools of Singing.* Metuchen, NJ: Scarecrow Press, 1997.

———. *On the Art of Singing.* New York: Oxford University Press, 1997.

———. "Historical Overview of Vocal Pedagogy." In *Vocal Health and Pedagogy.* Edited by Robert T. Sataloff. San Diego: Singular Publishing, 1998.

———. "The Odyssey of Orpheus: The Evolution of Solo Singing." In *Voice Perspectives.* Edited by Robert T. Sataloff. San Diego: Singular Publishing, 1998.

———. *Singing Schumann: An Interpretive Guide for Performers.* New York: Oxford University Press, 1999.

———. "Countertenoring." *Journal of Singing* 57: 2 (2000): 99–121.

———. *Training Soprano Voices.* New York: Oxford University Press, 2000.

Mills, Wesley. *Voice Production in Singing and Speaking.* 2nd ed. Philadelphia: J.P. Lippincott, 1908.

Minifie, Fred D., Thomas J. Hixon, and Frederick Williams. *Normal Aspects of Speech, Hearing, and Language.* Englewood Cliffs, NJ: Prentice-Hall, 1973.

Mori, Rachel Maragliano. *Coscienza della voce nella scuola italiana di canto.* Milan: Edizioni Curci, 1970.

Nair, Garyth. *Voice—Tradition and Technology. A State-of-the-Art Studio.* San Diego: Singular Publishing, 2000.

Negus, Sir Victor E. *The Comparative Anatomy and Physiology of the Larynx.* (1949). Reprint New York: Hafner, 1962.

Paget, Sir Richard. *Human Speech.* New York: Harcourt, 1930.

Pleasants, Henry. *The Great Singers: From the Dawn of Opera to Our Own Time.* New York: Simon and Schuster, 1966.

———. *The Great Tenor Tragedy: The Last Days of Adolphe Nourrit as Told (Mostly) by Himself.* Portland, OR: Amadeus Press, 1995.

Proctor, Donald F. "The Physiologic Basis of Voice Training." In *Sound Production in Man.* Edited by A. Bouhuys. New York: New York Academy of Sciences, 1968.

———. "Breath, the Power Source for the Voice." *The NATS Bulletin* 37, 2 (1980): 16–30.

Reid, Cornelius L. *Bel Canto Principles and Practices.* New York: Coleman-Ross, 1950.

———. *The Free Voice.* New York: Coleman-Ross, 1965.

———. *Psyche and Soma.* New York: Joseph Patelson Music House, 1975.

Robison, Clayne. "Beautiful Singing: What It Is and How to Do It. Implications of the New Interactivity (Chaos) Paradigm in Physics." *Journal of Singing* 58: 1 (2001): 7–28.

Rose, Arnold. *The Singer and the Voice.* London: Faber and Faber, 1962.

Rosselli, John. "The Castrati as a Professional Group and a Social Phenomenon." *Acta Musicologica* 60 (1988): 143–149.

———. *Singers of Italian Opera: The History of a Profession.* Cambridge: Cambridge University Press, 1992.

Rushmore, Robert. *The Singing Voice.* New York: Dodd, Mead, 1971.

———. "Indications for Surgery in Singers." *Journal of Singing* 56: 4 (2000): 43–45.

———. "The Nose." *Journal of Singing* 57: 1 (2001): 51–54.

Sataloff, Robert Thayer. "The Physics of Sound." In *Vocal Health and Pedagogy.* Edited by Sataloff, 2nd ed. San Diego: Singular Publishing, 1998.

Sataloff, Robert Thayer, ed. *Vocal Health and Pedagogy.* 2nd ed. San Diego: Singular Publishing, 1998.

———. *Voice Perspectives.* San Diego: Singular Publishing, 1998.

Sataloff, Robert Thayer, Deborah Caputo Rosen, and Steven Levy. "Performance Anxiety: What Singing Teachers Should Know." *Journal of Singing* 56, 5 (2000): 33–40.

Schutte, Harm K. *The Efficiency of Voice Production.* Groningen, Netherlands: State University Hospital, 1980.

Schutte, Harm K., and Richard Miller. "Differences in Spectral Analysis of a Trained and an Untrained Singer." *The NATS Bulletin* 42, 2 (1983): 22–26.

———. "Resonance Balance in Register Categories of the Singing Voice: A Spectral Analysis Study." *Folia Phoniatrica* (Basel) 36 (1984): 289–295.

———. "Breath Management in Repeated Vocal Onset." *Folia Phoniatrica* (Basel) 36 (1984): 225–232.

———. "Intraindividual Parameters of the Singer's Formant." *Folia Phoniatrica* (Basel) 37: 31–35, (1985): 289–295.

Seashore, Carl. "The Vibrato." In *Experimental Studies.* Ames: University of Iowa Press, 1932.

Seiler, Emma. *The Voice in Singing.* Philadelphia: J.B. Lippincott, 1875.

Sieber, Ferdinand. *The Art of Singing.* Translated by F. Seeger. New York: William A. Pond, 1872.

Shakespeare, William. *The Art of Singing.* Bryn Mawr, PA: Oliver Ditson, 1921.

Shipp, Thomas. "Vertical Laryngeal Position in Singing." *Journal of Research in Singing* 1, 1 (1977): 16–24.

———. "Effects of Vocal Frequency and Effort on Vertical Laryngeal Position." *Journal of Research in Singing* 7, 2 (1984): 1–5.

Smith, Ethel. "An Electromyographic Investigation of the Relationship between Abdominal Muscular Effort and the Rate of Vocal Vibrato." *The NATS Bulletin* 26, 4–6 (1970): 8–17.

Sonninen, Aatto A. "The External Frame Function in the Control of Pitch in the Human Voice." In *Sound Production in Man.* Edited by A. Bouhuys. New York: New York Academy of Sciences, 1968.

Stampa, Aribert Atem. *Sprache und Gesang.* Kassel: Bärenreiter Verlag, 1956.

Stanley, Douglas. *Your Voice—Applied Science of Vocal Art.* New York: Pitman, 1945.

Stark, James. *Bel Canto: A History of Vocal Pedagogy.* Toronto: University of Toronto Press, 1999.

Steane, J. B. *Singers and Critics.* London: Gerald Duckworth and Co., 1995.

Stetson, Raymond H. *Bases of Phonology.* Oberlin, OH: Oberlin College Press, 1945.

Stevens, Kenneth H., and Minoru Hirano. *Vocal-Fold Physiology.* Tokyo: Tokyo University Press, 1981.

Stockhausen, Julius. *Method of Singing.* Translated by Sophie Lowe. London: Novello, 1884.

Sundberg, Johan. "The Acoustics of the Singing Voice." *Scientific American* 236, 3 (1977): 82–91.

———. *The Science of the Singing Voice.* Dekalb: Northern Illinois University Press, 1987.

———. "Vocal Tract Resonance." In *Vocal Health and Pedagogy.* Edited by Robert T. Sataloff. San Diego: Singular Publishing, 1998.

Titze, Ingo. "How Can the Vocal Mechanism Be Tuned for Maximum Acoustic Output Power?" *The NATS Bulletin* 37, 5 (1981): 26.

———. "What Determines the Elastic Properties of the Vocal Folds and How Important Are They?" *The NATS Bulletin* 38, 1 (1981): 30–31.

———. *Principles of Voice Production.* Englewood Cliffs, NJ: Prentice-Hall, 1994.

———. "Acoustic Interpretation of Resonant Voice." *Journal of Voice* 15: 4 (2001): 519–528.

———. "The Larynx and the Ear—How Well Do They Match?" *Journal of Singing* 57: 5 (2001): 41–43.

Tosi, Pier Francesco. *Observations on the Florid Song.* (1743). Translated by J. E. Galliard. London: J. Wilcox, n.d. Reprint London: Stainer and Bell, 1987.

Van den Berg, Janwillem. "Some Physical Aspects of Voice Production." In *Research Potentials in Voice Physiology.* Edited by David Brewer. Syracuse: State University of New York Press, 1964.

———. "Myoelastic-Aerodynamic Theory of Voice Production." *Journal of Speech and Hearing Research* 1 (1968): 227–244.

———. "Register Problems." In *Sound Production in Man.* Edited by A. Bouhuys. New York: New York Academy of Sciences, 1968.

Vennard, William. *Singing: The Mechanism and the Technic.* Rev. ed. New York: Carl Fischer, 1967.

Von Békésy, Georg. "The Structure of the Middle Ear and the Hearing of One's Own Voice by Bone Conduction." *Journal of the Acoustical Society of America* 20 (1949): 749–760.

———. *Experiments in Hearing.* Translated and edited by E. G. Weaver. New York: McGraw-Hill, 1960.

Ware, Clifton. *Adventures in Singing.* New York: McGraw-Hill, 1997.

———. *Basics of Vocal Pedagogy.* Minneapolis: University of Minnesota Press, 1998.

Warman, E. B. *The Voice: How to Train It and Care for It.* Boston: Lee and Shepard, 1889.

Watson, Peter J., and Thomas J. Hixon. "Respiratory Kinematics in Classical (Opera) Singers." *Journal of Speech and Hearing Research* 28 (1985): 104–122.

Weiss, Rudolf, W. S. Brown, Jr., and Jack Morris. "Singer's Formant in Sopranos: Fact or Fiction?" *Journal of Voice* 15: 4 (2001): 457–467.

Westerman, Kenneth N. *Emergent Voice.* Ann Arbor, MI: Privately published, 1949.

Whitlock, Weldon. *Facets of the Singer's Art.* Champaign, IL: Pro Musica Press, 1967.

————. *Bel Canto for Twentieth Century.* Champaign, IL: Pro Musica Press, 1968.

————. *Profiles in Vocal Pedagogy.* Ann Arbor, MI: Clifton Press, 1975.

Wilcox, John C. *The Living Voice.* New York: Carl Fisher, 1945.

Witherspoon, Herbert. *Singing.* New York: G. Schirmer, 1925.

Wormhoudt, Pearl Shinn. *Building the Voice as an Instrument.* Oskaloosa, IA: William Penn College, 1981.

Zemlin, W.R. *Speech and Hearing Science: Anatomy and Physiology.* 2nd ed. Englewood Cliffs, NJ: Prentice-Hall, 1981.

INDEX

abdominal-wall (*see also* appoggio; breath management)
    anterior/lateral, 3, 4, 7, 24, 32, 40, 101
    hypogastric distention, 1–4, 16, 19, 20, 211
    inward thrusting, 19, 20, 210
    melismatic articulation, 33
Addison, Adele, 221
African American voice, 92, 218–222
aggiustamento (vowel modification: unified scale), 29, 51, 67, 74, 146, 161, 162–163
agility factor, 11, 12, 34, 60
American sound, 192–193
amplified performance, 220
Anderson, Marian, 221
appoggio, 5, 7, 11–12, 14, 16, 17, 19, 20, 34
    belly breathing, 1–4
    della nucca, 8–10, 43, 44, 56, 167–168, 170
    junior and senior high school students, 10
    lateral abdominal expansion, 20
    obesity, 174–175
    vocal-fold tension, 5

Arroyo, Martina, 221
Asawa, Brian, 156
aspirated insertions, 164–165
atmospheric pressure, 14

baritone 29, 131 *(see also* registration)
    changing to tenor, 132–133
    national timbre preferences, 192
baryton Martin (Jean Blaise), 158
basso cantante, 29. *See also* registration
basso profondo, 29. *See also* registration
Bauchaussenstütz, 1–4, 16
bel canto, 12, 33
belting, 151–152
Bjoerling, Jussi, 18, 150
Brahms, Johannes, 200
breath cycle, 14, 17
    breath column, 19
    duration, 19
    pacing, 25, 31
breath management, 14, 24, 28, 34
    breathy, normal, pressed, 15, 20, 21–23, 25, 28
    German School tendencies, 2–4
    high breath-emission rate, 26, 82
    natural breathing, 18–20